GEORGE WALTON

DESIGNER AND
· ARCHITECT ·

GEORGE WALTON

DESIGNER AND
· ARCHITECT ·

KAREN MOON

Published by

White Cockade Publishing
71 Lonsdale Road
Oxford OX2 7ES

British Library Cataloguing-in-Publication Data

A catalogue record for this book is available from the British Library

ISBN 1 873487 01 0
ISBN 1 873487 02 9 pbk

Jacket design by Gerald Cinamon
Typeset in 9.8 on 12 point Photina at the Oxford University Computing Service
Printed in Great Britain by Ebenezer Baylis & Son Ltd, Worcester

Front cover: Detail from a leaded glass door in Alma House, Cheltenham, *c.* 1904-5 (This England Ltd, photo Glasgow Museums and Art Galleries)
Back cover: Walton's interior for the Kodak showrooms at 72-4 Buchanan Street, Glasgow, 1900 (George Walton Archive, photo GMAG)
Opposite title page: Profile of George Walton (George Walton Archive, photo GMAG)
Page 10: George Walton in costume (George Walton Archive, photo GMAG)

Karen Moon trained in design at Birmingham Polytechnic and worked for the BBC, before moving on to study the history of design and architecture at the Open University and the Royal College of Art. She has worked for a number of museums and galleries on a freelance basis and has travelled extensively.

For Allister, Sam and Ben

CONTENTS

PREFACE

I first met George Walton's son, Edward, in 1979. Conversations with Edward were always stimulating and enlightening. Though his father died when he was still a child, Edward retained a deep respect and admiration for him, and held an excellent archive of his work; from time to time, he would dig amongst his treasures and bring out some jewel to show me. For many years, Edward strove to encourage public recognition of his father's work; what he looked forward to most was a book about his father, and an exhibition of his work.

The George Walton exhibition at Glasgow Museum and Art Gallery, with which this book coincides, was initiated through Edward's endeavour. So much greater was the tragedy of his death, in May 1991, when plans for the exhibition were getting underway, and his desires were so nearly achieved. His support was vital to this book.

I first turned to George Walton for study because he seemed to provide a useful introduction to a period of exceptional interest. This still seems true today. He was extraordinarily prolific in a remarkable range of media; his career neatly spans the central period of the Arts and Crafts movement in Britain, and reflects much of its geographical spread.

Yet to a great extent the personal life and private thoughts of George Walton were closed. He was a private man, not a talker, nor a writer. If he is to be understood, it is not through a search of written sources, for he wrote no diaries, no publications and few letters; it is primarily through visual reflection on his work. Today, much of this work is known only from photographs, and so some aspects of his work are lost. For instance, in his interior design work he was a colourist, from all reports, of great subtlety; evidence for this has barely survived.

What has survived is nevertheless compelling. We may have wished for more words, but as it is we must see to understand him; we cannot listen. This is perhaps how he would have wished it to be.

I would like to thank the large number of people who have helped me over the last fourteen years. Listing their names cannot do justice to the generosity and interest shown by so many. To any whose names I have overlooked I offer sincere apologies.

I am indebted first to those other members of the Walton family who have helped me so much and generously lent material for this book: Camilla Uytman, George Walton Scott (who has kindly added a memoir of his grandfather to the notes left by Edward), and Robin Hutchison.

Edward left his collection of material on his father in the care of Margaret Hall, Head of Design at the British Museum, who has worked untiringly to realise his aims. I am deeply grateful to her for all her help, and for making the collection freely available.

My warm appreciation goes to the following, who have provided particular encouragement and help at various times: the late Elizabeth Aslin, Roger Billcliffe, William Buchanan, Alan Crawford (who first initiated my interest in design history and has helped considerably in past months), Ieuan Hughes, Juliet Kinchin, the late Jocelyn Morton, Gillian Naylor, and the late Helen Weller (whose intention to write a book on the Walton family was sadly frustrated); to Professor Christopher Frayling, whose inspired tutoring has not been forgotten; and, above all, to Jill Lever who has been, perhaps without knowing it, the greatest support to me over the years, easing my life as a researcher, believing in my ability to write this book, and keeping me in touch with developments when I was abroad.

My sincere thanks to those who have opened their homes to me for purposes of research: Mr Barnes, C. Blinkhorn, Sir James and Lady Carreras, Tinsey Chan, Penelope Court, the late Miss Marjorie Dick, Doris Duncan, Mr and Mrs Hathrell, Mr and Mrs Harry Legg, Mr and Mrs Ronald MacDonald, Sir John and Lady Margetson, Mrs Morrow, the late Miss Violet Paterson, Felice Pearson, the late Mrs H. Purvis, and Mr and Mrs J. Thomas.

Among the members of the Davison family, I am indebted to David Davison, John Davison, Doreen Leslie Smith and Barbara Balkwill for their enthusiastic help and generous loan of photographs.

I also wish to thank for help of various but invaluable kinds Robert Aickman, Dr Brian Allen, John C. Annan, Douglas Annan, David Ball, Dr Steven Blake, Brian Blench, David Blinkhorne, John Brandon-Jones, Alan Broadfoot, Lance W. Brown, Gerald Cinamon, Brian Coe, Richard Cole, Stephen Downs, Michael Donnelly, Professor G. Eisler, Léone Ellyne, Tony Faiers, The Fine Art Society, David Fletcher, Rosalyn Gee, Devina Graham, G. E. Grainger, the Very Reverend Malcolm E. Grant, Rosemary Hayes, Kenneth Hinshalwood, Professor Thomas Howarth, Ellen Howden, Alwyn Hughes-Jones, Jan Hunt, Alan Johnson, James Judd, Jane Kidd, T. H. Kingerlee & Sons Ltd, Lyn

Kingsmill, Maureen Kinnear, Fiona MacSporran, David Martin, Rachael Miles, D. O'Callaghan, C. O'Donnell, Colin Osman, F. E. Owen, Alan Powers, George Rawson, Paul Reeves, Pamela Robertson, Francis Robinson, Sister Margaret Rose, Colin Rowntree & Partners, Ralph K. Rowntree, Elizabeth Rycroft, Olive Seabury, Ewa Suchorska, Ailsa Tanner, Jackie Tanner, Richard J. Taylor, Robert Tilling, Clive Wainwright, David Walker, A. J. Wallis, Sam Welford, Baroness Eirene White, Mrs Edna Williams, Paul Wood, and Miss M. D. Young.

The assistance I have had at the various libraries and collections where I have found material is impossible to acknowledge in detail but warmly appreciated; I am particularly grateful to the staff of the Mitchell Library in Glasgow, the British Architectural Library, particularly the RIBA Drawings Collection, and various departments of the Victoria and Albert Museum, including the Archive of Art and Design and the National Art Library.

I would like to acknowledge the generous financial contributions provided by Glasgow Museums and Art Galleries and the Paul Mellon Centre for Studies in British Art towards the production and travel costs associated with this book.

In the final stages, I have been indebted above all to Daniel Robbins, curator of the Walton exhibition at Glasgow Museums and Art Galleries, for the great energy with which he has supported this book by every means available to him; and to my publisher, Perilla Kinchin, for her patience, unwavering commitment and invaluable editorial advice.

I am deeply grateful to members of my family for their support and encouragement throughout; especially to David and Pauline Ripper and Keith and Ruth Moon; to my children, Samuel and Benjamin, who have put up with so many inconveniences and dull days cheerfully; and to my husband, Allister, to whom I owe, quite simply, more than I can say.

Karen Moon

Illustration Acknowledgments

T. & R. Annan & Sons Ltd, Glasgow 19, 61, 62, 127 (photo GMAG); Barbara Balkwill 190; Birmingham Library Services 29; H. Blairman & Sons Ltd, London 139; R. Brinton 192; British Architectural Library, London 25, 30, 57, 65, 102, 110, 111, 114, 130, 136, 167, 181, 194, 195, 196, 204, 207, 210, 211, 223, 228, 229; William Buchanan 18; Building Design Partnership (photo GMAG) 43; Alan Crawford 74, 75, 76, 79, 81, 123, 124, 126, 219, 220, 221; David Davison 142, 178, 179, 180, 189; Edinburgh City Library 134; Fine Art Society, London 55, 148 (photo A. C. Cooper Ltd); C. H. Fletcher, Silsden Ltd (photo Karen Moon) 225; George Walton Archive (photos GMAG) 1, 3, 4, 9, 11, 13, 41, 58, 66, 77, 78, 80, 82, 84, 89, 93, 94, 115, 117, 131, 135, 138, 140, 141, 144, 152, 153, 155, 156, 157, 158, 159, 163, 166, 172, 182, 183, 184, 185, 186, 193, 203, 205, 209, 212, 213, 214, 230, 231, 232; Glasgow Museums and Art Galleries 2, 15, 16, 23, 33, 34, 36, 38, 39, 47, 67, 132, 145, 217; Glasgow School of Art 150, 169, 171; Glasgow Society of Women Artists 42; Hunterian Art Gallery, University of Glasgow 95, 122; Anthony F. Kersting 187; Juliet Kinchin 170; Kodak Ltd (photos GMAG) 69, 70, 85, 86, 88, 100, 103, 105, 106; David Lloyd Jones (photo GMAG) 17; Fiona MacSporran 149; Karen Moon 12, 26, 31, 32, 35, 37, 40, 44, 46, 49, 60, 64, 96, 101, 120, 119, 125, 133, 143, 151, 154, 164, 165, 168, 173, 174, 175, 177, 191, 206; Mitchell Library, Glasgow 59, 68, 71, 72, 73, 92, 109, 116, 128, 129, 147, 188; National Library of Scotland, Edinburgh (photos GMAG) 27, 98, 99, 112, 113, 118, 146; National Museum of Photography, Film and Television, Bradford 48, 90, 91, 104; North Yorkshire County Record Office, Northallerton 56; Colin Osman 197, 199; Public Record Office, London 20, 87; Ann Reed 50; P. J. Reeves Ltd 54, 137; Royal Photographic Society, Bath 218, 222; George Walton Scott 6, 22, 107, 202; Doreen Leslie Smith 176, 198, 200, 201, 208, 215, 216; Sotheby & Co., London 63; Strathclyde Regional Archives, Glasgow (photos GMAG) 97, 121; Tate Gallery, London 24; Richard J. Taylor 51, 52, 53; This England Ltd (photos GMAG) 160, 161, 162; Victoria and Albert Museum, London 83, 224 (photo Daniel Robbins), 226 (photo Karen Moon), 227 (photo Daniel Robbins); Private Collections 5, 7, 8, 10, 14, 21, 28.

TWO MEMOIRS

My father, by Edward Walton

George Henry Walton was born in 1867 and, having married for the second time, fathered a son in his early fifties. The writer is that son. By the time the observer is fourteen years old, the subject has been dead six months or so. One must question what sort of impressions can be usefully recalled more than half a century later. And can these childhood pictures of a loving father contribute to the analysis of George Walton as an original artist?

Yes. There is a sense in which the childhood eye might be of great help. Had GHW been a scientist or other structured thinker the gap between man and work would have rendered the reminiscences nothing more than curiosities. But he was a creative artist, designer, experimenter, innovator; and a child's picture of such a man may correspond very closely with the spirit of one who attempted, very quietly, such daring experiments. Only a man with the innocence of a child himself could have offered such strange new alternative forms with such confidence when he was hardly out of his teens.

The George Walton I knew was already tired, and to what was a natural quiet and gentleness was added a quiet born of fatigue, of having lived on into a world in which, after the First World War, his art was being overtaken by political and technological forces of a scale and fierceness that he can never have understood.

He was six foot tall, and except in public had a slight stoop. I remember a physically quiet man, seated in a Morris ladderback rush-seated chair, his hair brushed forward from the back of his head, white and quite thick, with an amber tinge. He had a large, or rather long, nose, broken in play as a child, which added to the sculptured, formal look of his face, and gave him, with his quiet, an air of always 'thinking' – and I think he always was!

He spoke little and quietly, with a faint Scots accent, much less than that of his sisters. He was very long to reply. Reply was a serious, considered business. My mother had a story of seeing me seated facing him on his lap, thumping him gently and saying in exasperation 'Say words, Daddy!' But his smile and courtesy were always there, so that no one would consider him withdrawn, in spite of his silences.

His movements were, like all craftsmen's, very disciplined. On one occasion someone tumbled a clock

4. George Walton with his son Edward, *c*. 1930.

from a mantelpiece and he got his foot underneath it to break its fall. He always drew at a board, slightly sloped, on a plan chest or trestle, and always stood. He also drew and painted at an upright easel, or on a temporary studio partition, built on giant bamboos. At the end of each day's work he tidied his board, pencils and instruments and laid them out for the next day.

I see his clothes again, sometimes, in the photographs of older statesmen alive in the twenties: dark suits, waistcoat and watch chain, and the essential grey Homburg hat. His suits, made by Gunn & Colley, were carefully saved, lasting for twenty years or more, I think. Even when working he dressed formally. I understood that a tweed suit worn before lunch was, to my father, used in younger days to a morning coat, quite a daring and informal get-up.

These last sentences show how difficult it is for me to recreate the man and the atmosphere for others. If I refer to the *Punches* of the 1880s and 90s, a world in which my father in his twenties was already making a reputation, I see jokes, servants, classes, scenes which reflect the world in which my begetter and kind guardian and loving parent had his place, a world to which we can today only relate theoretically.

That he flourished for some thirty years, from say 1886 to the First World War, with so gentle a temperament must have meant a security from somewhere to back his native talent. (My mother said 'Your father wasn't a fighter, you know'.) That security came from a large and loving Scots family, twelve children in all, the eldest (Gilbert) having gone to Australia before my father's birth. Lack of funds, a good basic education, and the Scots need to succeed pushed them all forward. My grandfather, Jackson, a charming spendthrift, died when my father was quite a youth, and many of the children still training. My Aberdeen grandmother, a lady of gentle manner, but, I think, iron will, raised them all to success and even distinction in their careers. My impression is that they shared each other's success, like the members of a regiment.

Glasgow in the 1880s and 90s was a buoyant, expansive place, full of opportunity. The tobacco trade, then the shipbuilding on the Clyde, a diversity of manufacturing industries and Glasgow's role in the 'modernising' of Scotland under Victoria produced a stratum of wealthy entrepreneurs. Trains were thundering to and fro from England, and the gas-lit mansions of the new industrial masters were going up on the fringes of Glasgow and in the country nearby. Although George Walton was a quiet, modest man, he started work in an atmosphere where anything might be tried, and almost anything was possible. It was in this context that he worked his artistic revolution.

My grandfather, by George Walton Scott

I was twelve when my grandfather died in 1933. My mother was his daughter by his first marriage, Marguerite. His second marriage late in life led to the curious circumstance that his second child, my 'Uncle Edward', was only a year or so older than I. My own childhood memories of my grandfather overlap to a great extent with Edward's. Other reminiscences come mostly through my mother.

My grandfather spoke to me as an equal on my visits to his house in Sterne Street near Shepherd's Bush. He was never condescending to the young. As an infant I used to sit on his knee while he sang songs ('There was a wee cooper who came from Fyfe' was my favourite), recited poems, or played finger games, like 'Here's the church, and there's the steeple ...', which would always make me laugh. I remember the smell of to-

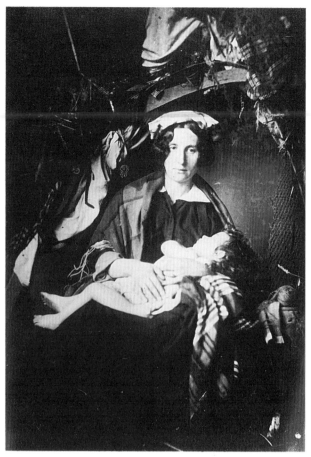

5. George Walton's mother, Eliza Ann Nicholson, and one of her many children posing for 'The Gipsy Tent', a photograph taken in 1859 by Jackson Walton.

bacco and fresh soap. He spoke with a slight but clearly recognizable Scots accent, pronouncing the 'h's in 'which' and 'when' and speaking vowels as pure sounds. He would slip from speech into silence but gave no impression that he was bored with me. I only remember that his silences seemed to produce a sense of peace with his surroundings. His movements and gestures were elegant and slightly formal; he had a presence which drew your attention as soon as he entered a room.

George Walton's manners and way of speaking were indeed those of an earlier age, inherited from his father and mother, directly and via his older brothers and sisters. His father, Jackson Walton, who died when he was a boy, was a man of strong will and charm. Born in 1808, he was already twenty-nine when Victoria came to the throne, and he retained the Regency manners of his youth throughout his life. When he married Eliza Ann Nicolson in 1844 the couple drove to church preceded by a carriage full of flowers, and followed by another similarly laden. The characteristically Victorian values of frugality and self-help would have seemed ridiculous to Jackson. He had considerable artistic talent and energy, but he was careless with money and the family depended very much on the determination and sense of Eliza Ann. She could trace her descent back to James IV of Scotland through the 4th Earl of Huntley and Margaret Drummond Stuart: the family came from the Orkneys. She was much younger than he was, almost twenty years. Margery Hutchison, a daughter of E. A. Walton, told me that she married Jackson against her will.

George Walton did not inherit much of his father's flamboyance, but he does seem to have adopted some of his mannerisms. His self-assurance and sophisticated yet natural good manners stood him in good stead after he moved from Scotland to London in 1897. He became acquainted with Princess Louise, a daughter of Queen Victoria, who was keenly interested in the arts and kept a studio in Kensington Palace where he was a frequent visitor. She commissioned him to design her dress for the coronation of her brother Edward VII. My mother told how Princess Louise was giving my grandfather a lift in her coach through Kensington Gardens one morning, when he saw his wife and daughter walking towards them. With great aplomb he lifted his hat ceremoniously as the coach passed them by.

On this occasion George Walton was no doubt wearing a morning coat, but I remember him only dressed in tweeds, with his tie sitting neatly on a stiff or semi-stiff collar, and shoes always brightly polished. Even when painting he remained smartly clad. There appears to have been little dressing in the bohemian manner in Scotland at the end of the nineteenth century: as the botanist Professor John Walton, son of George's brother, the painter E. A. Walton, wrote: 'All the artists wore conventional dress. They were too busy to be arty' (*Glasgow Herald* 6 October 1961). However the Waltons had a long tradition of dressing up for special occasions. They devised amateur theatricals to raise money for charity. Some of this was recorded by Jackson, who was one of the earliest amateur photographers. One series of daguerreotypes shows Eliza Ann and the family dressed as tinkers. The family also dressed up as 'Nigger Minstrels' and 'Chinamen'. In fact the Waltons would put on fancy dress at the drop of a hat.

This continued as a hobby for George Walton in later life. During the early years of this century J. B. B. Wellington, a well-known photographer and technical innovator, took a series of photographs of my grandfather and my mother in various guises – a Harlequin, a Russian, a Dutch girl, a princess. Wellington was a close friend of George Walton and one of his principal patrons.

Amateur theatricals and fancy dress entertainments were common pastimes in artistic circles at this period. My mother was a natural actress. Once George Bernard Shaw saw her in one of her amateur roles and asked

6. George Walton and his daughter Marguerite attired for one of J. B. B. Wellington's photographic extravaganzas: taken in the entrance hall of the Leys.

my grandfather whether she could appear in his play 'St Joan'. He refused to allow it: the daughters of those who belonged to what were called the professional classes did not go on the stage. Although he never treated anyone in a superior manner, George Walton adhered to some prejudices prevalent at the time. He certainly believed in a pecking order within the professions. I remember that he was shocked when, after a visit to the dentist, I mentioned that I was fascinated with the surgery and thought I might be a dentist when I grew up.

While George Walton was married to my grandmother, Kate Gall, there seemed no need for them to save money: her family was wealthy, and he was at the height of his career. Parties at their house at 44 Holland Street, Kensington, were frequent and spectacular, some in fancy dress. As my mother and friends of hers who were invited recalled, red carpets were laid out at the entrance to the house, which was festooned with a mass of flowers, and my grandfather would devise all kinds of other decorations. Dance orchestras were hired, and the parties continued into the early hours.

At this period Walter Crane lived a few steps away at 13 Holland Street and the Cranes and Waltons frequently visited one another. Walter Crane was very fond of my mother when she was a child and decorated the plain wallpaper in her nursery with beautiful drawings of animals and plants.

My mother's extravagant way of life continued in the twenties: my parents would dress up in exotic costumes for the Chelsea Arts Ball and other venues, and they entertained constantly, if a little less formally than my grandparents. Their house attracted many artists: my godfather Ian Strang, was a frequent visitor, also James Pryde and Augustus John. My mother's cousin Margery also came, with her husband W. O. Hutchison, later President of the Royal Scottish Academy and head of the Glasgow School of Art. There was more than a little of Jackson about my mother: she was gifted. She and Margery would paint beautiful decorations on plates, cups and saucers, with no thought of selling the designs.

The style of my grandfather's life however changed abruptly during the First World War when Kate died and the Gall money disappeared: as far as I know he was left nothing. And during the latter part of his life he found commissions hard to come by, as new concepts in design took over. He moved to a small house he had designed in Sterne Street, with his second wife Daphne. As a small boy I noticed the sharp difference between my parents' lifestyle and that of my grandfather. My mother and Daphne were also markedly different. My mother was spectacular, careless, spendthrift and sophisticated. Daphne was quiet and matter of fact. They were not compatible.

Designed for practical use and furnished with my grandfather's own work, the small rooms in the Sterne Street house were easy to run. The house was separated from his studio by a small courtyard with classical plaques on the walls. The studio was a place of great activity, full of finished and half-finished work stacked away neatly in corners. Sometimes my grandfather would be standing at a drawing board when I arrived. He would slowly lay down his brushes, and then lift me up into the air. Sometimes he would give me a piggy-back. His assistant Cassie Partridge would be nearby at her drawing board, helping him with his textile designs. I remember her bright red hair, but little else except that she seemed unobtrusive and gentle.

My grandfather used to make all kinds of paper hats and darts for Edward and me. He once made us two nearly identical castles out of orange boxes and brown paper. The buildings were placed on tall rocky foundations painted grey and brown. The paths serpentining upwards were made of sandpaper.

There were not many books at Sterne Street: my mother told me that her father rarely read. She could remember him sitting by the fire during winter evenings looking into its midst, lost in thought. Throughout his life he was interested in shapes, colours, and the construction of objects. Perhaps he saw some of these things in the flames and burning coals.

Although I always remembered George Walton as a grandfather who was close to me, I never really began to appreciate his kindness, nor understand his problems or his sadness, until long after he was dead. Now his old-fashioned manners and generosity of spirit remain deeply imprinted on my mind. As his friend C. F. A. Voysey wrote: ' He was the most gentle of men, with strong feelings always under control.'

But there is also another side to George Walton. He possessed much of his mother's grit and fortitude, as is illustrated by a letter he wrote in 1927. At this period when his fortunes were at a low ebb and his work not much appreciated he wrote to Morton Sundour Fabrics about a design the firm had found unsuitable: 'I thought I had arrived at a solution but it does one good to be up against difficulties and to solve them – I am having another go at it. I do not like to be beaten and I am most anxious to achieve a real success at this.'

As a young man of twenty-one with very little money George Walton abandoned a safe future at the British Linen Bank in Glasgow to set up his firm George Walton & Co. That determination and perseverance remained with him throughout his life.

I BEGINNINGS

Glasgow was the city of George Walton's birth. His father was from Manchester, his mother from Aberdeen, but by 1862 they had settled in Glasgow, one of the fastest growing of Britain's mid-Victorian industrial centres. Glasgow was a city of huge contrasts. On the one hand, its cholera epidemics drew national attention to some of the worst slum areas in Britain; on the other, it was a city bursting with commercial energy, a place where fortunes were made. For those with business skill and daring the possibilities were boundless.

Jackson Walton was fifty-three when he arrived in Glasgow with his wife and large family.[1] He had had no settled occupation for some years. The son of a wealthy cotton importer, he had inherited a flourishing commission agency in 1838, but the business succumbed to his indifference. Jackson was a flamboyant character, more Georgian than Victorian. He believed it to be a gentleman's right not to work, and he lived in style. His move to Glasgow in 1862 suggests that the pressures of the real world had begun to claim his attention. He now had eleven children; probably the nine born by his second wife Eliza moved with him to Glasgow and another would soon be on the way.

7. Jackson Walton, *c.* 1870.

Glasgow promised opportunity, and the hopeful gravitated to it from far and wide. The city's prosperity had come initially through the tobacco trade with the American colonies. Various manufacturing industries had grown alongside. Later the textile industry assumed greater importance and shipping, which had always been important for trade, combined with the new iron- and steel-making industries to make Glasgow one of the foremost centres of shipbuilding in Europe. Steam locomotive and coach-building had a parallel success. Iron foundries had gained prominence in the manufacture of architectural ironwork and constructional parts, which were exported worldwide. Carpets, fabric production and dying, threadmaking and the production of textile machinery would continue to prosper well into the twentieth century despite the general decline of the textile industry. Glasgow was remarkable for the great diversity of its manufacturing concerns. The rapid success of many new enterprises and the swift rise to prosperity of vigorous entrepreneurs were characteristic of the times.

Yet the tale of Jackson's stay in Glasgow is not a settled one. The family was uprooted time and again to different parts of the city while Jackson followed successive enthusiasms. His abilities were creative and practical, and though he tried for a while to re-establish his career as a commission agent, he eventually abandoned this for the manufacture of patented steam boiler coverings; five years later he had set up again as a manufacturing chemist. But if he had no talent for business, there were other pleasures. He had always enjoyed painting and had produced over the years a number of small, sensitive landscapes in oil. He also made successful forays into photography, creating carefully arranged subject pieces, sometimes with Eliza as model, which belong to the early photographer's search for a means of artistic expression within the new medium (pl. 5).

Despite its industrial bias, Glasgow was an ideal habitat for the artistically inclined. Photography as a science and a commercial enterprise of course had its place in Glasgow's industrial landscape. But Scotland was the home of some of the earliest photographers of the pictorial tradition, including D. O. Hill and Robert Adamson, and at this date Glasgow could boast Thomas Annan, who was becoming a significant figure. His business, established in 1855, specialised in the reproduction of works of art and the survey he would make in a few years' time of the city's slums would be an original and important contribution to his field.[2] In architecture, the original and eclectic work of Alexander Thomson demonstrated the vitality of Glasgow's Classical tradition. Avid collecting amongst some of the leading industrialists had encouraged the growth of a lively art dealing sector and, had Jackson idled his time in Craibe Angus's or Alexander Reid's gallery, he would have rubbed shoulders with shippers, warehousemen, and manufacturers of bleach, chemicals and pig-iron, creators of Glasgow's wealth. There was a growing number of better educated, more leisured and increasingly cultured men and women, the progeny of industrial success, for whom Glasgow would need to provide.

Opportunities for art training, however, were limited and the situation was exacerbated by Edinburgh's pompous insularity. The Royal Scottish Academy based in Edinburgh was the central exhibiting body for Scotland and long-established rivalry between the two main cities had led to an impasse: Glasgow artists were effectively barred from showing their work. Many of Glasgow's most talented painters left the city to settle either in Edinburgh or London, but by the time Jackson arrived a resistance movement had formed. In 1861 the Fine Art Institute (later the Royal Glasgow Institute of the Fine Arts) was founded to provide an alternative exhibiting venue, and soon the Glasgow Art Club would be set up as a meeting point for artists. Glasgow was fast becoming a progressive artistic environment.

Amongst his children Jackson was no doubt delighted to find signs of artistic talent. Helen was twelve years old when her family moved to Glasgow and within a few years it was clear she had inherited the creative side of Jackson's nature. She was the third child born to him by his second wife Eliza, and later would be an important influence on her youngest brother, George. In 1865 she was sent to Glasgow's School of Design.[3] Set up in 1840 at a time when efforts were being made to improve the standard of design (particularly for the textile industry in its competition with France), the School was originally intended for the training of working-class men and women for positions in industry. By the mid-1860s when Helen was enrolled, the type of training it offered – mainly in drawing and pattern design – had attracted growing numbers of gentlewomen in reduced circumstances to whom art teaching could offer a respectable source of income. Helen's attendance at the classes is likely to indicate her family's financial difficulties as much as their desire for her fulfilment.

The School of Design was hardly the most inspirational place for a young artist. Its training was stiff and traditional, offering classes in drawing and painting from plaster casts or copies, relieved for Helen by the plant drawing in which she excelled. She rose above the difficulties, and her ability was recognised in a series of awards culminating in the Haldane Prize in 1871, her last year of attendance.

By this year problems at home were on the increase. Jackson's commitment to steam boiler coverings was wavering and, worse, he was showing signs of increasing ill health. The Glasgow years had produced another three additions to the family: Hannah was born in 1862, Constance (or Connie as she was to the family) three years later, and 3 June 1867 had brought Eliza's twelfth and final child, George Henry. Jackson's young family was in no position to be abandoned, but in 1873 he became seriously ill and died of tuberculosis.

8. Eliza Ann Nicholson: a photographic portrait of his mother by George Walton.

Eliza Ann Nicholson, from a Quaker background, had married a man seventeen years older than herself, and now, at forty-seven, far from being worn down by constant child-rearing, she showed her strength of spirit. It was easy now to recognise how she had become the mainstay of the family, how her straight–forward determination to make things work, her perseverance, had held them all together through the years. Of the eight children who were probably still at home at this stage, Helen, now twenty-three, could provide the needed support in managing the family; Richard and William would have been settling into the insurance business in which they both found work; Dora and Edward Arthur were in their teens; and there were the three young ones, Hannah, Connie and six-year-old George.

How the family managed is not clear. The wealth Jackson and Eliza had known in their youth had dwindled over the years. He had been a capable man, but irresolute, and (it could not be denied) a spendthrift and a gambler. As the years went on the family's finances became increasingly strained.

1881 was the year of Richard's wedding. He had moved to Newcastle some years before, where he met Judith Crawhall, whose father Joseph was a distinguished woodcut artist and illustrator.[4] Their marriage underlines the fact that the family's income generators had by this time assumed their own responsibilities. William must long since have moved away. At home Eliza had five unmarried daughters, Edward and George.

9. George Walton in his early teens.

Glasgow Boys, Glasgow Girls

When Jackson died there had been no family business to pass on. His legacy came in a different form. Helen and the four children of his later years – Edward, Hannah, Connie and George – showed remarkable ability in creative work and the Walton house became a veritable art club on its own. Helen is likely to have been a powerful encouragement, and Edward's early drawings showed surprising assurance. Now in 1881 Edward was adult, making a career for himself in the arts. A few years ago in 1876, the family had managed to support him for a year at the Staatliche Kunstakademie in Düsseldorf. These days he was busy on sketching trips with his artist friends James Guthrie and George Henry, exhibiting where he could and selling work. The family association with the Crawhalls had brought a close friendship with Judith's brother, also called Joseph, who like them was committed to an artistic career, and the young men travelled together in the summer, working through the winter on canvases in preparation for exhibitions in the spring.[5]

At this stage Edward's contribution to the family purse is unlikely to have been significant, though he was beginning to attract attention in the local press. At home, his family struggled on in genteel poverty. Helen had already begun to take students for private drawing and painting classes, supplementing this income by the sale of pottery and glass decorated with her floral and insect studies transformed into delicate patterns. Thirteen-year-old George's school fees at Partick Academy could no longer be maintained and he was found a position in a bank.[6]

Edward was now the bright hope of the family and his career would be followed with much interest by his younger brother George. Although on his return from Düsseldorf in 1877 his application to the Glasgow Art Club had been rejected, he had found stimulating relationships with other painters, whose friendship offered mutual support. An older group of conservative historical and genre painters had settled in the Glasgow Institute and the Glasgow Art Club: at the one the young men were discouraged by criticism, at the other they were rejected. Edward and his friends soon met a variety of other artists who shared their views. Their disgust at the sentimental subject matter of their elders, and dislike of their muddy, overworked technique added to the bitterness of rejection and stirred their rebel instincts. They determined to learn nothing from the 'Gluepots', as they called the Art Club group, and looked instead for inspiration to the works from London, France and Holland which appeared from time to time at the Glasgow Institute, at Craibe Angus's or Alexander Reid's. Several of the Glasgow artists had worked in

10. Edward Arthur Walton. Note the Japanese print and a north country spindleback chair of the type used later in the Buchanan Street tea rooms.

11. George Walton (behind) with the Glasgow Boys on a sketching trip at Cockburnspath in 1883. Left to right: E. A. Walton, Joseph Crawhall, George, James Guthrie and J. Whitelaw Hamilton.

France, where their association with the English painters William Stott of Oldham, H. H. La Thangue, and George Clausen had encouraged a less provincial outlook. Their mutual desire for recognition was allied with a yearning to find an alternative manner of expression and they united in a search for fresher subjects and a brighter palette.

In France they were not attracted by the Impressionists so much as by Bastien-Lepage, with his loose brushwork, his stress on composition, and his straightforward approach to peasant subjects. The truthful recording of the Impressionists did not appeal to the Glasgow painters. They were keen to capture the effects of sunlight, but were not prepared to throw over composition as a tool in their search for beauty, even if this meant beauty at the expense of 'truth'. If the Impressionists influenced them it was to encourage an interest in light and an enthusiasm for working out of doors.

In this way Edward and his closest friends – Guthrie, Lavery, Crawhall and Henry – came to be associated with a wider movement among artists in Glasgow away from the Art Club's approved formula and style. They were a loose-knit, disparate group with varying styles of work, but for the aims they held in common they came to be known as the Glasgow Boys.[7] Their search was for a fresh means of expression, rather than a new theoretical framework, and a loose adoption of the 'Art for Art's Sake' doctrines of James McNeill Whistler and Oscar Wilde in London suited them well, freed them to search for themselves for beauty and decorative qualities unhindered by the Victorian yoke of moralistic sentiment. The Glasgow Boys were not confrontational.

They did not look for radical subject matter in the city streets around them, nor in their preferred country subjects were they concerned with the social comment of the French Realist painters; but from the stuffy works of the Gluepots they effected a transformation. By their lyrical harmonies of colour, their rejection of superfluous detail in favour of looser brushwork, and in the fresh open-air quality of their work they formed a coherent standpoint which could not be ignored. The Glasgow Art Club might not like the new style but they could no longer deny that the artists were a force to be reckoned with. From the mid 1880s the barriers weakened and the artists began to receive the recognition they had earned.

If Whistler's arguments were attractive, so was his work. His emphasis on the overall decorative qualities of painting rather than on particularities of subject appealed to the Glasgow painters. His influence was soon apparent in the arrangement of their compositions, in their use of colour and patterning, and, more widely, in a concern for the architectural setting of their work and an appreciation of Japanese art. In the later years of the 1880s the decorative aspect of the Boys' paintings was accentuated. New elements from the Celtic revival would be assimilated, together with the compositional lessons of Japanese art. Whistler's assertive personality and innovative work attracted a group of admirers who regarded him as master. Several of the Glasgow Boys, including Edward, were won. Stott of Oldham, a close associate of Whistler's until 1887, may have introduced them. He certainly encouraged their approbation.

The grievances of Edward's friends in London

13. George Walton on an outing with three of his sisters. Left to right Dora, Hannah and Helen.

against the exclusive tendencies of the Royal Academy paralleled the Glasgow Boys' resentment at the Art Club. In 1886 a number of the London artists joined to form a new exhibiting society which they called the New English Art Club. Many of Whistler's followers became involved and the Glasgow Boys were quickly invited to join. There were substantial showings of their work in 1887 and 1888. Edward's involvement ensured his knowledge of developments in the London decorative arts as in the same years a splinter group of the Art Workers' Guild (set up to unite 'craftsmen in architecture, painting, sculpture and the kindred arts') formed to organise exhibitions for the decorative arts, and there was some discussion between the two groups on the possibility of joint action. Instead, in 1888, the Arts and Crafts Exhibition Society was formed. The link between the Glasgow Boys and the London decorative artists would soon be openly declared in the headpiece

12. Frontispiece of the first issue of the *Scottish Art Review*, June 1888, designed by Selwyn Image.

of the *Scottish Art Review's* first number in 1888, designed by Selwyn Image, co-founder of the Century Guild.

For George, life in the 1880s was centred around the artistic interests of his family. It was clear the British Linen Bank held no attraction for him (he was later described by his son as 'not at all numerate'),[8] but he struggled on. Whenever there was opportunity he would be off with Edward, joining his sketching trips or dropping in to the studio at Bath Street. He was the impressionable teenager, absorbed by the artists' discussions on technique, informed by their views on developments in London, excited by their work, delighted at their success.

In 1884, there was a visit to London, when George, no doubt accompanied by Edward, stayed for a fortnight in the capital. Perhaps they went to Dowdeswell's gallery to see Whistler's latest triumph (his 'Notes' – 'Harmonies' – 'Nocturnes'); or called in to Morris & Co.'s showroom in Oxford Street. There were so many things to explore. It is likely that a generous amount of time was spent with a young lady called Kate Gall, for it was on this trip that she and George became engaged.[9]

Back in Glasgow, George was crushing as many art classes as he could manage and afford into his daily routine, both before and after office hours. Some of these were at the Glasgow School of Art (as the School of Design was re-named in 1869),[10] where Helen had trained and where Edward had studied for a while on his return from Düsseldorf. 1885 brought a change of principal at the School and a breath of fresh air. Francis - better known as 'Fra' – Newbery had arrived from

London, bringing with him from his previous post at South Kensington the news and enthusiasms of artists and craftsmen in the south, and an eagerness to develop the decorative arts at his new Glasgow School.

George was also attending classes with P. M. McGregor Wilson – an artist associated with the Glasgow Boys, though not closely attached to the group. With D. M. McKinlay he took students at his short-lived 'Glasgow Atelier Fine Arts', next door to Edward's studio at 162 Bath Street, from 1887-9.[11] Bath Street was teeming with artists and George had ample occasion to meet the other painters more widely associated with his brother's group, amongst them Whitelaw Hamilton, Alexander Mann, Arthur Melville, E. A. Hornel and David Gauld. At W. Y. MacGregor's studio close by he might have met James Paterson, and at Alexander Roche's, William Kennedy and Thomas Millie Dow.

Helen had settled seriously into art teaching, running her studio from the family home at 5 Belmont Terrace, Hillhead. She gave classes in drawing and painting, in watercolour and oils. She also taught her techniques of china and glass decoration.[12] Helen's work in these media was becoming known in Glasgow circles and there were numerous orders, which had to be fitted into the hours between classes. Hannah had already benefited from Helen's teaching. She had a special aptitude for fine work and with Helen's guidance, they could now collaborate on the decorative work, sharing ideas and sometimes working on individual pieces together. They bought porcelain tableware blanks, from the local J. & M. P. Bell & Co., sometimes tiles, and uncut glass vases, perhaps from the local firm

15. Glass jug decorated by Hannah Walton.

of Couper & Sons. To these they painstakingly transferred the details of their botanical sketches and underwater scenes.[13] Hannah's talent for detail made her ideally suited to miniature painting and she added to the skills of their studio when she began to work on cameo portraits and miniature repairs. Occasionally they would also collaborate on embroidery.

Helen's studio, established by 1881, was a precursor of the 'sisters' studios' which would blossom in the 1890s.[14] It set a precedent which encouraged others to follow. Though neither Helen nor Hannah (who became an official 'teacher' in Helen's studio in 1890) benefited from the instruction of the new Technical Art Studios which Newbery opened in 1892, and though their range of skills did not include the metalwork which featured so prominently in the 1890s, the decorative emphasis of their work was widely known and Helen's experience and abilities as a teacher of craftwork were publicly recognised when she was invited to join the School of Art staff in 1895.

Connie, meanwhile, was concentrating on her painting. In the later 1880s she had the opportunity to travel to Paris to study in Krug's studio and Colarossi's, though it is not easy to imagine how this was financed.[15] She was adept at flower studies, and her watercolours were exceptional. She had a bolder approach than her sisters and enjoyed working on a larger scale, though it was her watercolour painting which would gain her early recognition.

Of all George's many siblings Edward and Hannah were the closest to him in friendship. George and Hannah were closer in age; and in many ways they had the most in common. They shared an interest in

14. Helen Walton at work in her studio.

16. Tea cup and saucer with butterfly motif decorated by Helen Walton.

17. Ceramic tile decorated by Hannah Walton: a design after Burne-Jones.

decorative work and Hannah's admiration of the Pre-Raphaelites would be echoed in George's later work. He could not match her sensitive draughtsmanship, but her clear colours, sharp eye for detail and delicacy of touch were shared. While Edward and Constance both had the benefit of training abroad, there were no similar opportunities for George and Hannah, which must inevitably have encouraged the sympathy between them. And now Hannah was becoming a successful artist in her own right, which George could not have failed to recognise.

No doubt he often met other women artists of Glasgow through his sisters and friends. There was a great deal of talent among the sisters of the Glasgow Boys: the painter Maggie Hamilton, sister of J. Whitelaw Hamilton, for instance, was the same age as George and a family friend. Throughout the 1880s there was a strong movement amongst women painters for greater recognition, and the particular frustrations of being excluded from life classes on account of their sex, and of reliance on bazaars and the like as the only outlet for their work, prompted the formation of a society. The Glasgow Society of Lady Artists held their first exhibition in 1883. For some reason, possibly financial (the joining fees amounted to a guinea), Helen at first held aloof from their meetings, though those involved were doubtless known to her.[16]

George Walton had unusual opportunities through his family for acquaintance with a wide cross section of artistic Glasgow society. The School of Art links, the women artists, Helen's students and clients in and out of the studio at home, the Glasgow Boys and their supporters, were connections which gave access to many overlapping social circles, which in the future would stand him in good stead. By the end of 1887, on the eve of George's new venture, there were signs that the efforts his family had put into their individual artistic careers were bearing fruit.

Decorative Currents

During the third quarter of the 1880s, it is likely that Walton's aspiration to form a decorating company was becoming clearly defined. Perhaps McGregor Wilson or Newbery had recognised George's talents for what they were – he was no draughtsman, but he shared his sister Helen's skills in pattern making, had a remarkable sense of colour, a natural talent for handling form, and a practical capability inherited from his father. If they advised him accordingly, they might have prompted his action.

Yet Walton's direction to decorative work (rather than painting) is easily explained. His sisters' activities were an important stimulus, and the Glasgow Boys' emphasis on the decorative was inspirational: indeed it would lead many of their own number to an involvement with the decorative arts in the 1890s, Hornel and Macgillivray producing graphic work for *The Evergreen* and David Gauld, Harrington Mann, Henry, Hornel, Cameron, Guthrie and Millie Dow all generating designs for stained glass in the 1890s. There were other currents. The Aesthetic Movement had brought to Glasgow the inspiration of Morris's glass, 'Queen Anne' style fireplaces and Godwin furniture through the exploits of Daniel Cottier's firm.[17] Glasgow had lent some of its finest designers to the Aesthetic cause, among them J. J. Stevenson, Bruce Talbert, J. M.

Brydon, Christopher Dresser[18] and Cottier himself, several of whom returned from time to time to restore to Glasgow the fruits of their endeavours in the south. In the 1870s and 1880s stained glass and interior decorating firms like Cottier's had flourished, Adam & Small and J. & W. Guthrie among the most important. Cottier's jubilant collaborations with William Leiper (Glasgow's architectural Goth) outside the city, and with Alexander Thomson within, could hardly have passed by someone in Walton's circumstances.[19] Neither could Morris's regular lectures in Edinburgh and Glasgow, which ensured that his work and ideas were well known. As *The Studio* remarked in 1912, 'When William Morris first visited Glasgow to lecture, and sat with his young student host far into the night discussing ideals, even he with his big mind and hopeful temperament must have failed to grasp the length to which a decade or two of earnest art teaching and practice would carry the new movement': it is unfortunate that the identity of the student is not known.[20]

Amongst other influences from the south, the work of Mackmurdo and the Century Guild was currently reaching Glasgow through illustrations in *The Cabinet Maker* and *The Art Journal* in the years immediately preceding the establishment of Walton's firm.[21] Mackmurdo had links with Scotland through the work of the Home Arts and Industries Association of which he was founder, which had done much to encourage craftwork in Glasgow.[22] Periodicals like *The Magazine of Art*, *The Journal of Decorative Art*, *The Artist* and *The Art Journal* had spread the influence of the Aesthetic Movement nationally. The furniture and decorative work of E. W. Godwin would have been well-known for some time – illustrated frequently, available through William Watt's 1877 catalogue, *Art Furniture*, and widely plagiarised by the trade.[23] Godwin's connection with Whistler adds weight to the idea that Walton modelled himself to some extent on Godwin (who produced metalwork, carpets and stencilled friezes as well as furniture and buildings), or at least on the joint personality of the Godwin-Whistler partnership in design. Whistler had been involved in a series of decorative projects both with E. W. Godwin and Thomas Jeckyll, insisting this was all the Artist's domain. Edward's admiration for Whistler had infected his brother (Edward even called his white cat 'Dado' after Whistler's light interiors). It was Whistler above all to whom Walton pointed as the inspiration for his career.[24]

The current rage for Japanese art and design (not least in the form of the Anglo-Japanese furnishings and

18. Edward Walton's studio at Cambuskenneth, *c.* 1888. Could this be George's first fireplace decoration?

wallpapers of Talbert, Godwin and Dresser) stimulated the decorative instinct. Edward was a particular enthusiast, and his brother undoubtedly concurred. It was an enthusiasm shared with his sisters. While Edward had his own small collection of Japanese prints, Helen and Hannah's glass and porcelain decoration, with its butterflies, dragonflies and fish, often reflects the influence of Japanese woodcuts and sometimes the direct inspiration of items in the City of Glasgow's Japanese collection.[25]

Added together, the strength of these currents drew Walton. The wider possibilities of decorative work were known to him; funds for training as a painter were not available; and Whistler's decorative feats, the startling performances in colour of his exhibition interiors, he could not remove from his mind.[26] In Glasgow – that surprising city of art and enterprise, feverish with activity towards the end of 1887 on the eve of its own International Exhibition – the atmosphere was ripe for such a venture, and it was reasonable to assume that there would be a market for his work.

Some savings had no doubt been set aside, some decorative experiments carried out perhaps at Edward's studio or the family home. Whatever artistic work George had done over these years when the bank had stolen his time, no evidence of it now remains, but that it was sufficient in quantity and merit to prompt an unusual commission, cannot be questioned. In 1888, Catherine Cranston, a local restaurateur, offered him work on the redecoration of her Argyle Street premises and at the age of twenty-one, George Walton abandoned his career in finance, never to return.

II GEORGE WALTON & CO., GLASGOW

At the beginning of 1888, George Walton was a decorator only in aspiration, at most, an amateur. In taking him on, Kate Cranston showed her imagination. She was a lady of character. From a family of hoteliers and restaurateurs, she had flouted middle-class convention when, following the example of her brother Stuart, a tea dealer who had opened the city's first tea room, she set up her own business at 114 Argyle Street in 1878. This had been followed eight years later by a modest expansion to the ground floor of 205 Ingram Street. The city centre tea room was a brilliant solution, at a time of strong temperance sentiment, to the separate needs of businessmen and of ladies out shopping. Pioneered by the Cranstons in the 1880s, the Glasgow tea room was given a significant boost by the Exhibition of 1888: by the late 1890s and early 1900s it was a phenomenon for which the city was internationally renowned. Despite her brother's prior claim, it was Kate, the redoubtable 'Miss Cranston', who, with her emphasis on the best quality in catering and decor, became in public eyes the 'originator of the essential Glasgow tea room'.[1]

Kate Cranston's refurbishment of 1888 at Argyle Street was undoubtedly her opportunist response to the approaching International Exhibition.[2] She was not alone. Up and down the main streets of Glasgow, shop fronts were being painted, new businesses opened, every commercial operation finely tuned to the surge of business opportunities the Exhibition was expected to generate. Spurred by its burgeoning civic pride Glasgow had joined the ranks of ambitious cities keen to follow the tradition established by Prince Albert's Great Exhibition of 1851 at the Crystal Palace. Glasgow claimed recognition as a major centre of manufacturing and international trade, in the Empire second only to London.

Launching out

Early in 1888 Walton joined the mêlée, opening his own premises, 'George Walton & Co. Ecclesiastical and House Decorators', at 152 Wellington Street.[3] Though he may not have expected his new business to benefit directly from the Exhibition, the general atmosphere of insuppressible optimism about Glasgow towards the end of 1887 is likely to have been persuasive. The Exhibition was already providing new openings for Edward and his sisters. Helen and Hannah were busy preparing exhibits. Edward was hard at work on designs for a panel for the dome of the main Exhibition hall, a commission shared with James Guthrie, John Lavery and George Henry – the first sign of official recognition for the Glasgow Boys from the city.[4]

All in all, it was an auspicious year. In London, those of the Art Workers' Guild who preferred corporate action to talk were now well ahead with plans for their first exhibition to be held in the autumn at the New Gallery, an event which would consolidate the activities and direction of the new designers in London. Walton had perhaps already heard of another venture starting up in the south, Charles Robert Ashbee's Guild and School of Handicraft, a workshop and training school for the crafts.[5]

Part of Kate Cranston's undeniably successful business method was her considered combination of caution and nerve. So far her decorations had been Aesthetically artistic, not daringly out of line. By 1888 her business was sufficiently established to branch out – it was, after all, Exhibition year. Yet even now she took on the reputable but stylistically cautious Edinburgh decorators Scott Morton & Co. for her concurrent addition to Ingram Street.[6] Argyle Street was the venue for something different. George Walton was her intuitive choice.

All that survives now of Walton's earliest commission are two tiny photographs in a promotional booklet, produced by Miss Cranston's business c. 1898.[7] The first, showing a room in the prevalent Baronial style, does not seem particularly distinctive, though Walton's responsibilities may have stretched no further than the colour scheme, which the poorly reproduced monochrome illustration fails to transmit. The second, however, of a screened alcove decorated with floral patterns (pl. 19), gives a unique and revealing glimpse of Walton's decorative orientation at the outset of his career. Walton's briar and rose pattern, more open than the later wallpaper and textile designs for which Morris is so famous, was nevertheless close in conception to Morris's simpler patterns of the 1860s, a tradition continued in the painted interior decorations of Morris's firm. Based on the Tudor Rose, this type of design was by now common currency amongst the early Arts and Crafts designers.[8] Walton's interpretation of the motif – spare but decorative, ordered not distorted, bold in conception yet fresh and delicate in treatment – reveals characteristics of his approach to design which will identify his work in the future. The rose and briar is a connecting theme in Walton's output until the turn of the century.

19. A corner at Miss Cranston's Argyle Street tea rooms.

The screen and framework of the doorway may also be Walton's as a segregated area for ladies is a likely introduction at this stage of Miss Cranston's business. While the panelling design has indicated the direction of Walton's decorative future, the somewhat clumsy architectural detailing shows him, despite inexperience, ready to tackle three dimensional form. The heavy wood columns are capped with the exaggerated cyma recta moulding which later became integral to the Glasgow Style. The scrolled pediment and egg is especially intriguing. More sculptural than the 'Queen Anne' style detailing of the 1870s and 80s, can this show Walton's attraction (parallel to Mackintosh's of the early 1890s) to the more exuberant Baroque emerging in London? Such minimal evidence might perhaps be passed over were it not for Walton's personal connection with the breeding ground of the new Baroque, through the loose-knit circle of architects with Glasgow connections working in London. Walton's lasting friendship with Charles Edward Mallows, a Bedfordshire man working in William Flockhart's London office, is known to have started at this time. Flockhart was later recognised as a master of Edwardian Baroque. Mallows may well have been up in Glasgow early in this year working with Flockhart on Wylie & Lochhead's Exhibition display.[9]

A tea room on one of Glasgow's principal shopping streets made an appropriately public début for Walton's decorating career, and it was this for which, according to J. Taylor of *The Studio* in 1906, he abandoned his regular employment.[10] Yet it seems improbable that he would have left the security of his banking salary and taken on the burden of a rented showroom for this alone. Other commissions may well have been promised. Despite the difficulties of the Waltons' Glasgow years, the family was well-connected, and (no doubt because of the difficulties) there was a strong family loyalty. The clearer picture of 1891 shows Walton's company flourishing in the area of domestic decoration with a string of clients connected either directly or indirectly to the increasingly prosperous Glasgow Boys. The unknown jobs of 1888-90 are likely to have come from the same source. Certainly at the start, the advocacy of Edward is implied. The lack of available material on the first two years of Walton's practice suggests this work was small, private and domestic.

For this reason, the best-documented commission of the early years, the decoration of St Peter's Episcopal Church, Braid Street, from mid-1890, was probably not typical.[11] Nevertheless, it provides an illuminating view of how Walton's fledgling company could operate, particularly in its close collaboration amongst members of his family.

Constance had the major role, with responsibility for the decoration of the main walls of the building. Her scheme was a series of 'frescoes', for which she adopted a technique which had been developed by Puvis de Chavannes.[12] Gaining recognition as the first woman member of the Royal Scottish Society of Painters in Watercolour in the same year, Constance had a growing reputation and her collaboration may have lent greater credibility to the commission than George on his own could muster at this stage.

Walton & Co. were responsible for the decoration of the chancel roof, to which they applied a pattern of fleur-de-lis in green and gold on a light ground. A dove formed the central motif. The effect, executed in 'delicate tints' was 'mediaeval in character' and the surviving description suggests it was close to the type of decoration carried out by Morris & Co. in the 1860s at the Cambridge colleges and elsewhere. Walton's company was also responsible for the design of hangings for the altar. These, 'of pale green cloth worked in ivory silk' were the work of 'the Misses Walton' and of Mrs R. Y. Pickering (one of the group of lady artists intimate with the Walton family, who also worked the reredos to Walton's design).[13] 'The Misses Walton' are likely to have been Helen and Hannah – Constance clearly had enough to do. Hannah's involvement in her brother's company in its first few years reflects their affectionate relationship. It was her work which was sent, as one of two pieces, to convey the company's ethos at the prestigious Arts and Crafts Exhibition in London of 1890: whether or not she worked in an official capacity for the company, her connection was strong.[14]

Although Walton never learned a skilled craft like cabinet-making, his son reported of later years that when there was painting to do on stencilled friezes or murals, he was often to be found up on the ladder doing it himself.[15] With occasional help from his sisters, he is likely to have carried out the bulk of his earliest decorative work alone. The paint brush came easily to his hand. As the number of commissions grew, there was a need to employ others. The pattern began to change. By 1890, at the time of the St Peter's job, Robert Graham had joined the company. Walton & Co.'s second exhibit at the Arts and Crafts Exhibition of 1890 was a wallpaper, 'Lily and Rose', designed and executed by Graham. It may have been this design which Walton took the trouble to register. For Graham, it was a propitious start to a long association with the firm, culminating in his role as manager from 1903-5.[16]

20. A wallpaper registered by Walton & Co. in 1890; possibly the 'Lily and Rose' design which was exhibited at the Arts and Crafts Exhibition of that year.

Painting and paperhanging were the principal activities of Walton's business and it is likely that the wallpapers of a number of firms were available through the company's showrooms.[17] Graham's exhibit shows the firm designing and producing its own wallpapers, probably by block-printing – no doubt in emulation of Morris & Co. An experimental aspect of the early years, this activity was not maintained, but Walton's interests were expanding in other directions. In 1889 the work he submitted for exhibition at the Glasgow Institute was a design for stained glass.[18]

To complement the decorating and keep business flowing, there were various side-lines. In making picture frames Walton not only followed Whistler, but showed an astute grasp of his market.[19] He designed his own mouldings, took a fresh look at the construction, paid close attention to colour and finish, and sold them in the showroom. In Glasgow there was no shortage of demand.

Exhibition design had similar advantages. When Walton 'framed, draped and hung' W. M. Warneuke's photographic exhibition at Glasgow's East End Industrial Exhibition in 1890, it was probably one of several. Walton's association with this local photographer (whose wife was an artist) established his subsequent life-long link with the photographic world.[20]

For the Walton & Co. of 1888, decoration – the application of paint and pattern – was the first concern. The title 'Ecclesiastical and House Decorators' declares Walton's intention to compete on a modest scale with firms like J. & W. Guthrie, Cottier & Co. and Scott Morton for a share of the market in church and domestic interior work. Yet although the decorating was principally Whistler-inspired, from his earliest job at Argyle Street, Walton's eye to William Morris is evident. Events of the following years are likely to have attracted his attention more sharply to the Arts and Crafts movement of the south. Newbery arranged a series of lectures by leading lights of the Arts and Crafts at the School of Art: Walter Crane came to Glasgow for this purpose in 1888, William Morris in 1889 and Lewis Day in 1890, while a selection from the Arts and Crafts Exhibition Society's show of 1889 was set up at the Corporation Galleries in January 1890 a few months prior to the start of work at St Peter's.[21] Over the following months, the decoration of St Peter's was completed for all to see and George Walton & Co. underwent a transformation. The premises at Wellington Street were extended to the adjoining property, and the firm could now announce its skills and services as 'Glass Stainers, Embossers, and Gilders', and 'Furniture Warehouses', as well as 'Painters and Paperhangers'.[22] This expansion, which implicitly involved an increase of staffing and equipment, demonstrates Walton's growing commitment to the crafts.

Walton's choice of the rose as a motif initiating his decorative career appears with hindsight a symbolic gesture. With the new prominence given to it by Walton, the rose had arrived to oust the Aesthetic sunflower in Glasgow's decorative hierarchy – even as, in Walton's own work, the influence of the southern Arts and Crafts would grow to outweigh that of the Aesthetic Movement. By imitating the craft workshop ideal of Morris, with its associated themes of 'truth to materials' and emphasis on hand craftsmanship, funded by commitment more than cash, Walton brought the Arts and Crafts movement more fully to Glasgow than had Cottier before him. Planted in Glasgow's own distinctive environment, this generated the new decorative movement which grew on Glasgow soil.

The two years bridged by the St Peter's job (which ran from mid-1890 to February 1891) were crucial for establishing the company and its direction. Outside the firm, there were events of parallel significance.

Marriage, family matters and friends

They were important years for all the family. As Constance had gained from her mural work, so Hannah's confidence had grown and she was now operating as a teacher alongside Helen in the studio in Bothwell Terrace, Hillhead, where the family had moved in 1888.[23] The Glasgow Boys had benefited from the public opportunities of the International Exhibition and the bastion of the conservative establishment had at last been stormed: Edward followed Guthrie's admission as Associate of the Royal Scottish Academy in 1889. He was elected to the Glasgow Institute the following year. The Boys' success at the Grosvenor Gallery in London in May 1890 led to an autumn show in Munich and acclaim for their work on the continent. The last few years for the Glasgow Boys had meant not only greater recognition but subtle changes in direction. For Edward, Guthrie and Lavery, success would incline them increasingly to society portraiture and its financial rewards, but there were other drifts. The decorative tendency of their work had increased. Whistler and Japanese art were reaching the peak of their popularity: this was neatly underlined at the Glasgow Art Club's Fancy Dress Ball where Edward dressed as Hokusai while his fiancée Helen sported Whistler's emblem, the butterfly. (George appeared as a troubadour and his sister Dora as a milkmaid.) George Henry and E. A. Hornel began to experiment together on 'The Druids' with a greater emphasis on pattern and mural-like flattened perspective. They incorporated gesso, a medium exhibited recently in Glasgow by Walter Crane: the representations of the Arts and Crafts movement in the city, which had inevitably affected George, were not lost on the Glasgow Boys.[24] It was from this time that several of them began their involvement with stained glass design.

Edward had announced his engagement to the artist, Helen Law, née Henderson, at the Glasgow Art Club Ball. Helen was a Quaker, like his mother. She had been widowed after only a few months of marriage some years before and when Edward married her in June 1890, he adopted her eight-year-old daughter.[25] George was starting work at St Peter's at this time, and deep in plans for his own marriage the following year. Kate Gall was up from London from time to time, and, not long after Edward's wedding, she joined George and his Glasgow friends in rehearsals for one of their many social entertainments, a performance of *Twelfth Night*

21. Edward Walton and his wife Helen at their Glasgow home, decorated by Walton & Co. *c.* 1891.

in which Kate and Helen took the major parts (with Fra Newbery in a supporting role).[26] Kate's parents were very wealthy, established in fashionable society in London. Their agreement to the marriage would seem entirely improbable were it not that Kate's father was himself a self-made man with a strong interest in art objects (especially antique silver), which lends some credibility to his sympathy with George. It is likely there was a substantial marriage settlement intended to secure their future. How else can the company's recent confident expansion and the couple's implausible accommodation in the newly-built, enviably-modish Charing Cross Mansions be understood? The ceremony was performed on 3rd June 1891.[27]

In their Shakespearian revels, George's eyes may have been all for Olivia, but in Sir Toby Belch he had found an artistic conspirator and an important new friend. Fred Rowntree (from the large and well-known Quaker family in Yorkshire) had worked in Leicester and London before returning home to set up his own practice in Scarborough in 1885. In 1890 he moved to Glasgow to form a partnership with the local architect Malcolm Stark. Here he fell in quickly with the smart artistic set centred round the Glasgow Boys, probably through his connection with the Henderson family, to which Edward's wife belonged. He and Walton would

22. George Walton and Kate Gall, in their engagement picture.

remain close for many years and would collaborate on a number of commissions from 1895.[28]

Though no part of *Twelfth Night*, James Craig Annan had by this time become another key figure of Walton's most intimate circle. They shared similarities of temperament, and, along with Warneuke and Rowntree, an admiration for the Glasgow Boys and their prophets (Whistler, Velazquez, the Hague School and Japanese Art), and a desire to take their teaching beyond the easel. For Annan, initiation into the technique of photogravure (a photographic process related to etching) and close study of the Old Masters in his father's fine art reproduction business, were enough to set him on the road. Soon he was producing sensitive prints which revealed his artistic capabilities. By 1891 James Craig Annan's reputation had already placed him on the selection committee of a local photographic exhibition; later his fame would spread far beyond Glasgow.[29]

While the society of Annan could enhance Walton's appreciation of fine degrees of colour and tonal contrast, of surface and of balance, Walton could offer Annan his intimate knowledge of the Boys' painting and a supporting framework for Annan's art in the design of its setting. When Annan called in at 152 Wellington Street (where T. & R. Annan's goods entrance was adjacent to Walton's shop) they could exchange news: Walton might thumb over the prints of his latest interiors which Annan had brought, and Annan (a regular customer) could pick up his order of frames.[30]

1891: a busy year

James Craig Annan's periodic record of Walton's work from 1890 to 1895, which survived into the 1950s, has since been largely lost. Without some details of its accompanying location list, there would be little known today of the 1890-95 output of Walton's business as he made the rounds of the elegant but ultimately private residences of Glasgow's discriminating élite.[31] And after a century of use it is not surprising if the rooms have been repainted when we get there, the wallpapers stripped or the windows broken. Walton's work in most cases has succumbed to the inevitable fate of a decorator's *oeuvre*. These early interiors of his apprenticeship are now represented by a few disconnected remains. Nevertheless the more enduring items – chiefly fireplaces and stained glass – give some indication of his developing directions.

The hectic programme of 1891 justified in retrospect the company's expansion. There was Edward's new home to be decorated, and Guthrie's, and Whitelaw Hamilton's Helensburgh retreat; beyond these, shipowners, merchants and industrialists jostled in the queue.[32]

By far the most exciting area of development was Walton & Co.'s stained glass. The company's eventual involvement in stained glass was to be expected. The decorating firms Walton would have watched – Cottier's and J. & W. Guthrie – were both deeply committed to stained glass production. Besides its importance in church commissions, it was essential to the new style interior, influenced by Morris's productions, which Cottier had brought to Glasgow.

Walton's earliest interest in stained glass, revealed in his Glasgow Institute exhibit of 1889, coincided – perhaps not by accident – with the new involvement shown in the medium by the Glasgow Boys David Gauld and Harrington Mann, who would go on to produce a significant body of work for J. & W. Guthrie over the next few years.[33] Similarities in the output of Gauld and Walton in 1891 suggest some dialogue between the two.

1891 was the first year the company could have a hand in the execution of its own designs. For any process which could not be carried out in the workshops, there was a vast array of possible alternatives. Had Walton scanned the listings of specialist Glass Stainers in the Trades Section of the local directory, out of the thirty or so firms he might have selected William Meikle & Sons (whose window he could inspect from time to time as he strode down Wellington Street), or perhaps the equally reputable Stephen Adam, always sensitive to Pre-Raphaelite subjects or the Anglo-Japanese.[34]

It would be odd if there were not inconsistencies in the firm's first efforts. The results show an appropriate diversity and a vigorous, experimental outlook.

For James Gardiner – patron of the Glasgow Boys and relative of Edward's close friend James Guthrie – Walton produced an unexpectedly assured set of panels for the oriel window of his house in Grosvenor Crescent, Hillhead. The influence of Morris & Co.'s glass is clear, particularly its windows by Burne-Jones for the Green Dining Room at the South Kensington Museum, which Walton had probably seen on a trip to London. Instead of keeping the abstract pattern and the pictorial section separate, Walton merges them in the central panel, though not altogether smoothly (pl. 32). The figures, with their long, lightly patterned robes, the individual plant motifs, tufts of grass and the architectural background all relate to the Morris & Co. panels, yet the effect is different. The trees, because of their lightness of tone, are characterised by the bulging, irregular lines of the leading; in combination with a cloud to the right, they seem to float, giving the picture a dreamy quality quite unlike the windows at South Kensington. There are close parallels, however, with David Gauld's painting of 'St. Agnes' of 1889 and his stained glass panel 'Three Musicians' for Hugh McCulloch, probably made in the same year as Walton's window.[35] The exceptionally long trunks, and solid, outlined tops of the trees, with the block-like treatment of buildings behind, connect Walton's window with Gauld's 'St Agnes'. The colour combination Walton used – green and turquoise with a fragment of purple – became strongly associated with the later Glasgow Style.

For James Gardiner's brother and shipping partner, Frederick (who simultaneously requested a face-lift for his own city home), Walton designed a delightful decorative panel. It was in stark contrast to his window at Grosvenor Crescent. Here he used only plain frosted glass, with the lead cames forming the pattern (a method repeated at James Guthrie's house in a much less startling way). There is no trace here of Morris. Instead, Whistler's influence prevails. Both George and Edward were enchanted by Whistler's decoratively painted picture frames. Edward often sketched similar patterns round the borders of his drawings at this time.[36] At Frederick Gardiner's, Walton transfers the inspiration to a medium of his own without a qualm. Yet he is careful to credit the source. Walton's explicit reference to the Japanese wave motif adopted by Whistler is identified with a butterfly. This is the earliest indication of the tendency to transfer an idea, without regard for convention, from one medium to quite another, which here brought about a remarkably innovative design.[37]

23. Butterfly panel in leaded glass at Frederick Gardiner's house, 5 Dundonald Road, Glasgow.
24. Painted decoration on the frame of 'Nocturne in Blue and Gold: Old Battersea Bridge' by James McNeill Whistler.

Although in his butterfly window he was responding to Whistler's interpretation of the Japanese, Walton kept his own set of authentic Japanese pattern books, which he would have picked up easily in the city.[38] Glasgow was a major centre of the lively trading exchange with Japan currently under way. Japanese goods could be purchased at the City Oriental Warehouse in St Vincent Street. A no doubt more sophisticated selection could be explored at a gallery set up in Renfield Street by one of the Boys, Grosvenor Thomas, who dealt in Japanese curios.

At Whitelaw Hamilton's Thornton Lodge, Helensburgh, Walton produced a fireplace for the drawing room with a plain black-and-white-tiled surround set off with touches of gold leaf on the mantelpiece. His early interest in fireplace design reflects the historic dominance of this feature of the interior. Control of the fireplace was almost as essential as control of the walls if the effect of his schemes was to be carried through. The fireplace would soon become a focus for the company's craft skills and for some of Walton's most inspired designs. To re-cover the artist's settee, he selected a printed cotton velvet which had been exhibited at the 1890 Arts and Crafts Exhibition by Thomas Wardle.[39] Wardle worked closely with Morris, and his 'Wardle Art Fabrics' could be procured from Liberty's or directly from the works at Leek, Staffordshire. The pattern was repeated at the window as a gauze, above which was set another of Walton's experimental linear glass panels in the form of a dove.

For the walls, Walton devised his own design, possibly a block-printed wallpaper, perhaps stencilled directly on the wall. (Stencilling, a technique common in Scotland at the time, was a medium to which Walton was increasingly attracted.) This dynamic pattern links Walton with the revived interest in Italian Renaissance designs. Walton's friend James Morton (son of Alexander Morton, the local textile manufacturer to whom Walton would later turn for the production of his own textile designs) himself formed an early fascination for Renaissance fabrics and there are clear parallels between Walton's design and some of the textiles in James Morton's collection.[40]

The surviving photographs of Walton's drawing room at Thornton Lodge give a rare insight into the overall effect he was attempting at this date within the limited production capabilities of his own workshop.[41] While certainly refined, the room has not the restfulness which Walton later declared as an aim. Allowing for the fact that he had little control over the furnishing of this room, it is nevertheless evident that Walton had not yet discovered a principle which he would later employ to such good effect: in his own words, 'the first thing to consider is the proportion of bare spaces rather than the proportion of ornament for the effect of ornament greatly depends on the value of the bare spaces surrounding it'.[42] Thomas Howarth's comments on the (now missing) Annan photographs show that Thornton Lodge was typical of Walton's early interiors: 'Walton seemed content to follow the prevailing fashion for highly decorated wall surfaces, and in nearly all the examples wallpapers and stencilled mural decoration played an important part. These were usually of vigorous but inoffensive floral patterns with acorns, pineapples, leaves and so forth – and if any opportunity occurred similar patterns were applied to ceilings'.[43] Despite his admiration for the economy of Whistler's exhibition designs, in his domestic decorations Walton was in a field pervaded by convention, to which he was himself subject. From the perspective of 1900 he could feel 'my first attempts in design ... shew many failures'; but comparison with contemporary interiors – for instance William Leiper's room for John Anderson at Park Circus of the same year – demonstrates that his urge to simplify was already apparent.[44]

In view of Howarth's remarks, Walton's more

25. Drawing room at Thornton Lodge, Helensburgh, the home of J. Whitelaw Hamilton. Photograph by James Craig Annan.

sparing pattern for Edward of the same year (pl. 21) was unusual. While it may have been influenced by Mackmurdo or the earliest patterns of C. F. A. Voysey,[45] this design may equally have been reached by a conscious simplification of the pattern structures typical of seventeenth-century Italian silks, perhaps encouraged by his appreciation of the stencil technique with its traditionally more open effect. Whatever the source, it represents a novel line of thought and a further display of Walton's concentrated efforts at reduction.

This historic source of inspiration is paralleled in another early design of repeated grass tufts. Owing its origin to the individual plant studies displayed without perspective on the flat ground of mediaeval tapestries, this motif was undoubtedly mediated through the fabrics and windows of Morris & Co. Removed from its context it makes a startlingly original design. Variations on the grass-tuft theme recur frequently in Walton's stained glass and stencil designs.[46]

26. A dressing table by Walton, with a grass-tuft design on the wall, and a carpet possibly inspired by Whistler's paintings (see p. 108).

William Morris had concentrated much of his effort on the design of flat pattern and stained glass and his company was the most influential producer in these areas during the last decades of the nineteenth century. An obligation to Morris was common to all progressive designers of Walton's period. Walton was exploring alternatives. His move towards a lighter style was probably influenced by the less elaborate wallpapers of the time, like Walter Crane's 'Alcestis' for Jeffrey & Co., several of Lewis Day's block-printed velveteens for Turnbull & Stockdale (such as 'Daffodils'), and the early designs of C. F. A. Voysey with which he may have been familiar. Walton's grass-tuft pattern, however, and the design for Edward, despite their origins, are in no way derivative. They signal a creative, individual mind. While the fragmented picture of Walton's work of 1891 shows him in some ways a man of his times, formed by the influences of prominent con-

temporary designers and styles of work, the variety and unusual qualities of his output already mark out his unconventionality.

1891 was an action-packed year: the company's expansion, the wedding, the stream of decorating commissions already explored. And there were others which have been lost – work on a shop for the fashionable drapers and silk merchants Neilson Shaw & MacGregor, and the decoration of 'The Glen', a large house in Paisley, for Sir James Fulton, an industrialist connected with the textile industry – and, inevitably, with the Glasgow Boys.[47]

1892-5: experience, experiment, growth

In 1892, James Craig Annan, now wholly committed to Art Photography, left Glasgow for a trip to Holland with his friend the Glasgow artist D. Y. Cameron. Travelling to Amsterdam and Utrecht, and along the coast to Katwijk and Zandvoort, Cameron worked his etching plates and Annan, wielding his hand camera, produced startling and unconventional photographic images, which for their subject matter, format, composition and atmosphere might be taken for the work of Glasgow's guru – Whistlerian 'arrangements' in grey and black.[48]

On their return to Glasgow, an exhibition was planned to coincide with the opening of T. & R. Annan's newly-acquired premises at 230 Sauchiehall Street. For this daring joint exhibition, where Annan's photographs were given equal status as art objects with Cameron's etchings, the design of the new gallery and the framing was put in the hands of George Walton.[49] Walton's interiors, so carefully recorded by his friend, provided inspiration for Annan. 'We must surround ourselves with the most beautiful objects which we can procure', he declared, for 'By accustoming oneself constantly to see things of beauty, one becomes more sensitive and more able to discriminate rapidly ... the most useful attribute a photographer can possess'.[50]

The effect of the interiors at Sauchiehall Street resembled an oasis in the desert, according to one midsummer visitor.

'Abandon heat and glare, all ye who enter here', might well be written over the portal ... The light is subdued, the greens and browns and creamy paint are restful and cool; on the walls are low-toned carbons of classic pictures, mellow mezzotints, and rich etchings – all the delight of the senses.[51]

The hallway frieze was decorated with Walton's wallpaper design from Thornton Lodge, but in the other rooms, where there was no wood panelling, plain painted wall surfaces predominated. The fitted cabinet in the reception room had simple recessed handles and an arched opening. The rooms were sparsely furnished with rugs strewn on the waxed wood floor. By com-

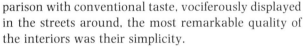

27. Reception room in James Craig Annan's photographic gallery, 230 Sauchiehall St, Glasgow.
28. 'A Dutch Dog Cart' by James Craig Annan, the frame almost certainly by George Walton.
29. W. M. Warneuke's photographic studio, 153 Sauchiehall St, Walton's first shopfront.

brother's clients. Though the company's identifying label has rarely survived, Annan's and Edward's early frames provide a plausible if limited picture of the company's output. These frames are often finely moulded, finished in 'ivory' or pale tones; others, broad and dark (like the frame for Annan's 'Sybilla') rely for their effect on the quality of the wood and the craftsmanship of the joints.[53]

In Glasgow, George Walton was responsible for the public image of progressive photography: Warneuke was another satisfied customer. He had returned to Walton in the preceding years for a second all-inclusive exhibition design, and soon followed Annan in requesting the redecoration of his own spacious studio on Sauchiehall Street.

In contrast with the quiet elegance of Annan's rooms, Warneuke's had an oriental theme.[54] Walton rigged up a series of receding fretwork screens, dominated by an ogee arch, to embellish the original entrance arcade, with his own bold and decorative lettering announcing the proprietor in a swirling metalwork frame: here he was again, experimenting with style. Liberty's and H. & J. Cooper's of London had been producing Arab- and Moorish-style interiors for some years and an eclectically oriental style had presided at

parison with conventional taste, vociferously displayed in the streets around, the most remarkable quality of the interiors was their simplicity.

For the frames, Walton and Annan developed a style to suit the occasion: 'Several of the pictures square in size have been surrounded by a square, flat, broad frame, the whole carrying out the idea of a Dutch tile'. Others were distinguished by unusual reeded mouldings or by their colours – subtly harmonised with the photographs, which Annan had printed in tints of brown, grey-green or 'Bartolozzi red'.[52]

Annan relied on Walton's framing skills for half a decade, and Edward must have been chief among his

30. Stair window for William Burrell at 4 Devonshire Gardens, Glasgow, *c.* 1892-3, filled with Walton's favourite motifs: doves, peacocks, tulips, roses and the recurring grass tuft. This aging photograph by J. C. Annan is the only record of the complete window: the lower peacock panels have since been destroyed.

Glasgow's 1888 International Exhibition. Walton shared his brief enthusiasm for the oriental (here and at East Park in Barrhead of 1893-4) with the Glasgow Boys, for whom, in these years, Morocco was as likely a destination for pilgrimage as Japan.

Warneuke's metalwork signboard is peculiarly at odds with the overall theme, and its freely undulating linear rhythms have little connection with the company's work examined so far.[55] The only metalwork produced by the company before 1892 (excluding perhaps the decorative light fitting at Edward's house, pl. 21) was a wrought-iron gate apparently designed by Walton for Thornton Lodge – presumably in 1891 when the interior was completed. A free interpretation of the eighteenth-century scrollwork adopted by architects of the 'Queen Anne' style, the gate retains a sense of tradition which the signboard lacks.[56] Can it be coincidental that in the same year Warneuke's signboard was produced, the metalworker William Kellock Brown had set up his workshop a few doors down the street from Walton & Co.? Kellock Brown, originally from a metalworking background in Glasgow, had spent some years in London, where his continued education in sculpture had run alongside a brief career as chief metalworker (with George Esling) of Mackmurdo's Century Guild.[57] The lines of the Warneuke signboard – more clearly 'Mackmurdo lines' than anything Walton had produced so far – prompts the interesting suggestion that he was in contact with Kellock Brown at this stage and may even have had his metalwork parts made up in Brown's workshop, conveniently located at 138 Wellington Street.

As Walton accumulated experience and the company's reputation grew, Walton & Co. began to attract larger and more prestigious jobs. During 1892 the ship-

32. Stained glass panel of *c.* 1891 for James Gardiner's house, 15 Grosvenor Crescent, Glasgow (see p. 28).

ping magnate and connoisseur William Burrell flattered Walton with a commission for the large stair window in his own private house. It was the first time Burrell bought the work of a contemporary Scottish artist and in this instance it may have been George who attracted a client for the Glasgow Boys rather than the other way round. Much more ambitious than Walton's figure panel for James Gardiner, his window for Burrell is also less conventional. Unlike a lancet panel he produced in the same year, the glass painting is reduced as much as possible, most notably in the figure panels.[58]

William Burrell's window is an extraordinary combination of different styles and effects. It acts as an introduction to Walton's preoccupations and sources of the period, announcing several themes which will recur. The top panels are striking, naturalistic representations of vases of flowers ranged in a row in the Persian manner, perhaps inspired by his sisters' flower paintings. They reappear later, in 1896, as a mural decoration in Miss Cranston's Buchanan Street tea rooms (pl. 61), and (greatly simplified) in a stained glass window of the same year at William Rowntree's (pl. 125). The central figure panels, much more diagrammatic, are topped with a floral frieze which relates to the favoured rose and briar used for windows, stencils and mosaic. The two left-hand figure panels again recall Gauld's hieratic figure compositions, while the right-hand panel, in a sudden burst of movement, declares

31. Central upper panel from Walton's window for Burrell, perhaps inspired by his sisters' flower paintings.

Walton's knowledge of the most recent work of E. A. Hornel. Hornel's painting 'Summer' shown at the Glasgow Institute in the early part of the year, and even more 'The Dance of Spring', have interesting parallels with this design in the area of figure composition. The individual tulips in the central panel set the pattern for a series of separated floral motifs on windows, fabrics and stencils in future years. The lowest panels, an entirely decorative display of doves and peacocks, again announce recurring themes. Doves, used previously at St Peter's and at Thornton Lodge (1891), are repeated at Drumalis in 1893 and later at The Leys (1901). Peacocks become the emblem for Walton's firm.[59]

Drumalis

In the following year, Walton was invited to decorate 'Drumalis', a grand mansion house in Larne, Northern Ireland, for Sir Hugh Smiley, who had family and business connections in Glasgow. Drumalis is by far the most complete company job to survive from this early period. Some of the work – the passage to the billiards room (exhibited early 1894 at the Glasgow Institute) with its internal glazed doorway (photographed by Annan in 1893), and the windows in the hall signed with the company's name – can be deci-

sively dated and attributed to Walton.[60] Yet for most of the decorative work there is no such documentation. There could be little doubt of the authorship of the passageway with its moulded panels, barrel-vaulted ceiling (often used later), emphasized cornice and distinctive glazing. Elsewhere, the connecting theme of curving, linear patterning used throughout the house makes it seem likely that Walton was responsible for the entire scheme. There is some indication of the firm's attentions after it became a limited company in 1896, but stylistically, most of the work is from the 1893 period.[61] There are, however, some curious anomalies. The house is full of surprises.

At Drumalis, Walton's versatility is everywhere apparent. He is as successful with his plainer glazing as he is with the more complicated figure panels. He attends to the smallest details (even the door handles are individually designed) and yet can follow through a theme in a way that unifies the whole. Drumalis shows the professionalism Walton had achieved, the size of his operations and the range of artifacts produced by his company by 1893.

33 and 34. The central figure and an adjacent decorative panel from the hall window at Drumalis, *c.* 1893.

35. Detail of the decoration of the hall ceiling, Drumalis, its background pattern based on a stylised grass tuft.

The hall gives the clearest view of the overall effect of Walton's work. The greens and reds of the windows are picked up in the ceiling decoration while the honey colour of the central figure links up with the woodwork. The subtlety of the relationships in this colouring hint at the special harmony of Walton's interiors.

36. One of a set of windows overlooking the courtyard at Drumalis. The inverted hearts are made of copper.

In the rich upper glazing of the windows of the hall, Walton again sets an abstract pattern of circles against the figures as he had at James Gardiner's, though here the figures themselves have become more dominant through their proportionate enlargement within the frame. The greater emphasis on decorative panels expresses Walton's move in this direction, apparent in the surviving internal windows of the house. The combination of bold leadwork patterns in plain glass with highlighted spots of clear colour is widely used in the many internal windows; and there is one set of panels, with swirling lead lines like the Warneuke signboard (pl. 29), which substitutes copper inserts for the coloured fragments: an important step.

The painted and stencilled ceiling of the hall has survived in excellent condition. Divided into panels by the mouldings of the ceiling, a design of flowers and foliage is applied to a stencilled background grid. While the painted foliage remains close to Morris's patterning, the grid shows the beginning of Walton's search for a more personal idiom.

37. A window panel at Drumalis.

The surprising inlay of the hall and landing – almost Art Deco in effect – could be rejected as part of Walton's scheme were it not for the close relation of the patterning to some of Walton's leaded windows elsewhere in the house, and for the continuous foliar device below the cornice, which directly repeats a motif of the ceiling. This inlay – if it is indeed his – makes explicit Walton's open-minded and exploratory approach to design work as he sought to establish his own style: the experiment was never repeated.

The fitted cabinet in one room at Drumalis is the only surviving piece of furniture attributable to Walton from before 1896 which can be confidently dated. The broken arched pediment, with its brass finial and cartouche, is a far more elegant and sympathetic rendering of early eighteenth-century detailing than his earlier woodwork for Miss Cranston. Fred Rowntree may have had something to do with this. He was at present involved with his partner Malcolm Stark on

38. Ceiling light in the billiards room, incorporating thistles for Sir Hugh Smiley's Scottish wife.

39. Fitted cabinet at Drumalis, *c.* 1893.

holes and recessed brass grips. His source for the chest (similar to the one at Annan's) is not hard to find. Ford Madox Brown, Pre-Raphaelite painter and designer for Morris & Co., had shown a related chest of drawers (based on rural eighteenth-century precedents, but stained green) at the Manchester Jubilee Exhibition of 1887 and again in 1890 at the Arts and Crafts show. All in all the Drumalis cabinet with its 'architectural' details above, its prominent arcade and its plain chest below, reads as an essay in 'Queen Anne' under the influence of Charles Locke Eastlake, whose 'reformed' furniture had been publicised in *Hints on Household Taste*.[63]

40. Roundel over a stairway at Drumalis.

Furniture

The description 'Furniture Warehouses' applied to the company in 1891 suggests it had been at least re-tailing furniture by that date. This may have included Walton's own designs made up outside, as well as the regional country styles favoured by Morris & Co. and popular with architects of the Art Workers' Guild. Rush seats, spindlebacks and ladderbacks were becoming increasingly common. Ford Madox Brown produced a ladderback chair *c.* 1860 and Morris & Co. had for some time been producing its own version of the Sussex chair. James MacLaren (one of the Glasgow-trained Scots working in London) 'discovered' the Ledbury chair bodger Philip Clisset *c.* 1887, and his 'rush-bottomed chairs' had since reached the attention of the Art Workers' Guild.[64] Ernest Gimson had begun to learn the craft. Perhaps regional chairs like the Yorkshire or Lancashire spindleback which Edward included in his painting 'The Girl in Brown' of 1888, were amongst the company's early stock (pl. 10). This type of chair was still being used lavishly in the firm's interiors as late as 1896 (pl. 61). A more satisfactory arrangement for the making of furniture was soon in force, however. In

Gray Dunn & Co.'s biscuit factory extension in Stanley Street. Showing his keen interest in the 'Queen Anne' style, its arcaded front, Flemish gable and obligatory 'Queen Anne' bay echo the London Board Schools to which J. J. Stevenson had contributed. A slightly later shopfront by Rowntree for Walton's former clients Neilson Shaw & Macgregor confirms this current tack, with its broken pediment, urn, and arched window openings – like Walton's cabinet – supported by intri-cately turned columns (delicate to the point of spindliness).[62] The contrast in approach between Walton's rendering of the Baroque with its implicit re-spect for the period, and the more fluid and flamboyant interpretation of a comparable set of designs at the Glas-gow Art Club by the young architect Charles Rennie Mackintosh, already indicates differences of tempera-ment between the two designers which would become more marked in the future.

Walton's glazed cabinet and arcaded recess is set atop a far less sophisticated chest with cut-out handle

1892 Walton & Co. took on its own cabinet-makers and announced its skills accordingly in the Glasgow directory.[65]

The Drumalis cabinet and Edward's spindleback suggest the early direction of Walton's furnishing interests. Supplementary evidence is provided by a collection of old glass slides, some of which show furniture probably dating from this period. They include a glass-fronted cabinet with circular glazing bars – a simplified version of the type exhibited by George Jack at the first Arts and Crafts Exhibition in 1888 – and another piece of clearly eighteenth-century derivation. A further slide shows a heavy, rather clumsy sideboard, perhaps the one made for F. C. Gardiner and shown at the Glasgow Institute in 1893. Other experiments – plain, solid forms using the the plank construction popular since Charles Lock Eastlake recommended it in 1868, and the simplified spindleback in the Annan reception room (pl. 27) whose date is unfortunately unclear – show a freer mind.[66]

East Park

In 1892 Miss Cranston had married a wealthy industrialist, John Cochrane, owner of the Grahamston Foundry and Boiler Works. They had moved by 1893 into East Park, a semi-detached house on the Carlibar Road in Barrhead. Walton was called in to decorate. His eagerness to make the most of the new woodwork skills of his firm, demonstrated in the panelling of Drumalis, is still marked. East Park's drawing room displays his latest experiment – rather more conventional – in the fireplace ingle seat, with its bracketed-out shelf and 'oriel' cupboard, in the manner of Shaw. The bay window recess was a different matter. Here traditional ceiling mouldings vie with an ogee arch and a horizontal strip of fretwork which one might have taken for a piece of garden trellis. Walton for one was not dissatisfied with the result. Six years later he still liked it enough to allow its publication.[67]

Perhaps this was the reason. In the East Park drawing room he had made his first real attempt to integrate the woodwork elements, including the furniture, with the room scheme as a whole – a new challenge only timidly considered before, now more confidently explored.[68] From the viewpoint of 1899, when Walton was reaching the zenith of his career as an interior designer, he could look back fondly to East Park with its integral window seat, its fireplace ingle, its slenderly emphasised verticals, the gentle curves of the woodwork profiles sympathetically echoed in the lines of the leaded glass. It represented the germination of an approach to interior work which he had developed ever since with such sophistication and success.

Other surviving glimpses of the 1893-4 interiors at East Park give hints of Walton's current sources of inspiration: in a wall stencil, a curious design based on a conventional foliar pattern jostles for attention with the Tudor rose of Argyle Street and a series of Japanese *mon* motifs; and in the painted decoration of the piano, there are putti reminiscent of Walter Crane.[69]

While one can credit the individuality and enthusiasm of the East Park interiors, it is clear that Walton's ideas have not quite come together. Shooting off in several simultaneous directions, he was not yet in full command of his imagination.

Glasgow Life

The first years of any new company are crucial. With so many jobs to keep under control, Walton was fully occupied. Life must have been exhilarating and exhausting. Over this time, he was also adjusting to new circumstances at home. A daughter, Marguerite, was born in late 1892 and Kate's attentions were in demand. She was a devoted mother: the bond between her and her daughter had an intensity which lasted into Marguerite's adult life. Unlike so many of the Glasgow women Walton knew, Kate was not an artist. She was, however, a capable embroideress, shared Walton's enthusiasm for theatrical events and entered fully into Glasgow life.[70]

The Glasgow art world was full of activity. Great excitement was caused by George Henry and E. A. Hornel's departure for Japan in 1893 and their return was eagerly awaited. Fra Newbery, now well-established at the School of Art, began to set up courses in the decorative arts in 1892. His new 'Technical Art Studios' offered classes in stained glass, metalwork, ceramic decoration and bookbinding, and his wife Jessie set up her famous embroidery class in 1894. Unusual talent was stirring amongst the new students, for it was around 1893-4 that the first of the 'Spook School' graphic work of C. R. Mackintosh, Margaret and Frances Macdonald and Herbert MacNair began to emerge. The Glasgow Institute exhibitions were a vital source of publicity for Walton and his associates. There Helen and Constance exhibited watercolours and the occasional decorative piece, George, examples of his interiors, and Malcolm Stark and Rowntree samples from their developing practice in public and domestic buildings in Glasgow and Yorkshire.

In April 1895 Walton was busy preparing his exhibits and designing the programme for a grand exhibition of Arts and Crafts to be held at the Queen's Rooms beside Kelvingrove Park. It was considered 'the first Arts and Crafts Exhibition on a large scale which has taken place in Glasgow'.[71] Most of the leading designers in the country were invited to exhibit: Morris sent examples of books from the Kelmscott Press, 'Harry' (presumably Henry) Holiday stained glass and cartoons; Walter Crane and the Silver Studio were also represented. Amongst the Scottish designers, Robert Lorimer, Phoebe Traquair and Robert Burns brought work from Edinburgh, while from Glasgow, Guthrie & Wells and Stephen Adam showed glass; Mackintosh contributed seven wallpapers and, with MacNair, some cabinets 'notable for design'; Jessie Newbery exhibited needle-work, and Helen Walton (newly engaged by Newbery as a teacher at the School of Art) some of her pottery, while Constance's 'very charming decoration' occupied a prominent place on one of the walls. In the 'Crafts-men at Work' section, Walton & Co. lent John Shedden to demonstrate glass-staining, but Walton's main ex-hibits were 'a massive sideboard' ('one of the most no-table specimens in the furniture department'), stained glass and cartoons. It was an important opportunity for publicity for the company and promised to put Glas-gow on the map for the rather too southerly-oriented arts press.

Throughout this time Walton's friendship with Rowntree was growing. At the Arts and Crafts exhibi-tion they took joint responsibility for the decorations – the first recorded design job on which they collab-orated. They had reached a consensus on art matters. Together they admired 'Queen Anne'; together they applauded Voysey; both delighted in the possibilities of architectural form and structure; both were caught up in the feeling for craftsmanship and materials encour-aged by Morris; and both, united in their rejection of Victorian over-ornamentation, preferred a plainer and more restful style in furniture and interiors.

For the exhibition, some light-hearted scheme of decoration was expected: Walton and Rowntree pre-sented a bazaar in a southern Spanish town, with the various exhibits arranged in stalls. The divisions were formed by plain uprights, each decorated with a shield representing one of the crafts, executed by students from the School of Art. The arrangement was gener-ally pleasing, though criticisms were levelled at the pic-ture show: it was in reality more of an exhibition of crafts than of arts and Walton had been unable to de-velop his enthusiasm for hanging pictures, as the wall space provided was totally inadequate.

A few months later Walton and Rowntree's talents were again in demand for the arrangement and deco-ration of the Lady Artists' Club's Art Exhibition and 'Fancy Fair', a typical entertainment of the period, held in order to raise money for a gallery extension to the Club's premises at 5 Blythswood Square. Walton and Rowntree were required to transform the Fine Art In-stitute into an old-world street with the stalls decorated to represent artists such as Gainsborough, Wilkie,

41. Programme by Walton for the 1895 Arts and Crafts exhibition in Glasgow, in the manner of Walter Crane.

Landseer and Marcus Stone. There were special entertainments:

> The two architects designed a suitable stage in the large gallery, and electric light was laid on. The Misses Jessie Keppie, Ruby Pickering, Jane Aitken, Katie Cameron and Agnes Raeburn painted the scenery for a series of nursery rhymes and also acted in them. The stage arrangements were in the hands of Mr W. B. Miller and Mr Charles Rennie Mackintosh, the latter, as stage manager, tapped with a stick in true French fashion when the curtain was to be drawn. There were also other *tableaux* such as *La Belle Dame Sans Merci* acted by Mrs Rowntree and Mr J. Craig Annan, and beautiful costumes were lent by Messrs. E. A. Hornel, George Henry, Duncan McKeller, Grosvenor Thomas, and Dr. Alex Frew.[72]

42. The Glasgow Society of Lady Artists' 'Fancy Fair', December 1895, designed by George Walton and Fred Rowntree.

Walton's and Rowntree's decorations were a resounding success. *The Gentlewoman* was effusive – 'nothing so effective has ever been seen in Glasgow' – and concerned that its readers should not miss an unadvertised attraction at one of the stalls, where Kate and Mrs Fred Rowntree 'attired in costumes à la Caldecott of patterned chiné silk', provided confidential 'instruction in the Waltonian art'.[73]

Besides affording a colourful glimpse of the activities of the group, this speedy repetition of Walton and Rowntree's team work shows their collaboration had been a success. The following year, their partnership became a customary arrangement as they worked together on a number of more serious commissions: on the Lady Artists' Club's new gallery, on Annan's house at Lenzie and on two cafés in Scarborough for Rowntree's cousins, William and John.

Walton's contact with London over this period should not be underestimated. As with many of his friends and associates, a multitude of circumstances drew him south. Edward's group of contacts in London had been growing, particularly his friendships with artists in the Chelsea group, which included the magnetising figure of Whistler. He and the Glasgow Boys found increasing opportunities to exhibit, at the Royal Academy, the New English Art Club, and at the Grosvenor and Grafton galleries.

Warneuke and Annan had also been communicating for some time with photographic colleagues in London. Annan showed work with a group of rebel photographers who had recently seceded from the Photographic Society, at their first exhibition in October 1893. In February 1894 he committed himself to his avant-garde associates by joining 'The Linked Ring' – an élite photographic society which would be of considerable significance to Walton in the future.

Walton himself sent work to the London Arts and Crafts Exhibitions in 1890 and 1893. The exhibitions would have formed a strong attraction to him and it seems unlikely he would have missed these prime opportunities of acquainting himself with developments in the vanguard of his own field. It was perhaps at the 1893 exhibition that he met C. F. A. Voysey for the first time. He had undoubtedly kept an eye, with Rowntree, on *The British Architect* and early copies of *The Studio* and would already have been familiar with his work. It may have been this new connection which encouraged Voysey to exhibit at the Glasgow Institute from the following year. A close friendship developed between the two designers from this time.[74]

Walton would have visited London also for family reasons, initially to see his in-laws, but from 1893 to visit his brother Edward in Kensington. Edward had begun to tire of the limitations of Glasgow for a painter with ambition. A move to London would greatly increase his opportunities for new work. By 1893 these ambitions and the encouragement of London associates combined to produce action. After a warm send-off, he departed with his family for the south. Edward's move left a deep impression on his brother George.

III TEA ROOMS AND INTERIORS, 1896-1897

On the way home from the Lady Artists' 'Fancy Fair' of December 1895, those who walked past 150-152 Wellington Street might have stopped to gaze; and, almost a hundred years later, we can make a fairly confident guess at what they saw – furniture and perhaps fireplaces, stained and leaded glass, original designs for stencils, wallpapers and tiles. Drawn inside, the visitor could view the company's skills and its style of decoration, apparent in the scheme of the showroom's interior. Emphasizing its integrated approach, imaginative designs for architectural woodwork, fitted cabinet-work, wall-framing, and even speciality door furniture may have been on show. Fashionable fabrics from the best sources could be supplied (Thomas Wardle's Art Fabrics, designs by William Morris) and traditional country chairs from regional makers. No doubt Annan's photographs of Walton's interiors were thoughtfully arranged along the walls. The exclusive work of a number of individuals and companies could be obtained through the showroom. Hand-painted china and glass, needlework and tiles from the Walton sisters' studio were doubtless there,[1] alongside Edward's or Connie's paintings in their special Walton & Co. frames. Perhaps the brand-new range of 'Clutha' glass vases designed by Walton for the local James Couper & Sons could be examined (pl.144).[2] The variety of work the seven-year-old company could supply was surprising. Walton & Co. offered services in complete domestic and commercial interior work, shopfront and exhibition design.

Along with the showrooms at Wellington Street, there were a few other locations in Glasgow where Walton's work could be seen: at Miss Cranston's in Argyle Street, at Annan's and Warneuke's galleries, and at Neilson Shaw & MacGregor's draper's shop. But the vast majority of the company's decorative schemes had been carried out in the privacy of the home. Through the powerful medium of personal recommendation, Walton's work was sufficiently known to have gained him a succession of commissions, so that by mid-1890 the company was consolidating its position as a source of exclusive interior work for a growing clientele, its busy workshops spilling out into Renfrew Street and Sauchiehall Lane.[3] Yet comparatively few of the company's jobs were open to the public gaze. Despite its evident success, Walton & Co. was still a small concern in the busy metropolis of Glasgow, the position of its showroom on Wellington Street – outside the main shopping thoroughfares – not guaranteed to attract the greatest attention.

1896 presented Walton with the opportunity to give his company's work a more public face. Like 1891, it was a year full of new openings and change. The company was reaching a stage where the question of expansion naturally arose; Walton's association with Fred Rowntree opened a number of opportunities of a new order; and in general the type of work taken on over the year represented a major switch from the current concentration on domestic interiors to commissions of a more public nature. This change of emphasis coincides with the increased accessibility of contemporary photographs, and there is a sense in which from 1896 the present-day spectator of Walton's career no longer has to peer between the folds because the curtain rises.

For the change in profile, it was partly to Miss Cranston that Walton would again be indebted. But Miss Cranston was no longer hazarding the unknown. She could return to Walton with confidence, as she had in the decoration of her own home, East Park, in 1894. It was the turn of another to be tested. As she had taken a risk with the unproven Walton in 1888 amongst a group of more established workers, so she would speculate again in 1896 with the young architect Charles Rennie Mackintosh, whose recent graphic adventures showed him to be a decorative artist of promise. He would be given the opportunity to show his skills on the walls of her newest tea rooms at Buchanan Street, currently under construction, where Walton & Co. would now operate in a major role.

Walton's new working association with Fred Rowntree brought commissions of a similar nature, but further afield. Stark's practice had evidently benefited from taking Rowntree into partnership, for a good number of their exhibits at the Glasgow Institute of the Fine Arts between 1890 and 1895 had been generated by Rowntree's connections in Yorkshire.[4] In 1896 Walton also benefited. Rowntree proposed his collaboration on a café interior for his uncle in Scarborough – Walton & Co.'s first job in England. Such assistance was probably reciprocal: it seems likely that Walton recommended Rowntree to his close friend James Craig Annan, as Annan considered the alteration and decoration of his own home, on which Walton and Rowntree worked together later in the year.

For Walton these jobs were all, one way or another, collaborative commissions. Four were completed with Fred Rowntree. Buchanan Street was a more complicated affair: there was Mackintosh, with whom Walton had a more ambivalent relationship; and co-operation with other contractors was required – with J. & W. Guthrie, and the architect of the building, George Washington Browne.

Joint ventures: a gallery and a home

The Fancy Fair of December 1895 had been a great success. With capital now available for building, there was no longer any doubt about the acquisition of 5 Blythswood Square and the new year saw the gallery pass from the stage of proposal to practical planning.[5] In order that preparations would be ready for the completion of purchase in November, no time was lost in setting the designers to work. Fred Rowntree's plans were submitted to the building authorities on 2nd April 1896 and it is reasonable to suppose that Walton's interior scheme originates from this time.[6]

Rowntree's drawings (in the name of the Stark & Rowntree partnership) incorporate the primary alterations intended by the Lady Artists: a top-lit gallery space and improvements to kitchens. He proposed that the back of the building on the ground floor be extended to form an L-shaped room with roof lights, approached through a new doorway formed in the hall. With Walton's contributions, the finished interior displayed exposed timbering beneath the roof light, pale green panelled walls, a large stonework fireplace, and lighter decorative notes in the touches of stained glass. The expenses of the Club on the alterations amounted to £1,430 19s. 5d.[7]

The focal point of the gallery was the dominating fireplace – the sculptural strength of its stonework and the unusual form of the metalwork below. The carved stone headpiece, unique in Walton's work, is no more typical of Rowntree. That it was Walton's contribution is confirmed both by family tradition and the *History of the Lady Artists' Club*, and merely underlines Walton's ability to produce widely varying styles of work during the more experimental phases of his career.[8] A fireplace by Ernest George and Peto, illustrated in *The Studio* in 1893 (and again in April 1896 just as Rowntree was drawing up the plans) is a possible source of inspiration.[9] More important to Walton's developing practice is the new emphasis on metalwork in the fireplace ornament below. The firedog finials can be understood as a development of some of Walton's motifs at Drumalis (especially the swirling tendrils and flattened heart shapes of his glass and copper window), but the hood and backplate have no precursor in the firm's output. They show Walton's awareness of the type of metalwork being used in Morris & Co. interiors to the design of George Jack, which, to any observant student of design, was available from a browse through the pages of *The Studio* or the exhibition rooms of the Arts and Crafts Exhibition Society in Glasgow or London.[10]

43. Stone fireplace surround in the Lady Artists' Club, with exciting new metalwork developments by Walton & Co. below.

44. The raised metalwork of this fireplace by George Jack exhibited at the Arts and Crafts Exhibition Society show of 1893 may have inspired Walton's backplate at the Lady Artists' Club.

46. Leaded glass window at the Lady Artists' Club.

Walton's use of relief patterns on the cast-iron backplate of the Lady Artists' Club follows up Jack's idea, and becomes a basis for later designs.

The decorative glass at the Gallery continues Walton's commitment to simple, decorative patterns using coloured and plain glass, with the design formed entirely by the leading. The forms used (bows, scroll-work, hanging flowers, rose garlands) recall the Crane-influenced graphic style of Walton's Programme for the Glasgow Arts and Crafts Exhibition of 1895 (pl. 41) and some of the internal glasswork at Drumalis. These experimental efforts at purely decorative (as opposed to pictorial) panels, somewhat naïve in character, soon lead with increasing confidence to the mature style he reaches by 1898.

None of Walton's glasswork is evident at Glen Bank, the house in Lenzie which James Craig Annan was oc-cupying in 1896, close by the carbon printing estab-lishment set up by his father nearly twenty years before. Nor does the fireplace continue Walton's experimenta-tion with metalwork parts. Below dark ceiling rafters, the flat, decorative fireplace, with patterned tiles, be-trays no obvious sign of Walton's hand. Yet there is no doubt that Glen Bank was a collaborative commission: Rowntree's and Walton's initials, with its owner's and the date, '1896', are engraved on a brass panel set into the fireplace surround. Though a pair of dividers marks out Rowntree as architect and a palette (rather signifi-cantly) distinguishes Walton as 'Artist' of the interior, responsibility for the internal work is difficult to appor-tion. It is likely to have been the architect's choice to expose the roofing timbers in the drawing room exten-

47. Part of the chimney piece at Glen Bank. This brass plaque records the close relationship between Walton, James Craig Annan and Fred Rowntree, which was at its strongest around this date of 1896.

48. In the drawing room at Glen Bank: a photo-graph by James Craig Annan.

sion. Rowntree was working along these lines in his more public commissions,[11] yet this was hardly foreign to Walton. At the Annan Gallery (where there is no indication of Rowntree's involvement) Walton had combined exposed ceiling beams with fitted cabinet-work so similar to that at Glen Bank that the rest of its interior woodwork can safely be assumed to be Walton's design. Besides, the quality of this woodwork is not reflected in Rowntree's later output. There is a finesse in the proportions and detailing of the panelling and fitments at Glen Bank, a subtlety of approach, which already distinguishes Walton's handling from the more commonplace manner of Rowntree.[12]

Though the exposed beams might also suggest the inspiration of Baillie Scott, in fact the house at Lenzie breathes the Voysey influence. Rowntree's cottage porch at Glen Bank owes much to Voysey's at Walnut Tree Farm, and an upstairs fireplace, probably Walton's, to one in Voysey's house at Frensham. Voysey's influence in Glasgow was strong. He was exhibiting regularly at the Institute, where the 'House at Frensham' was shown in 1895. Walnut Tree Farm was illustrated in *Academy Architecture* (which gave wide coverage to Scottish work at the Edinburgh R.S.A. and Glasgow Institute exhibitions) in the same year.[13] The understated drawing room fireplace at Glen Bank is also more in sympathy with Voysey's than Baillie Scott's work. Where Walton's interiors already differ from Voysey is in his more sophisticated integration of the furnishing with the fabric of the building. Already apparent is Walton's determination to create a fully-considered interior scheme.

49. Advertisement by Walton for John Rowntree's café, with the galleon motif used on the façade.

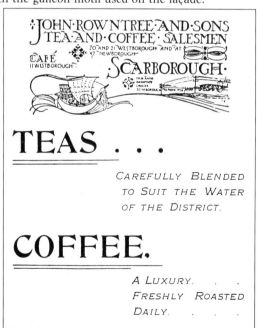

50. Fred Rowntree.

The Rowntree Uncles

Rowntree's home town, Scarborough, was a fashionable resort for the Victorian holiday-maker who fled the polluted atmosphere of his industrial city for the invigorating attractions of the seaside town. Scarborough's rising popularity in the nineteenth century was marked by the completion of the seven-storied Grand Hotel (by the architect Cuthbert Brodrick) in the 1860s, and the more recent opening of an expansive department store, by the flourishing business of Rowntree's uncle, William Rowntree & Sons.

The Rowntrees were a widespread and prominent Quaker family of the region, now remembered, alongside their confections, for their more serious interests both in architecture and social reform.[14] The original business activities of the Scarborough branch of the family had divided in the 1820s into two separate ventures. For more than half a century John Rowntree's (a grocer's) and William Rowntree's (a draper's) had been developing side by side.[15] By the 1890s the current generation of Rowntrees was well known for the quality of their merchandise and for their adoption of the most advanced technical developments. John Rowntree had the edge: his had been the first shop in Scarborough to be lit by gas, then the first to be lit by electricity; he had telephones installed by 1881. William Rowntree's drapery shop had swollen to the scale of a department store, where, with an eye to his predominantly female clientele, he provided the most comfortable surroundings, with all modern conveniences – 'lighted by electricity and warmed throughout with hot water'.[16]

John Rowntree's business had developed a speciality in tea and coffee importing. His decision to open his own café was a predictable step, perhaps prompted by his knowledge of the growing success of such refreshment rooms in Glasgow. His Quaker background made him naturally sympathetic to the temperance movement, of which coffee and tea rooms were an integral part. When, towards the end of 1895 he was ready to fit out his newly-purchased premises at 11 Westborough, John Rowntree turned to his cousin Fred, and with Fred took on his unofficial partner George Walton.

The pattern of work took the usual direction, with Walton responsible for the entire decoration and furnishing of the interiors (including – as we had suspected at Glen Bank – 'practically all the woodwork').[17] Rowntree's energies were expended on the street frontage, the modernisation of the services and the overall layout of the rooms. Naturally ideas would be shared: Walton already had a keen interest in shopfronts, and their joint porings over Walton's copies of *The Studio*, their admiration for Voysey, so involved with decorative work, had given Fred a corresponding appetite for details of the interior scheme.[18] The start of the commission may well have pre-dated the designs for the Lady Artists' Club as the work was well in progress by the end of March.

The bold arch of Rowntree's front, cut by the horizontal band of an extending balcony, surmounted a recessed bay with small leaded window panes and tiled stall-board below. The effect was quaint, old-world, countrified, and inviting. Walton extended the concept inside by fitting it out in rustic style, using oak panelling and exposed ceiling timbers, a cornice shelf sporting Delft tiles, antique plates and vases (plus his own Clutha glass), with sturdy tables and rush- and leather-seated chairs. The 'cottage inglenook with its broad brick hearth, its wide settee and roughly hewn oak beam', lauded in *The Studio* by Baillie Scott only a few months before, was the obvious focus.[19] Revived initially for the cosy interiors of Nesfield and Shaw's 'Old English' style, the fireside recess or inglenook had become an essential element of the Arts and Crafts vernacular style. Walton had built in a fireplace settle at

52. Inglenook at John Rowntree's café.

East Park and the same concept is apparent in a drawing room for James Marshall (pl. 59),[20] but the ingle details at John Rowntree's imply the more specific inspiration of Scott's *Studio* article: half-timbering with ogee braces above, the use of brick on the surround as well as the hearth, and large, ornamented, wrought-iron firedogs 'dumbly expressing the love of the workman for his work'.

Upstairs was an assortment of rooms each decorated in an individual manner – one entirely plain except for

51. John Rowntree's café front, designed by Fred Rowntree with brasswork by Walton & Co.

a narrow band of stencilling, one with a stencilled repeat pattern probably on fabric, and one with plain panelled walls topped with a boldly painted frieze. This latter (clearly aligned with the newest ideas in decoration) attracted adverse comment in *The British Architect* the following year.[21] While ambiguous in his final judgement, the critic was evidently alarmed by its disregard for convention.

Despite this sparing use of pattern, something of the startling plainness of these interiors to contemporary eyes can be understood by comparing them to the typical bourgeois Victorian room, with its rich surfaces and colours, and its tendency to elaborate pattern. The apparently puritan spareness of the café interiors (perhaps not immediately attractive to the average Scarborough resident) was allied with elements of Aesthetic charm. Details of the decorating procedures, which have survived in the form of Walton's invoices to John Rowntree, indicate how novel and fresh the colours and finishes must have seemed.[22] This, combined with the more obvious 'Art' embellishments (panels of Japanese matting, Chinese vases, stencilled wall-hangings and avant-garde furniture), goes to explain the attraction of the John Rowntree rooms, to which this contemporary comment bears witness:

> Now, Scarborough is the epitome of the common place 'proper thing'. There are, or there were until Walton appeared, certain rules to be observed in dress, in demeanour, and even in one's decorations. To have omitted in the domestic embellishment of a Scarborough house, a German print of the Prodigal Son was as serious an offence – and what could be more serious? – as to appear on the evening promenade in flannels and a blazer. Since the beautified Rowntree's Café I do not suggest he has influenced to any marked degree the dress or demeanour of Scarborough visitors, nor has, perhaps, the Prodigal lost all sympathy, but still there is George Walton everywhere; and now the rank and fashion of Scarborough refuse to sip tea except within George Walton clad walls.[23]

Walton's recipe for success was a subtle blending of ingredients applied with the panache of a Whistler devotee. He brought together the fashionable elements of the simpler Morris & Co. interior – coloured stains on wood, fabrics hung on walls, flat floral patterns of cottage-garden flowers set off with intriguing metalwork fittings and unconventional furniture – but they were assembled under an artist's eye. Whistler's sensitivity to colour and surface had been hyper-developed. His canvases have been compared to the enigmatic surfaces of the oriental ceramics he so eagerly collected: 'thin layers of shadowy, evocative colour ... half concealing, half-revealing, like the endless depths of glazed ceramic surfaces'.[24] His paintings were open to view. However publicly inaccessible his interior schemes, his repute as a decorator, often in collusion with the architect Edward Godwin, had certainly reached Walton's ear, if not his eye. Their colours were faded pastels, clear and translucent celadon hues, vegetable yellows and greens – painstakingly mixed by the artists themselves. Walton's repute as a colourist, as a master of materials, was well-established with contemporaries. His attention to surface quality at the Rowntree's café (in delicate combinations of rose pink and purple set off by white) is marked: wood was lightly waxed to bring out the grain or treated with judicious layers of stain and varnish to contrive subtle variations in colour. While the influence of the Glasgow Boys and of Whistler's painterly attitudes is clear, Walton also belonged to a strong Scottish tradition in interior design (of which Cottier was part), renowned for its emphasis on colour.[25]

Within this painterly environment, Walton added his own distinctive touches: innovative metalwork and an individual style of furnishing. The passer-by encountering the café front on the street (pl. 51) was greeted by hand-beaten, repoussé metalwork advertising the name of the proprietor, decorated with a galleon in full sail (an appropriate symbol for an importer, and a chosen emblem of Arts and Crafts designers in the south). Whether or not Walton had contributed to the architectural conception of the shopfront, the brasswork was the product of his firm, as the cost of 'making, designing and supplying' this panel was

53. Part of the company's bill to John Rowntree showing the types of materials and finishes used.

charged at £9 10s. on his bill.[26] The light fittings round the building with their elaborate, curling leaf forms, finished in 'Berlin black', show Walton experimenting more widely with metalwork techniques. Though the company did not list themselves as 'Smiths' in the Trade section of the Post Office Directories until 1899, it is clear they were producing significant pieces of lighter metalwork by 1896.[27]

The current rage for repoussé work which began in the previous decade, was keenly supported by *The Studio* and promoted in Newbery's new Technical Studios at the School of Art.[28] This was principally in brass and copper: from 1893 attention was beginning to turn to silver. With C. R. Ashbee in the lead, designers like Alexander Fisher, Arthur Dixon and Nelson Dawson began to develop a new aesthetic which combined marks of clear hand-finishing with the brightness of semi-precious stones and enamelling, in the production of tableware and jewellery.[29] These developments almost certainly added their force to Walton's later use of colour in metalwork, but perhaps more significant at this time was Ashbee's use of enamels and gemstones on the pewter and copper repoussé ceiling roses of his own home. These had been publicised in that essential manual of the Arts and Crafts, *The Studio*, as well as in *The Art Journal*, in 1895 some months before the execution of Walton's work at John Rowntree's.[30] This gave Walton time to digest and consider the implications. For in the John Rowntree's inglenook there lurked

a surprise. That disregard for convention which so upset *The British Architect* is again apparent: curving arms of metal supported strange copper-work creations, in which were embedded not enamel or precious stones but something much more accessible in Walton's workshops – pieces of coloured glass. These curious firedogs are the first example of his use of copper and glass in fireplace design and properly begin Walton's remarkable career in the production of decorative fireplaces – certainly amongst the best and most original of the period.[31] Baillie Scott and Ashbee would soon be surpassed.

Despite these intriguing developments in Walton's metalwork, by far the greatest significance of John Rowntree's is in the appearance of new furniture designs. Miss Cranston's tea rooms at Buchanan Street would provide a showcase for these developments in Glasgow, but they were not opened until the following May. It was Scarborough which saw the début of a new phase of success in Walton's furniture-making.

Walton had used country-style chairs at his brother Edward's home and in Annan's gallery. For the downstairs café at John Rowntree's he turned to the *caquetoire*, a French Renaissance style which spread to Britain during the later sixteenth century. There were close links between the French and the Scottish courts at this time, and the Scots developed a particular liking for the style, which continued to flourish in Scotland in the seventeenth century; in Walton's time surviving

54. These country-style chairs, designed by Walton for the John Rowntree café, echo the outline of the French *caquetoire* style popular in Scotland in the seventeenth century.

examples could be seen in the more aristocratic Scottish homes. Of joiner's rather than cabinet-maker's construction and of distinctive sculptural form, the *caquetoire* made an ideal prototype for a new Waltonised 'regional' style. William Watt had drawn attention to it in recent years when he commissioned a near-reproduction from Godwin, which appeared as part of the 'Shakespeare' dining room set in Watt's catalogue of 1881. It could hardly have been missed by Walton as it was 'in every upholsterer's showroom' by the middle of the decade.[32] In outline Walton's version is not dissimilar, but the solid panels of seat and back and the heavy turning of the legs are replaced with a lightweight rush-covered open framework of more delicately turned uprights, finished with a flourish to the curve of the arms. Though a highly personal interpretation, this chair is still basically traditional. The 'Abingwood' upstairs is far less conventional.[33] It uses *caquetoire* features of construction – the plank back extended below seat level, the arms with their welcoming semi-circular curve, the trapezoid seat narrowing towards the back – but it emerges in a different class: the back is now tapered and angled, the arms flattened and cantilevered in a quite individual arrangement.

Other chairs at John Rowntree's show the same new confidence in Walton's thinking. All three strands of development distinguishable in his earliest furniture –

55. One of Walton's most distinctive chairs, the 'Abingwood', used at John Rowntree's café and in the billiards room at Buchanan Street (pl. 64).

the country style, plank construction, and finer eighteenth-century derivations – can be seen again at Rowntree's. A tall-backed elegant chair with black-enamelled finish (pl. 63) also makes its appearance in the Rowntree's Café in contrast to the rustic style of his rush-seated chair downstairs and the plank construction of the Abingwood. While the structure of the arm and the outward-curving legs, as well as the finish, of Walton's enamelled chair are directly derived from the Sheraton and early Regency styles, these also link it, with its elongated proportions, to the Aesthetic movement.

Although for most mid-Victorians the fashion for Sheraton and Regency was long since passé, amongst those of more eccentric taste there had always been enthusiasts. In more recent years, in line with the interests of the 'Queen Anne' revival, such fashionable figures as Rossetti and Godwin had declared an interest in the late eighteenth century and Whistler had sought out Regency and Empire styles for furnishing his own home (for they were in direct contrast to the 'elaborate contrivances by which the modern upholsterer encourages lounging in the drawingroom. When you wanted to lounge, he said, the time has come to go to bed').[34] Both Rossetti and Godwin produced their own designs including Sheraton and early Regency features of style in the 1860s and '70s, while precedents for the arrangement of Walton's narrow, caned splat can be found in the sketches of Godwin's friend, Thomas Jeckyll. Walton's adoption of the Sheraton chair is thus comprehensible in context, as well as in keeping with his new-style decoration of the Rowntree café.

From a surviving invoice it can be seen that the work on John Rowntree's was in progress for the greater part of 1896, adding to the coffers of the company the better part of £1000. The effort was worthwhile. The crush of furniture in the rooms when they were recorded in photographs six years later shows that the extent of their popularity was hardly anticipated.[35]

Not to be outdone, William Rowntree, a few doors down the road at 33-9 Westborough, decided it was time to engage the Walton-Rowntree partnership for himself, intending to set up his own refreshment area in the heart of his store. It was an ideal opportunity for Walton to excel. William Rowntree's was the prime Scarborough location for the fashionable shopper, filled with such attractions as Aesthetic furniture and accessories, and Liberty Art Fabrics. William Rowntree was currently adding an extension to his building, to Rowntree's design, and there are indications that his commission to Walton stretched beyond the confines of the tea room to a series of new rooms within the store.[36]

The tea room Walton produced was in complete contrast to the downstairs coffee room at no. 11. The

56. Fashionable Scarborough ladies sipping tea in William Rowntree's store.

rigid distinction between sexes in the Victorian era was strongly reflected in the design of its rooms and Walton responded to expectations by giving the downstairs coffee room at John Rowntree's (the venue for a businessman's lunch) a certain rough chunkiness, while in the sophisticated department store down the road (a ladies' domain) the atmosphere was delicate and refined. This sensitivity to requirements had been evident in his design for the Lady Artists: the gallery there was more formal than the tea room and more 'artistic'

than the café. Walton rarely found expectations a constraint. He could consistently provide interiors which were both imaginative and appropriate: a strong card in the development of his decorating business.

In his tea room for William Rowntree, the gentle curves, the light colour scheme, the fine surface of the fielded leather panels, the slender Godwin-inspired tables and the stylish seating (another idiosyncratic but modern rendering of an earlier style) are carefully combined.[37] The unity achieved is partly a result of attention to architectural elements: the modulation of ceilings and columns to escape the rigid right angles of the ordinary room and echo the character of the decorations. At William Rowntree's we see Walton's horizons extending. A new interest in problems of form suggests that his close collaboration with an architect has had its effect. Even the fireplace demonstrates Walton's absorption of Rowntree's lessons: its relationships of positive and negative values closely parallels Rowntree's handling of form and void on the John Rowntree Café front.

Walton's interest in the manipulation of the contours of the room now becomes a particular preoccupation. At James Marshall's house of *c.* 1896-7 he uses the decorator's rather than the architect's tools to this

57. A corner of the William Rowntree tea room showing the leather-panelled walls.

58. Stone chimneypiece in William Rowntree's tea room, with stencilled tulips above, 1897.

59. Drawing room for James Marshall, c. 1896-7. The ceiling beams are unlikely to have been structural.

60. Detail from a stained glass window at William Rowntree's store (see also pl. 125).

end, but it is yet a further example of the workings of a new frame of mind. The drawing room for James Marshall prompts an interesting speculation.[38] Marshall was a partner in the building firm of Hunter & Marshall and is known to have been involved in Walton's company from 1897: in later years John Hunter was also a shareholder. How did Walton come to know these builders? Could they have been on the lists of the Stark & Rowntree practice? Who, for instance, executed the work on the Gallery and at Glen Bank? It is not unreasonable to wonder whether Walton's close association with these builders contributed to his growing architectural awareness.

One of the features emerging in Walton's style was his use of restrained ornament set off against plain surfaces. Following the wall pattern of Edward's Glasgow home, and the grass-tuft repeat of an early interior (pls 21, 26), the type of simple stencilled pattern on the walls of the upstairs room at John Rowntree's begins to replace the elaborate overlays of the Drumalis ceiling or the Italianate wallpaper at Thornton Lodge (pl. 25). The frieze stencil at William Rowntree's (pl. 58) goes further: economical, open, it shows a new tendency to give individual treatment to separated motifs. A fabric at Glen Bank uses the same method – single pinks or carnations in a regular repeat.[39] This new style begins to appear in Walton's stained glass: the carnations of the Glen Bank fabric, the tulips of the Burrell window (pl. 30), a single twisting spray of briar and a vase of

flowers are the elements used to decorate the windows of the new Rowntree extension. The impact of these motifs is enhanced by their deliberate contrast with plainer surfaces around.

Buchanan Street

What the Rowntree establishments did for Walton's reputation in Scarborough, the Buchanan Street tea rooms would do supremely in Glasgow. Miss Cranston's individual taste in the decoration of her tea rooms, her consistent attention to the quality of food and service, had ensured the success of her business. Marriage in 1892 enabled her to expand with financial confidence. Her latest project, under way by 1896, was a five-storey establishment on Glasgow's premier shopping street. Despite the narrow frontage, the scale of the premises at 91-3 Buchanan Street meant a dramatic extension of her tea room empire, already established on two small but successful sites on Argyle and Ingram Street. In November 1896, while work on John Rowntree's was still in progress, Walton was busy with the interiors.[40]

Amongst the contractors Miss Cranston employed at Buchanan Street was the young architect Charles Rennie Mackintosh. Whilst various theories have emerged on the source of his involvement, it only remains certain that Miss Cranston took him on. That Walton had met Mackintosh before is not in doubt. They had both been involved in the Lady Artists' Fancy Fair of 1895, but it was not until this point that their careers began to overlap. Their ages were close (Walton was barely more than a year older), but their backgrounds were different. Walton had led his well-established company, patronised by a range of prominent Glasgow figures, for most of a decade. He had worked consistently on interior decorations and was a successful and experienced designer of furniture and stained glass. From the practice of these skills he earned his living. Mackintosh's energies, in the architectural offices of Honeyman & Keppie, had been largely directed to the furtherance of his architectural career, supplemented by classes at the School of Art. By 1896, he had had time for only a few decorative experiments on the side.

The unfamiliar distortions of the graphic work of 'The Four' (the Macdonald sisters, Mackintosh and MacNair), as shown at the Glasgow Art Club in 1894, had already met with disapproval.[41] Walton, from a family of artists in which conventional figure drawing was highly esteemed and who later expressed a strong dislike for the stylisations of Art Nouveau, is likely to have found himself out of sympathy. From the architectural office in which he had worked since 1889, Mackintosh's viewpoint and influences were different. Despite his association with the Glasgow Boy David Gauld, the training in a discipline which stressed relationships of form and precision of line led Mackintosh to admire the more severely stylised forms and decorative manipulations of Beardsley and the Dutch Symbolist Jan Toorop. Walton shared a regard for the more decorative aspects of Beardsley, but, in the main, different sources appealed: the Pre-Raphaelites, the Glasgow Boys, the work of Whistler and Walter Crane. These would be the most obvious sources of inspiration for his work on the walls of Buchanan St. The uncertain response Mackintosh's early graphic work received might have persuaded another architect to keep to his own specialism. It is difficult not to see Newbery's support and that of his fellow students at the School as crucial to Mackintosh's confidence. Newbery's hand in recommending him to Miss Cranston is not unlikely.[42]

Even so, Miss Cranston's keen eye could hardly have missed the controversial posters and graphic work emerging from 'The Four' at the School of Art. Mackintosh had produced very little furniture by this stage and it was not easily encountered. She may have noted his pieces shown at the 1895 Glasgow Arts and Crafts Exhibition, perhaps others elsewhere, but her employment of Mackintosh on mural designs at Buchanan Street – on two dimensional rather than three dimensional work – indicates that she was mainly familiar with his graphic experiments.

At Buchanan Street, Walton had the lion's share of the decorations and responsibility for the furnishings throughout, some if not all of the light fittings, the table settings, the stationery and the hoarding outside. The two lower storeys and the billiards room on the upper floor were entirely his domain. In the luncheon room, the ladies tea room and smoking gallery, he would need to co-operate with Mackintosh, to whom three large wall spaces had been allotted.[43] Walton's work would be executed by Walton & Co., Mackintosh's by Guthrie & Wells.

Walton may have had ambivalent feelings about Mackintosh, but he was not so proud or narrow-minded as to have overlooked the young architect's talents, even if his own tastes ran in a different vein. With no surviving contemporary record, it is now impossible to explore the relationship between the two designers. Yet their personalities were different and their directions opposed: they were not well matched.

This ill-assorted partnership came up with surprisingly satisfactory results. The emphasis in the interiors was on eye-catching wall decorations and Mackintosh's murals in both the Ladies' Tea Room and the Luncheon Room, strikingly conceived, co-ordinated pleasantly with Walton's furniture. His elongated trees match the straight, high-backs of Walton's cane chairs in one room; in another, the curves of his formalised vegetation link with the arched shaping of Walton's ladderbacks. Miss Cranston's trust was vindicated. Walton's wall decorations, in a more naturalistic style – a hunting scene, delicate floral patterns, vases of flowers and fruit (pls 64, 62, 61) – looked strangely naïve by comparison. A sprinkling of familiar motifs proclaims his loyalties: a butterfly for Whistler and a carnation declaring his links with the Arts and Crafts in the south (Ashbee used it as an emblem of his Guild). Walton furnishings – a selection of traditional country chairs and a number of his own designs – tell the same tale.

Despite her advanced approach to interiors Miss Cranston had commissioned a somewhat conservative Edinburgh architect to design the façade. George Washington Browne was not perhaps the best choice: he chose the revivalist idiom of François I, and scattered ungainly chunks of Rococo ornament around the inside, to the decorators' dismay. By the time of the opening in May 1897, Miss Cranston might already have regretted her decision. Gleeson White, in his *Studio* review in July gave Browne and his heavy-handed woodwork a hard time: 'ornate and superfluous ... these costly additions are eyesores, and mar the effect of an otherwise completely satisfactory experiment.'[44] It is Browne's intrusions which spoil the elegant simplicity of Walton's dining room (pl. 62) and represent the type of problem with which Walton must have been only too familiar. He had learnt to adapt. He succeeded here in painting over much of the woodwork, including the fireplace surround, with a light colour, interspersing the strapwork of the ceiling with delicate petals and flowers. Running a decorating business was not always easy, but Walton had learnt to cope with difficulties and usually came out on top.

Walton developed his use of stencils at Buchanan Street. The Scarborough rooms have already demonstrated that by this stage Walton had abandoned wallpapers in favour of this versatile technique, which he used on fabrics, ceilings and friezes. Stencilling had a

61. Tea room by Walton at Buchanan Street, with painted and stencilled wall decorations, magnificent brass electrolier, and traditional country spindlebacks.

number of advantages for Walton. First was the increased control it offered over buying from another firm's catalogue (for he had long since opted against producing wallpapers himself). It carried the prestige of a more exclusive form and suited his painterly hand.

Walton had involved himself in hand-painted wall decorations and stencilwork from the earliest years of the firm, gaining experience and expertise which he would later share fully with his Glasgow audience in a lecture.[45] He discovered that the use of transparent stains combined with resists was one of the most effective ways of colouring a plaster surface: it ensured the greatest possible use of the background colour and texture of the plaster, which in his estimation was essential to the balance and harmony of the whole. As a method it had close parallels with the watercolour technique used so effectively by his brother. Walton limited himself to a few colours, which, carefully blended in different combinations, gave a unity to the overall scheme. Darker stains or touches of body colour were used to bring out the pattern, and the need to make final adjustments as the work neared completion was

recognised. The development of this technique can be seen at Drumalis, where the background colour of the plaster is used as a basis for a scheme designed with a clearly restricted palette.

Walton made no secret of his successful formula. When opportunity arose he shared the fruits of his experience and the intricacies of his technique. Part of the making of Mackintosh was inevitably his absorption of what practitioners around him had already achieved. At Buchanan Street, Walton was the professional, Mackintosh the novice. Gleeson White's description of Mackintosh's technique shows a remarkable concurrence with Walton's and suggests that, if he was not learning on the job, he had taken earlier opportunities to examine Walton's work.

At Buchanan Street Walton varied the effect of each room, as he had at John Rowntree's, by using different techniques. One room was hung with a woven tapestry, one decorated with a simple stencilled repeat. In another, painted panels were set against alternating bands of stencilling, and in the billiards room (pl. 64) the two techniques were combined in a pictorial mural. While the design of Walton's woven tapestry belongs to the pattern-making tradition of Morris (though in a style more open and delicate than Morris' compa-

62. A luncheon room by Walton at Miss Cranston's Buchanan Street premises, lined with the silk and linen tapestry he used on several commissions.

rable 'Medway' or 'Flora'), his murals place him within the long-established tradition of interior painting of which Cottier had been part.[46]

Walton's natural sensitivity to techniques accorded with the Arts and Crafts concept of 'truth to materials'. In wall decorations he developed a style of pattern design which was sympathetic to the methods employed. The woven silk and linen tapestry has a flowing character which reflects the technique of weaving, while his stencilled patterns on fabric clearly reflect the method of printing in sections (cf. pl. 83).

Despite the incongruence of Washington Browne's woodwork, Walton's new furniture designs are much better integrated than they were in the upstairs rooms of John Rowntree's. Walton's attention to the harmony of the components of his interiors is visible in the tapestry dining room, where the gentle curves of the textile pattern are reflected in the lines of the light fitting and the slender undulations of the furnishing.[47] An armchair much closer to the Sheraton style than his chair for John Rowntree is paired here with another with an unusually extended back. The back of this chair flows –

like the wall pattern – in an elegant linear design, producing a new form of high-backed chair, linked by materials and construction to both the Aesthetic movement and early Regency furniture, but at the same time distinct. This emphasis on sinuous verticality is paralleled in Walton's earliest upholstered chairs, particularly an armchair used at Glen Bank, and the later Ledcameroch (pl. 73), and shows his ability to produce quite unconventional designs, which still retain traditional links. Verticality was an important component of the Glasgow Style, as it had also been of the '80s aesthetic. Godwin, Dresser, Mackmurdo and the teetering fabrications of trade 'Art furniture' all contributed to its tenacious popularity. Mackintosh's unapproachable ladies in the luncheon room, like the elongated figures of his poster work, demonstrate that he was already a master of extended form. Walton introduced this element into the art of Glasgow Style furniture.

The country chairs Walton used at Buchanan Street were just as carefully selected. Standard ladder- and spindlebacks of Lancashire origin, they were chosen for their qualities of line and form including a strongly vertical character. Despite the fact that Walton's company was expanding vigorously in the area of furniture making at this time, Buchanan Street shows that he

63. The black-enamelled chairs used at John Rowntree's café and Miss Cranston's Buchanan Street tea rooms, and frequently thereafter, occasionally in other finishes (*cf.* pl. 84).

was still prepared to use 'ready-mades' when they suited his purpose. With the John Rowntree and William Rowntree jobs overlapping in the later part of 1896 (perhaps with the Buchanan Street work already in hand), Walton & Co.'s workshop capacity was undoubtedly full. If it was a choice between contracting out his own designs to local makers, and choosing from among the many regional styles, he evidently preferred the latter.

The use of heavy furniture for the billiards rooms was the accepted way of marking out its masculinity. Perhaps the pyramidal tendency of the billiards-table legs and the flat, non-perspectival decorative arrangement of the wall paintings were what prompted Edwin Lutyens to see in it shadows of Egypt, when he breakfasted at 'these queer, funny rooms' in June 1898. More

of Japan and Degas (the presence of which he also noted) might have inspired the careful arrangement of the mural composition, with its 'figure groups always thrust well to the side of the panel or spandril, with an effect which one would suppose to be far from restful'. Lutyens was delighted with the spectacle of the tea rooms: the 'greens, golds, blues, white rooms with black furniture, black rooms with white furniture', with the peonies on the tables, the green- and purple-handled knives, (and with his 'tea, butter, jam, toasts, baps and buns', sausages and eggs – not to mention the moderate price) even if he found it all, from the southerner's viewpoint, a little 'outré'.[48] A visiting critic from *The British Architect* (at a preview of the tea room decorations in Walton's Glasgow Institute exhibit in early 1897) also appreciated the billiards room mural, which

64. Walton's murals and furnishing in the billiards room at the Buchanan Street tea rooms. The distinctive Abingwood chair was used also at John Rowntree's café (pl. 55).

combined both painterly and decorative traditions, with its 'open contempt for convention ... but perhaps something fantastical is not altogether out of place in a place of entertainment'.[49] Hints of Voysey's wallpapers, especially those illustrated in *The Studio* earlier in 1896, can be detected in some of Walton's motifs, but most of the details – the stylised trees, for instance – were in common use among other designers whose work appeared in that journal – the design by Henry Wilson illustrated in 1893 is a prominent example.[50]

The jaunty spots of colour at Buchanan Street, remarked by Lutyens, were as apparent in Mackintosh's as Walton's work. Walton's palette derived from sources which included the Glasgow Boys, Whistler, and strong links with the Aesthetic movement as a whole. When Oscar Wilde, that evangelist of Aestheticism, crossed the Atlantic to convert America ('I am here to diffuse beauty, and I have no objection to saying that'), he had worn a green dressing gown to greet the press, and his get-ups for the trip – vital to the promotion of his aesthetic philosophy – included a coat lined in lavender and a prominently displayed yellow silk handkerchief.[51] If dandyism was to be avoided, the colours of the Aesthetic movement held an irresistible charm. Mackintosh's and Walton's colour combinations demonstrated shared ancestry. Mackintosh's earliest graphic works, 'The Descent of Night', 'The Tree of Per-

sonal Effort', 'The Shadow', bi-chromatic studies, emit echoes of Whistler's 'Nocturne in Blue and Green: Chelsea', or his 'Nocturne in Blue and Gold: Old Battersea Bridge'. Mackintosh's 'greyish-greenish yellow' walls at Buchanan Street recall the infamous 'greenery-yallery' of the Aesthetic movement. The flat (poster-like) background tones, combined with small, jewel-like spots of vivid colour, recorded by Gleeson White, parallel Walton's approach to stained glass.[52]

One of the most important lessons Walton had to teach was his concept of unity. It was clear in the luncheon room as it had been in the William Rowntree tea room. It was a lesson Mackintosh fully absorbed. Buchanan Street demonstrates Walton's artistic effort to touch everything – even the hoarding outside was an overture to the harmonies within.

The mood he wished to create in the tea rooms was appropriate to their function – refreshing, entertaining perhaps, but restful. The peacock design of Walton's hoarding is similarly the result of his acute sense of occasion, its dynamism making an effective advertisement. Walton's peacock is clearly derived from published sources which were readily accessible – from

65. Walton's powerful hoarding with its Whistlerian peacock stood outside the Buchanan Street tea rooms in late 1896 and early 1897.

Beardsley's graphic work (especially 'The Peacock Girl' reproduced in *The Studio* in 1894) and the Whistler-Jeckyll decoration of The Peacock Room (illustrated in *The Art Journal* in 1892); but the thoughtful transition to stencil, the impulse and imagination needed to take on such a mundane object, are Walton's own.[53] The hoarding was dramatic, intriguing: it could not be passed by. Walton's sense of theatre was deeply embedded, the passion of a reticent man who could not express his imagination in words. Even now Walton was indulging his predilection, appearing as the Red Haired Sorcerer at Glasgow's Fancy Costume Ball.[54]

Edward in Chelsea

While Walton was working on Buchanan Street, his brother Edward had settled in a studio room in the house of C. R. Ashbee.[55] 'The Magpie and Stump', 37 Cheyne Walk, was in the heart of London's Chelsea Bohemia, the artists' enclave along the river studded with studio houses, where Carlyle, Rossetti and Wilde (now in Pentonville prison) had lived, and which had among its residents the artists George Clausen, Walter Sickert, Philip Wilson Steer, and Whistler himself. Godwin, Webb, G. F. Bodley and Norman Shaw were among the architects of its buildings, and Ashbee, that 'studio-building gent', as E. A. Abbey labelled him in a letter to Edward, was just now starting out his modest practice in the building of artists' homes.[56] Exactly when Edward formed an acquaintance with Ashbee, already emerging as one of the more significant figures of the Arts and Crafts movement, is unclear. Ashbee exhibited regularly at the Arts and Crafts Exhibitions, and had strong contacts with the New English Art Club patronised by the Boys. This is where Edward is most likely to have met him. Frustratingly, Ashbee's intimately-recorded private life suffers a period of comparative obscurity at this time, just as the Waltons (Edward and his wife, Helen) enter the scene. Though there is no documentary evidence of a personal friendship between Ashbee and George, some contact between them seems probable and the path of the next few years is strewn with tokens hinting at Walton's familiarity with Ashbee's work.

What would have interested George Walton most about Ashbee was the Guild of Handicraft, set up in the same year as his own company. He could have examined its productions from time to time at the Arts and Crafts Exhibitions or in reviews in *The Studio*. At this stage the repoussé work would have caught his eye – and Ashbee's light fittings. It would be technique, images, proportions, ideas for new combinations of crafts that Walton would have looked for: the deeper currents in Ashbee are likely to have passed him by. Then there was the business side. Walton did not find this aspect of company matters inspiring (the success of his company had come more from his artistic individuality and his understanding of clients), but he would have a natural curiosity about the Guild's commercial standing. As he turned over in his mind the future of his own company, Walton must have found encouragement in the success of the Guild.

There was overlap in their output, but the Guild of Handicraft was rather different from Walton & Co. Walton had started his company as a decoration business, so his first aims had been general, not particular – which had necessitated the buying in of wallpapers, furniture, etc. available on the market. With Walton, the broad brush came first (walls, ceilings, floors), and when he could he took up the finer brushes (metalworkers, glass-workers, cabinet-makers) to work up the detail. His aim was not to train the workers, like Ashbee, or to revive a craft, but to add to the effect of his overall scheme. For this reason there were different emphases in their output. Ashbee produced furniture, though he did not excel; stencilling and stained glass did not figure at all. Silver and jewellery were far more important and later there would be the Essex House Press. Ashbee's interiors could not be described as harmonious (interior design did not come first on his list, so it was not to be expected). Muthesius would have put him with the group of designers whose rooms were 'not so very different from the old idea of assembling good interiors from whatever scattered material happens to be available', in the comforting company of Voysey and Morris.[57]

Edward had moved into the studio at Cheyne Walk during the autumn of 1896. Walton was working in Scarborough then and busy with his plans for Buchanan Street, but in those quiet moments when he pondered the future, his thoughts strayed to London.

IV TRANSITION

It was just at this point, as the work on Buchanan Street was drawing to a close, as Walton's prominence in Glasgow was reaching new heights, that he was arranging his removal from the scene. Negotiations to sell his private business, to set up a new limited joint-stock company, had begun in the summer of 1896. It was the end of May 1897 – the month in which Buchanan Street opened – which would mark Walton's release from full-time attendance at the Glasgow premises. He had been preparing the move for some time.

Walton could hardly have exhausted the market for his interior work in Glasgow. On the contrary, a new awareness of design amongst the Glasgow public was growing, to which the Buchanan Street tea rooms contributed. The founding shareholders' confidence in the new company, George Walton & Co. Ltd, is expressed in its terms of agreement.[1] It claimed a monopoly on business attracted by Walton over an area covering the whole of Ireland as well as Scotland, Lancashire and Yorkshire. The capital raised from the sale of shares would be used to finance an expansion of the business: new workshops and the opening of a new office-showroom in York. Walton's company was thriving.

The reorganisation of the company increased its prospects. It brought into formal arrangement the advice and experience Walton was gaining from a small band of intimates. Chief among these was Fred Rowntree. The strength of Rowntree's friendship and identification with Walton at this stage is underlined in his commitment to the new firm. He held only five less shares than Walton, so that, with over 50% of the shares sold in the first year between them, they controlled the business. William Gray, Rowntree's brother-in-law and also a Quaker (connected by marriage to Walton through the Hendersons),[2] and James Marshall were two of the firm's founding shareholders and initial directors. Gray brought to the firm business experience from his own company, Gray, Dunn & Co., biscuit manufacturers, whose factory extension was still in the hands of the Stark & Rowntree partnership. Marshall's involvement has already raised the suggestion that some of his firm's contracts may have coincided with Walton's commissions. The new company's declared competency as 'Builders, Plumbers, Gasfitters (and) Electrical Engineers'[3] implies an arrangement with his firm, Hunter & Marshall: certainly in the future Marshall's building knowledge would support the increasingly ambitious work the company was taking on. Others involved at the outset took less major roles. To

66. George Walton photographed by his friend James Craig Annan.

find James Craig Annan's name on the list is hardly surprising. Annan's colleague at T. & R. Annan & Sons, Alexander Mackendrick, and Rowntree's partner Malcolm Stark complete the group.[4]

Walton's projected move was one of the reasons underlying the reorganisation of the company. But why Walton should want to leave Glasgow, at the inception of this new and promising era for the firm, might not have been immediately obvious. Consideration of his personal and professional interests rapidly reveals his motives. What more than London could have attracted Walton to move from Glasgow? Much of his inspiration had come from that source: the Arts and Crafts exhibitions, William Morris; even the Aesthetic movement, though widely spread, had emanated primarily from London. Personal friendships – Whistler and associates at the New English Art Club – with the attraction of better long-term prospects, had drawn his brother Edward south. There is no reason to suppose that George's case was different. C. F. A. Voysey, whose architectural practice was London-based, had become a personal friend and his encouragement may be assumed. And what of Ashbee, Edward's landlord? Had he some influence on the decision? Both Ashbee's association with Edward and A. H. Mackmurdo's friendship with Whistler are intriguing connections: the possibility of their personal encouragement to Walton to move to London must be taken into account. Clearly Edward's experience had been positive. James Guthrie took on a London studio in 1897. John Lavery would soon do the same: he and other Glasgow painters who as yet remained north of the border, with the photographers James Craig Annan and W. M. Warneuke, made frequent forays into London to associate and exhibit with like-minded colleagues. They had found that publicity and acclaim came more readily from that quarter than from their own city. In London, the new decorative movement was better established and the market larger. Walton would understandably have felt that his professional prospects were greater too. Kate, who would have been returning home, is unlikely to have demurred.

By August, preparations were complete. George, Kate and five-year-old Marguerite moved to a good-sized house, 16 Westbourne Park Road, London, with a studio in the garden.[5] It was not quite the artists' enclave of Holland Park, or Chelsea, but it was the nearest thing – a good base for future work and a location less likely to be a drain on resources at this delicate stage in his career. The property was rented from Arthur Bolton, an architect much the same age as Walton, who had set up his own practice in 1890.[6] On the face of it, Walton was in situation remarkably similar to his brother's.

Like Edward, too, Walton came under 'Artists' in the Post Office Directories. In Glasgow he had been a decorator, in London it was to be 'George Walton, Artist'.[7] The significance of this must not be overlooked. It is understandable that a certain veneration for artists had resulted from Walton's youthful admiration for the Glasgow Boys and this is not refuted by his realistic choice of a decorating career. As we have seen, Whistler's approbation was vital. Whistler had made it ac-

ceptable, respectable, even fashionable to take up a career in decoration. He claimed to attach as much importance to his interior decorations as to his paintings, insisting that 'to be a painter, one must be a decorator, able to make of the wall, the room containing it, indeed, the whole house, a harmony, a symphony, an arrangement'.[8] Perhaps Walton, with his Glasgow company, did not feel he had become quite the right sort of decorator. After all, those he admired were first (or had been first) artists or architects: William Morris, Voysey, Mackmurdo, Ashbee, Godwin, Whistler ... and even the architects viewed themselves as artists. Their reaction against the earnest Gothicism and dry professionalism of an older generation, against the increasingly technical and commercial outlook of the R.I.B.A., had led them to shun a 'tradesman's approach'. Looking back, Ashbee expressed this feeling:

> I was ... [at Toynbee Hall] the only architect in residence. I came across some of the others, the great professional architects from time to time, the men who regarded themselves first from the point of view of a profession or business. We were always out of sympathy.[9]

And why? Because he and his progressive colleagues had different perceptions, 'higher' ideals. Architects like Burges, Godwin, Nesfield and Webb had mixed in the same artistic circles as Rossetti, Morris, Burne-Jones, Whistler and Albert Moore. They considered themselves artists not professionals. It was an attitude of mind common among Arts and Crafts architects, which had every attraction for Walton. (Though somehow, with their qualifications, it was easier for them to castigate 'professionalism': Walton never forgot his lack of training.) Those whom Walton hoped to join aimed at a unity in the arts. They sought a marriage between art and handicraft, rejecting the hierarchy of the 'greater' (fine) and 'lesser' (applied) arts of the old system – the denigration of architecture and the decorative arts. Instead, they were all artists as they were all craftsmen ('craftsmen in architecture, painting, sculpture and the kindred arts').[10] This was what the Art Workers' Guild stood for, an organisation to which the greater part of them belonged.

In London Walton was virtually unknown. Yet his position was far from insecure. Walton had not severed links with the company: instead, he was committed to the active role of Managing Director for the first five years. Without special dispensation from his Directors, he was obliged to give the making up of any newly-acquired work to the company workshops. He retained control over artistic decisions and would be acting to all intents and purposes as an agent for the company in the south. He had a regular salary – £100 a year basic, with a scheme of profit- and commission-related bonuses.[11] It was an arrangement which combined his

67. Insignia by Heywood Sumner for the Arts and Crafts Exhibition Society, 1888: there is no doubt here about the superior status of architecture and the fine arts.

personal inclinations with the benefit of an enlarged field of operations for the company. Most of all, it provided Walton with an assured income over the transitional period and the backing of the company's expertise in the production of his work.

Into the limelight

To find this new work, his reliance would be entirely on personal connections: and, of all Walton's friends, it was the photographers who proved most significant in this respect. For the first three years in London Walton's work came almost exclusively from the photographic world, the world from which he gained the most important clients of his later career.

W. M. Warneuke and James Craig Annan were competitors in Glasgow, but in London they were colleagues. Exhibiting regularly at the Royal Photographic Society's annual exhibitions, they had become involved with the agitated debate on the Society's future. Annan, particularly, had enlisted with the Secession movement in photography when he joined 'The Linked Ring' in 1894. It was part of the more general revolt against convention in the arts with which Annan was familiar from the Glasgow Boys' struggle with the R.S.A. Not unaccountably, The Linked Ring was likened by critics to the New English Art Club, with which they shared exhibition rooms.[12]

It had happened like this. In 1891-2 a group of respected photographers resigned from the Royal Photographic Society (the R.P.S.) after a row, purportedly over the showing of a late entry by one George Davison. A split had been imminent, the reasons for it running much deeper than this question of the late entry. Davison and his supporters represented the belief in photography as an art form, while the hierarchy at the R.P.S. was preoccupied almost exclusively with the scientific and technical aspects of the medium. It was not unlike the artistically-minded architects' repudiation of the R.I.B.A. Davison, H. P. Robinson, and others, formed The Linked Ring for the purposes of exhibiting together and giving mutual support. They called their exhibitions, held at the Dudley Gallery from 1893, 'The Photographic Salon'. Annan was closely associated with events and elected a 'Link' in February 1894. While his influence grew, his international reputation became established.

The Photographic Salon attracted at least as much attention as the R.P.S. itself. The group's artistic inclinations went further than the photographs. Their concept of the photographer as artist-craftsman gave them new horizons: they became increasingly interested in presentation and display. The distinguished photographer H. P. Robinson assumed the office of 'High Executioner' with Davison and Henry Van der Weyde as deputies, responsible for the 'hanging' of the exhibitions. Even before Walton arrived, their awareness of Whistler's exhibitions is evident, as they extended their attention to catalogues, posters and admission tickets as well as the mounting, framing and hanging of the photographs – all considered part of an integrated whole. By the time Walton arrived in London in 1897, The Linked Ring had already attracted praise in the photographic press for its tasteful arrangement of pictures. In November 1896 Annan used his influence as 'Centre Link' to press for further improvements. The walls of the Dudley Gallery had for long constrained the Linked Ring exhibitions to 'harmonies' in 'Maroon and Brown and Black'. The broad dark frames which Walton pioneered (now the established fashion amongst Links), however tastefully arranged, were inevitably set against these sombre walls. What had seemed at first to add to the 'quiet Dignity' of their exhibitions was now to Annan a 'maroon Dungeon', depressing, gloomy, encroaching on the possibilities of his pictures. With stirring suggestions of softer, more delicate colour combinations ('light brownish or greenish grey') Annan urged his colleagues to provide their own decorations for the Salon the following year. A lighter colour scheme would afford new opportunities, 'the Invention of dainty Designs and exquisite Mouldings in light Colours'.[13] It is not difficult to imagine where Annan – so long reliant on Walton's decorative abilities for framing and gallery decoration – had found his inspiration.

Annan's arguments prevailed. For the 1897 show, Walton was engaged and the interior of the Dudley Gallery left in his hands. The decorations immediately became a focus of attention for the press:

> Mr Maskell always appears to keep a reserve of attractions up his sleeve … This year he stages Mr George Walton, an art designer and decorator, and the bichromated gum process. These, so to speak, are the star turns of an entertainment that may or may not satisfy the shilling public, but which is bound to lead to a great amount of discussion among photographers.[14]

Walton's design of the gallery caused a stir – a response to his scheme of decoration combined with several innovations. On the arrangement of the display, *The Photography Annual* declared it to be 'the first time the geometrical, symmetrical, traditional manner had been completely abandoned'.[15] In placing the pictures in groups and sub-groups in an irregular pattern with varying spaces between the frames, Walton rejected both the traditional practice (employed by the rival R.P.S.) of 'skying and diving' – simply covering every available wall space with pictures regardless how high or low – as well as the popular alternative of arrangement in symmetrical groups. Despite the Salons' earlier efforts at improvement, recognised in their time,

68. A wall at the 1897 Photographic Salon. Walton's decorative touches on the wall were controversial.

Walton's sensitive arrangement was regarded as a complete innovation. It was indeed a wholly sympathetic display. It relied for its effect on rejection of all but the highest quality pictures (for this he was dependent on the concurrent policy of the Selection Committee), and aimed to accentuate the individual qualities of each.

Walton lined the walls with burnt sienna canvas. Its texture related to the new rough-textured photographic surfaces favoured by the Links and the colour subtly complemented and gave warmth to the prevailing sepia browns and greys of the photographs. There were paler tones of brown and green above and drapes of cheesecloth at one end. The arrangement was enhanced by decorative touches, all but unheard of in photographic displays: the field of vision above the display was separated by a decorative shelf fixed at cornice height on which were placed 'pale green glass vessels' holding bunches of dried honesty pods at tasteful intervals, while, here and there, to the critics' surprise, small decorative devices, of scroll, leaf or flower form, were applied.[16]

Not all reviewers were kind. Some derided the flower motifs as 'puerile' and the 'haphazard system of hanging' as a 'deliberate attempt to be carelessly artistic, not wholly free from affectation'. Others, however, claimed Walton had 'converted the somewhat sombre

Dudley Gallery into an apartment of sweetness and light' and thought the arrangement showed taste, skill and judgement. Either way, the more relaxed atmosphere provided unexpected relief: 'jaded exhibition-goers as we are, we certainly experienced less fatigue in examining the well-spaced out frames ... than we have known at any previous Exhibition'.[17]

The reviews imply that, to London critics at least, the artistic decoration of a photographic exhibition was a complete novelty (though we should note the positive reference to Annan's recent exhibition 'of limited publicity' by *The Amateur Photographer*).[18] Some less insular minds recognised the relationship of Walton's exhibition to 'Mr Whistler's "Mustard Pot", Mr Mortimer Menpes' Japanese Show, and several other painting exhibitions in London, Paris and New York'.[19] The 'Mustard Pot' would be Whistler's exhibition at the Fine Art Society of 1883 where the dominant colours were yellow and white, colours carried through in 'the costume of the attendant at the door, the flowers, the pots, the chairs, the assistants' neckties and even Whistler's socks'.[20] This was but one of a series of exhibitions by Whistler which made a radical departure from earlier shows with their typical drapes in rich dark hues designed to set off the paintings' ornate and gilded frames. It was the 'Mustard Pot' to which Walton later referred as 'the most remarkable event of the time', bringing a 'gaiety into all contemporary decorations', though the colours of his 1897 Salon were in fact closer to Whistler's exhibition at Dowdeswell's Gallery of 1886.[21]

There is no doubt about the 'whirlwind of criticism' the exhibition provoked. Not one of six major articles on the 1897 Salon failed to discuss Walton's contribution and though, according to one critic, opinions seemed about equally divided for and against, it should not be forgotten that many of the reviewers would have belonged to a group out of sympathy with the latest artistic developments *en bloc*.[22]

The 'artistic' faction was delighted with the results. The 'typical London decorator' had not in the past proved sensitive to their purposes: 'just as the average joiner breaks down hopelessly when required to build a light-tight dark room or a photographer's studio ... the photogram framer and photographic gallery decorator needs to have some intimate acquaintance with the general character of the works he is to surround'.[23] Now they had found their man.

George Davison and the Eastman exhibition

'Deputy High Executioner' George Davison, was particularly taken with Walton's work. A controversial figure, a distinguished amateur photographer at the centre of the Secession movement, Davison had made a stand for 'impressionistic' photography (the communication of the photographer's artistic impressions through the image) at a lecture he gave to the Royal Society of Arts in 1890. His experiments with blurred or softened images (in particular his alternately praised and derided 'Onion Field'), were at total variance with the more conventional photographer's regard for definition. Shortly before the opening of the Salon, Davison had left his job in the civil service to become assistant manager of the new Eastman Photographic Materials Co. (later Kodak Ltd) in Holborn: he had been a member of the company's Board for some years. He may by this time have already engaged Walton's offices for the decoration of his new home 'Beechcroft', the step which initiated his personal dependence on Walton's skills.[24] It is difficult to know when Walton and Davison had first met: perhaps as far back as 1893 when Annan and Davison were showing work at the first Photographic Salon and Walton was exhibiting at the London Arts and Crafts. It is likely that Davison asked Walton to design the Eastman Company's Exhibition before he saw the Salon – as it opened on 27th October 1897 at the New Gallery, Regent Street, only three weeks after the Salon had opened on the 4th.[25]

The Eastman Exhibition was rather a different affair from the Salon. It was much bigger; and, it was a commercial enterprise. Walton's responsibility was chiefly for two rooms: the West Gallery, where enlargements of the work of well-known photographers were on display, and the North Gallery, filled with thousands of prints sent in in response to a competition, including some by members of the Royal Family. Walton's decorations were much more elaborate than at the Salon, reflecting the no-expense-spared attitude of the company. In the West Gallery, the walls were swathed in purple. Gatherings of white cloth with a border design bearing the word 'Kodak', were used to break up the display. Drapes were also carried across the ceiling, forming a velarium, which distributed softly coloured light from the windows above.[26]

The North Gallery was more restrained. The white linen covering the walls was embellished with a repeat of stencilled motifs complemented by a central potted palm. Walton solved the problem of unifying thousands of small exhibits by using large decorated frames and providing portfolios through which the public could browse. It was different, more restful, but quite as successful as the West Gallery.

Regarded as a whole, the exhibition was considered by the press to be 'the biggest and best thing ever done in this country in the way of photographic exhibitions'.[27] It was an extravagant display. Davison had given Walton a free hand and Walton had amply rewarded his trust. He had understood the necessity of making a grand impression for the benefit of the company; he had resolved the not inconsiderable display problems into a unified whole; he had created dramatic interiors which gave the exhibition a sense of occasion; and he had caught the attention of the crowd with his hand-beaten medallions and his novel use of the company's name as chief decorative device. The exhibition was a huge success. 'The practically free admission, the general interest in the subject, the work of the Royal Family, and the charm of good music in the afternoons, all combine to attract a photographic and fashionable crowd', 20,000 in all, according to the Eastman Company.[28]

69. The West Gallery at the Eastman exhibition, 1897.
70. *Below*: The North Gallery of the Eastman exhibition.

The success of this exhibition was crucial to Walton – more crucial than he could know. Davison quickly commissioned him to design the new head office and showroom of Eastman's European operation, in London's Clerkenwell Road. It was the beginning of a relationship in which Davison was to become patron as much as client, a patron who was to commission most of Walton's major architectural work. But this is to anticipate events which belong to a later chapter of Walton's life.

It was nearing the end of the year. Walton's first few months in London had not gone at all badly. Although the publicity gained had hardly spread beyond the photographic press, it had already borne fruit.

Ledcameroch, Bearsden

Kate was in Glasgow towards the end of the year.[29] If George was with her, there would have been much to discuss and plan at the company. At the end of 1897, the hall and drawing room for J. B. Gow in Bearsden outside Glasgow, would have been nearing completion. He would need to get together his submissions for the next exhibition at the Glasgow Institute. And of course there was the new London work to discuss: details to be sorted out on his new chair designs for Clerkenwell Road, the metalwork of the light fittings, the display

cabinets, the carpets to order, the details of stencils and fireplaces, the ticklish problem of transport to arrange.

In the end there were two exhibits at the Glasgow Institute: a view of the Eastman exhibition and an illustration of the interior of Ledcameroch, Bearsden for J. B. Gow. Excluding the exhibitions, Ledcameroch was the first job for some time on which Walton had worked on his own.

The hall at Ledcameroch is striking. Overall there is a lightness of touch which reflects Walton's recent experience in exhibition design. The large scale pattern of the frieze relates to the emblematic repeats of the North Gallery at Eastman's, though the subject is not foliage, but a butterfly in yellow and brown. Windows at both ends of the hall, the oversize white surround of the fireplace combined with the plainly-filled, light-toned panelling accentuate the feeling that the room is filled with light. The glazing was of the style into which Walton was settling: 'essentially in mosaic and no painting ... with hammered copper bands inserted'.[30]

The staircase provides another dimension. A remarkable balustrade with a wrought-iron handrail forming a transparent screen adds to the delicacy of touch. The tall, tapering newels, topped with flat caps, mark Walton's developing relationship with Voysey, who had in turn adopted the device from Mackmurdo. It was the first of a series of occasions on which Walton placed the handrails horizontally, ignoring the rake of the stair, echoing Voysey's balustrade at 14 -16 Hans Road, Knightsbridge: in the future he would develop this further, to great effect, at The Leys.[31]

As at Glen Bank, Voysey's influence is elusively in the atmosphere. Some have compared the hall fireplace to Voysey's shown at the Arts and Crafts Exhibition of 1896, though both in the scale of its surround and the details of the grate Walton's matches the Lady Artists' fireplace at Blythswood Square, which has much less

71. Staircase in the entrance hall at Ledcameroch, Bearsden, 1897.

72. Fireplace in the hall at Ledcameroch.

connection with Voysey.[32] The scale and simplicity of the chimney piece is not so very different from George Jack's fireplace of 1893 (which, as we saw, may have inspired the raised metalwork of the backplate), nor, for that matter, from the type of white fireplace surrounds Shaw had used in his saloon at Lowther Lodge or in the morning room of 185 Queen's Gate. There is a similarity in approach to an earlier fireplace by Walton for Frederick Gardiner, where a traditional form is simplified, rationalised and – regardless of any sense of displacement – re-scaled to suit the interior scheme. While a relationship with Voysey cannot be denied, Walton drew on many sources to create designs which are always personal.

wish to mould the architectural components of the interior into harmony with his decorative forms, Walton combined this new idea with his own personal style of glasswork. It was an important contribution to the new style of work developing in Glasgow, which had begun to blend its own distinctive manner with Arts and Crafts ideals. The drawing room fireplace, on the other hand, with its small groupings of dentils (relating to an earlier fireplace at Glen Bank), reflects the mannered use of Classical forms Walton increasingly adopts in his work after 1900. Although Walton links the gentle curves of the armchair with the delicate lines of the tapestried frieze, as he had in a Buchanan Street dining room (pl. 62), the room seems cluttered and confused –

73. The drawing room at Ledcameroch for J. B. Gow, 1897.

Turning to the drawing room at Ledcameroch, it is clear there were frustrations in this commission: Walton had to accommodate some of Gow's own furniture. In the hall it is not intrusive, but in the drawing room it impinges on the overall effect. Of the furniture, only Walton's elegant upholstered chair belongs visually to the scheme. In addition, the drawing room represents two different traditions which Walton continued simultaneously, making it less well integrated. The carved woodwork of the door in its arched architrave and with its panels of leaded copper and glass emphasises the hand-finished craftwork of the Arts and Crafts. The Glasgow designer, Herbert MacNair, had made recent experiments with flowing woodwork forms of which Walton was evidently aware (*cf.* pl. 147). Ideally suiting Walton's feeling for movement and his

partly because of the the foreign items of furniture and carpets, but partly because of this conflict of styles.

Expansion in Yorkshire

There had been other work in hand during 1897. William Seaton's Cabin Tea Room chain was floated as a public company and Walton & Co. were approached for the refurbishment, now sadly obscure, of four of its Glasgow premises: 'The Cabin', 'The Mecca', 'The Orient' and 'The Anchor and the City'.[33] William Gray took advantage of his association with the company at about this time, commissioning decorations and furniture for his house in Pollokshields.[34] And now the company's tea rooms in Yorkshire were beginning to attract new work. Francis Bedford and Sydney Kitson, architects in Leeds, had a job on in Perth in 1898, where

74. The hall at Elm Bank, 1898, with stencils, fireplace and furnishing by Walton & Co., including the Beechcroft chair. The carpet was designed by Robert Paterson.

Walton & Co. were subcontracted some glazing.[35] A major commission from Sidney Leetham to redecorate and furnish his house Elm Bank, in York, was on the books,[36] and the directors of Walton & Co. were seriously considering a showroom in York.

Elm Bank was another joint commission for Walton, but the first time he collaborated with W. G. and A. J. Penty, an architectural partnership (father and son) based in York. *The Studio*, in its description of the interiors, went some way towards establishing the division of work.

> the architectural work, including the details of wall framing, chimney-pieces, staircases, gallery, and portion of the fixed furniture, are due to Messrs. W. G. and A. J. Penty, while to Mr George Walton belongs the credit of the tasteful colour scheme, the decorative work, such as the drawing-room frieze and the mosaic panel over the chimney piece in the same room, and other mural decorations and most of the furniture.[37]

In addition to the architectural framework, the major decorative responsibilities given to the Pentys ensured that their work would considerably influence the overall effect of the rooms. As an interior designer, Walton had always had to take account of the architectural setting, but he knew the difference between working within an existing building and sharing responsibility for a new design with another creative force. Working with the Pentys on Elm Bank must have stirred memories of Buchanan Street and George Washington Browne. The partnership with Rowntree – now

disturbed by his move to London – had been different, had been a choice. Compatibility with the Pentys was essential for a satisfactory result.

Father Penty's work of the previous decade had been Gothic in tone. By the mid 1890s when his son Arthur began to influence the practice, their work moved more to a Shavian style featuring both 'Old English' and 'Queen Anne'. Fortunately for Walton, Arthur Penty, eight years his junior and with considerably less experience of interior work, found himself attracted to Morris and the work of the Arts and Crafts Exhibition Society, to which Sidney Leetham was also drawn.[38] All in all, Leetham provided a better basis for co-operation than Miss Cranston had at Buchanan Street.

How did it work out? Happily Elm Bank, now a hotel, can still be visited, and a tour of the building, *Studio* article in hand, proves both pleasurable and instructive.

The entrance hall, the main hall and dining room were all panelled in oak. Although the Pentys' interiors were noted for their 'light – abundant light', this had more to do with their handling of glazing than their partiality for woodwork – though, of course, the panelling of dining room and hall had such a long history that, to all but the most imaginative, it must have seemed obligatory. The hall – a magnificent, double-height space in the centre of the building – was dominated by the Pentys' wall framing, chimneypiece, staircase, and gallery. A comparison of the woodwork with their Davy Hall Restaurant of 1900 (where G.

Milburn of York did the carving), shows how typical it is of the Pentys' style – the turned balusters, the curved handrail of the gallery, the carved foliage on the fireplace surround, all favoured devices repeated elsewhere.[39] Walton might have chosen plain oak panelling himself (he did so in subsequent years quite independently), but his response to the elaborately carved and turned details of the Pentys' hall was to produce large, lively stencil patterns, bolder and more dominant than we find elsewhere in his domestic work. The stencils, in yellow, black, red, green, blue and chocolate, are now gone: Thomas Howarth, who visited Elm Bank in the 1950s, found them 'rather garish'.[40] Elaboration was not restricted to the walls. The extraordinary light fitting Walton had designed for the Buchanan Street Tea Rooms (pl. 61) was hardly out of place and the floors were richly carpeted with an award-winning design by Robert Paterson, a recent recruit to the Walton & Co. staff.[41]

The entrance hall, described by *The Studio* as 'restful', had similarly vigorous stencilling, while the dining room was dominated by vivid murals of mediaeval theme – shadows of the Buchanan Street billiards room murals in a more Pre-Raphaelite mood. Henry Wilson's scheme for the library at Welbeck Abbey, Nottingham-

shire, is recalled,[42] while Crouch & Butler's hall at The Anchorage in Birmingham, and Baillie Scott's and Edgar Wood's recent interiors in the Midlands and North of England are also brought to mind. The Penty-Walton dining room at Elm Bank strikingly parallels the work of other provincial architects of the mid-1890s inspired by Morris and the Arts and Crafts.

For the present-day visitor to the dining room (pl. 80) it is better to imagine the atmosphere than judge the details. The decorations, excepting only the ceiling and a panel above the fireplace, have been 'restored' with licence, hiding from view the quality (sometimes questionable, it must be admitted, in Walton's mural work) of the original painting.

Walton's handling of the glass at Elm Bank was far more sensitive. He relieved the dark woodwork with delicate panels of glass, decorated with flowers and leaves in blues, pinks and different shades of green. The large window over the staircase, one of Walton's most powerful decorative panels, shows his inability to design for a particular medium without carefully considering its relation to the whole. This window (with the

75. *Above*: one of a set of windows in the drawing room at Elm Bank, its rose motif in carefully selected pieces of glass echoing the Eros panel over the fireplace (pl. 81).
76. *Left*: central panel from the large window in the hall at Elm Bank.

others at Elm Bank) conforms clearly to Walton's later-stated ideals:

> The glazing of windows ... should always be considered with due regard to their purpose of letting in light. The filling of windows with rich glazing should be confined to recessed spaces where light may not be of special necessity. Simple glazing for domestic purposes is advisable in most cases – especially when rich decoration or colour is used on the walls, carpets, or furniture. Rich glass is much more pleasing when surrounded with colourless framing or colourless walls.[43]

The glazing of Elm Bank is both innovative and effective: Walton carried through his development of combined copperwork and glass, creating superbly confident panels in a distinctly personal style. The facility with which he produced the numerous internal and external windows of Elm Bank – mostly simple, linear patterns on a plain ground with jewel-like beads of glass and deep-coloured details – is extremely impressive (cf. pl. 124).

The furniture of the hall was comfortable and stylish – the 'Beechcroft' buttoned-leather chairs, with their curious finials and attractive geometric inlay. The complementary inlay of the table echoes the chequered or herringbone stringing revived and popularised by George Jack in his furniture for Morris & Co., though

77. The hall fireplace at Elm Bank, showing off the company's repoussé metalwork.

78. The Beechcroft chair, probably designed for George Davison's house, was used to furnish the hall.

Walton's enlargement of the pattern is rather more expressive.[44] The repoussé panels and prominent fire-dogs of the fireplace, now characteristic of the firm, lie uneasily beside the more traditional carved foliage of the Pentys' woodwork. And, if we take this opportunity to compare the quality of the Pentys' and of Walton's furniture and woodwork, like Rowntree, the Pentys lose out. Their coarser detailing of hinges, handles and carving (on the fitted furniture of the smoke room for example) compares badly with Walton's fine furnishings – fine both in design and execution.

While the hall, entrance hall and dining room belong to the heavier, Gothic lineage of the Arts and Crafts, the 'ladies' rooms at Elm Bank display an altogether different tradition: the elegance of the drawing room, morning room and bedooms is in deliberate contrast with the more 'masculine' dining room and hall. This dual personality of the Victorian interior had been clearly reflected in the furniture output of Morris & Co., where the rough and ready furniture of Ford Madox Brown, the mediaeval cabinets painted by Burne-Jones and Morris, were produced alongside George Jack's and W. A. S. Benson's more sophisticated cabinet work of late

79. *Above*: The Elm Bank drawing room, decorated by Walton in rose-pink and ivory-white, with purples and touches of green. Above the fireplace is the Eros mosaic panel (pl. 81).

80. *Below*: The dining room, in the tradition of Morris & Co., with Pre-Raphaelite-style murals and vigorous patterns. Note Walton's characteristic stencilling on the ceiling straps. For the fireplace see pl. 135.

81. *Above*: The 'Eros' mosaic in the Elm Bank drawing
room, in green marble and slate, coloured and opalescent glass, crystal, mother-of-pearl and touches of silver.
82. *Right*: Desk from the morning room in Elm Bank,
with stencilled linen panels on the wall behind.

seventeenth- and early eighteenth-century inspiration.

The delicacy of the drawing room is pronounced.
The scheme has the pastel colouring of Walton's earlier work: rose-pink and purple, ivory woodwork, with
a deep red carpet bordered in soft green. All is elegance
and refinement – the mahogany glass-fronted cabinet,
the watered silk of the lampshades, the white-enam-
elled, Sheraton-style chairs and the gentle outward
curve of the high-backed settee, the carefully-painted
stencil motifs on woodwork and ceiling straps, the delicate patterns of the frieze and the silk and linen tapes-
try-covered walls. The colours are taken up in touches
in the mosaic panel over the fireplace and in the closely-
related pattern of the decorative glass. Here, too, there
is less evidence of the Pentys' hand.

In this drawing room, as elsewhere in the lighter
rooms at Elm Bank, are hints of Japan, in the pale lac-
quered surface of the furniture, in its asymmetric arrangement, in the stress on broad planes of colour and
empty spaces. The textured plaster left in its natural

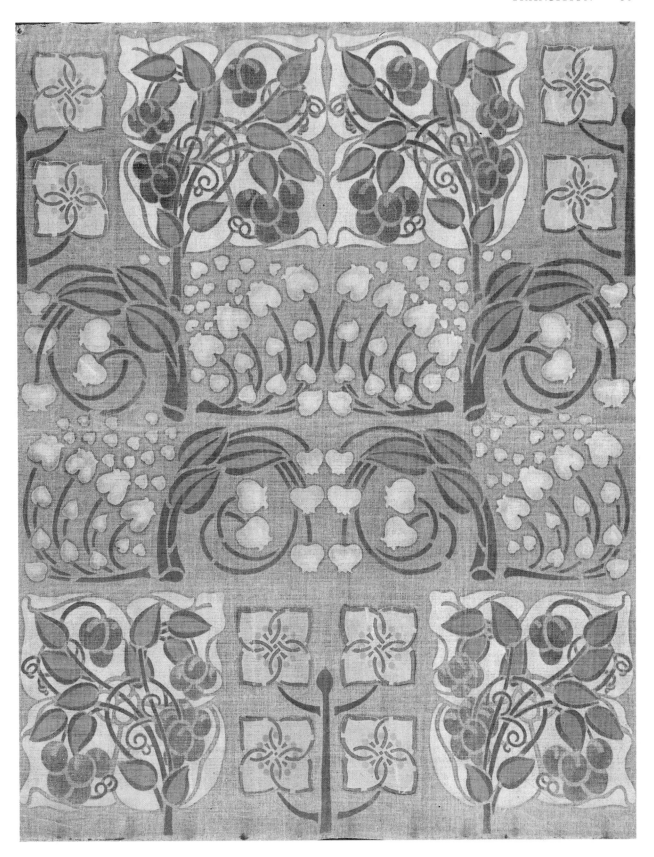

83. Detail of the stencilled linen used on the frieze in the morning room (pl. 82), 1898.

colour reflects the character of the Japanese interior, as does the quality of light from the windows screened in translucent gauze; so too, more directly, the simple grids of wall-framing with their fillings of Japanese matting. The Elm Bank drawing room in particular is highly effective. Walton's collaborative efforts with the Pentys on the hall and dining room are of somewhat uncertain result: in the delicate atmosphere of the drawing room he perhaps felt more at home.

Ledcameroch of 1897 showed Walton still struggling to clarify his ideas about the design of domestic interiors. While his work at Elm Bank of 1898 shows a new assurance, it also underlines the difficulties of collaboration. Yet these were important commissions. The Ledcameroch staircase makes clear the advance of Walton's architectural thinking; the light-toned Ledcameroch hall and the Elm Bank drawing room, a maturing of expression in interior design. Together these commissions reveal a greater sophistication in the company's craftwork. Both, especially Elm Bank, would be recognised as significant achievements in the national press, bringing the wider recognition for which the company was waiting.

A site was chosen in Stonegate, in the centre of York (no doubt with Rowntree's encouragement), and a new showroom was opened. Walton's move to London had not detracted from his attention to commissions in the north. Nor had the pressure of managing the company with only two months in Glasgow prevented him from making a dynamic entry to the London scene.

84. White paint, fitted cupboards and light stencilling in a bedroom at Elm Bank. The chair is a version of the design used in the tea rooms (see pl. 63).

V 'DECORATOR-IN-CHIEF TO PHOTOGRAPHERS'

In 1898, when Elm Bank was executed by the company in the north, back in London Walton was engaged in something quite different: work commissioned exclusively by a growing circle of photographic admirers. Relations with George Davison were going particularly well. 41-3 Clerkenwell Road, London, was to be the new European headquarters of the Eastman Photographic Materials Co. (soon to be re-named Kodak Ltd), an aggressively ambitious American company, set to expand itself on this side of the Atlantic. The job was vitally important for Walton. There was already talk of a showroom in Regent Street: if the Eastman Kodak venture was successful, there would be more showrooms – for Walton, the possibility of more commissions and a more certain future in London.

85. Interior of 41-3 Clerkenwell Road, London, head office of the Eastman Photographic Materials Co. (later Kodak Ltd), opened in the spring of 1898.

Building a reputation: the first Kodak showrooms

At Clerkenwell, completed by April 1898, there were two principal areas: a boardroom, and a showroom for the wholesale department, with display cabinets and seating.[1] Behind a rather nondescript façade (this was after all a location for business not style), the decorations of the showroom were surprisingly energetic. At frieze level, the theme of the design was the circle or semicircle, complemented by gentler curves and arches in the furniture. The stencil design was based on the signs of the zodiac, a circular pattern surrounded by vigorous stem and leaf forms and herringbone banding. It was a large pattern with strong tonal contrasts, one of Walton's most dramatic stencil designs – if anything, with the strong tones of the carpet, rather too dominant in the slightly crowded showroom. In contrast to the Salon and Eastman exhibitions of the previous year, the atmosphere was racy rather than restful.

86. Doing business in style: the boardroom at Clerkenwell Road.

The furniture was specially designed: in the showroom, arch-topped display cabinets echoed the passageway arch; the sturdy, functional chairs had a good deal of character. The 'Cholmondeley' chairs in the boardroom were equally appropriate: more sumptuous, with padded seats and sinuously curving lines, they had an elongated elegance which relates them to the highbacked, caned chair of Buchanan Street.[2] Although the stencilled frieze in the boardroom, too, was prominent, the reduced tonal contrast combined with the more open space made its tone less imperative. It was on the whole a more sophisticated and successful room.

George Davison was delighted with the results. Though the juxtaposition of patterns might seem discordant to the modern eye, there is little doubt that the rooms were quite remarkable in 1898. The showroom cabinets were not as finely proportioned as the Elm Bank designs, but the interiors, like the exhibitions, were well thought out, imaginative and functional; and the rooms had a personality of their own.

The new showroom at 171-3 Regent Street was opened a few months later, again to Walton's design. It was a more demanding commission, one of the largest spaces Walton had to deal with, to include a new shopfront for a difficult site. Considerable alteration was needed in order to transform the interior into a completely open-plan space with the ceiling supported by large, tapering columns.[3] Walton must inevitably have been involved with structural alterations before on interior work, but there were usually architects to hand. Even when alone on a job, he had always had Fred

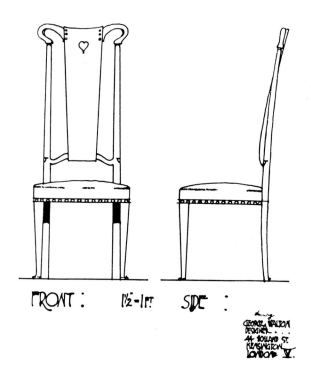

87. The 'Cholmondeley' chair, with its slender, padded back, is one of Walton's most characteristic designs. First used in the boardroom at Clerkenwell Road, the design was registered by the company in 1902.

Rowntree to turn to for advice. It was clearly the distance from Glasgow which in this case made him look elsewhere.

To take on an architectural student seemed the best decision all round. The job went to Edward Spencer,[4] found perhaps by Walton's landlord Arthur Bolton, whose scholarly interests kept him in touch with the architectural schools. (Bolton liked Walton and was making an effort to be helpful in other directions: he passed to Walton some of the wrought-ironwork on his current project in Paddington in the same year.)[5]

Spencer settled in to work at the studio in Westbourne Park Road. In some ways it was Walton who was the student. He had worked closely with architects in the past and had much practical experience – several shopfront alterations, staircase balustrades, ceiling modifications, etc. already to his credit – but mostly his single-handed alterations had been superficial. Davison was asking for more: *The Building News* reported unequivocally that the constructional alterations were in Walton's hands as well as the decorations and furniture. The Regent Street premises were Crown Property and detailed proposals had to be submitted and approved before alterations could commence.[6] Without Spencer, Walton would have had difficulties producing drawings of an acceptable standard.

The distance from Glasgow presented other problems. All the furnishings and fittings for the Regent Street shop were being made up by Walton's company in the workshops in Glasgow; no doubt for Clerkenwell the pattern had been the same. The drawings could be made in London and then sent north; when necessary, Walton could travel with them. But inevitably there would be crises: thank goodness for the telephone, installed at Wellington Street by 1892. Rail was the nor-

mal means employed for the long-distance transport of furniture, which William Gray, used to the distribution of his own products, could be relied on to arrange. Timing might prove to be a problem. Walton had of course had experience of this with the Scarborough work, but that had been 'in the family', so to speak: there was need for more professionalism here. From the station, one of the carriage operators could be hired, perhaps Liversidge & Son, popular with the furniture trade, who advertised in *The Cabinet Maker*. In the spring of 1898, such concerns as these would have been running through Walton's mind.[7]

At Regent Street, Walton again employed a decorative hoarding to whet the appetite while construction was in progress. Made of yellow pine, with fine tapering columns, it was painted an eye-catching bright apple-green. A lady photographer graced one end (perhaps the very first 'Kodak girl' in Europe), and the name of the company was prominently, and decoratively, displayed. *The Amateur Photographer* thought the hoarding showed 'what a vast improvement upon the usual rough poster-covered hoarding may gradually come into general practice as public appreciation develops, and firms like the Eastman Photographic Company have the taste and enterprise to cultivate it'. Walton may not have been the first in London to treat a hoarding artistically, but his designs were certainly inventive. As *The Amateur Photographer* continued: 'Several times lately we have noticed marked improvements in some hoardings where Messrs. Warings have been at work, but the greatest advance has been left for the Eastman-cum-Walton affair'.[8]

The removal of the hoarding would reveal a design required to satisfy two pressing conditions. It must provide a new public image for the Eastman Kodak expan-

88. The Kodak shop at 171-3 Regent Street, opened during the second half of 1898.

sion, and a shopfront to suit the vast columnar arrangement of one of London's most prestigious shopping streets. There would be many prepared to criticise.

For the entrance, Walton set a lunette over the recessed doorway. There were show-cabinets in oak, to mask the classical columns behind, and connecting the separated doors and windows an exaggerated cornice in characteristic Walton style. *The Building News* was not entirely won, though it thought the result worth illustrating and reporting in detail.[9] Its critic did not voice the nature of his doubts, but may have noted the lack of sympathy between Walton's individual front and the adjacent buildings. He may also have been unsure of the distinctive Glasgow flavour of the design. *The Architectural Review* was more positive: 'One of the earliest, if not the first example of [the] most commendable endeavour to enlist the services of design as a power of attraction may be noticed in the Regent Street shop, remodelled for the Kodak Company by Mr George Walton. How uninspiring was the occasion, and how successful is the result, is easily seen by comparison with the unreformed fronts of its neighbours.'[10] Considering Walton's restricted experience, the results were indeed creditable.

Inside, a showroom less insistent could hardly be imagined. The spaciousness of the Elm Bank drawing room was repeated: groups of tables and chairs were set out casually on the polished parquet floor on which

Robert Paterson's patterned rugs were strewn. The studded leather chairs designed for John Rowntree's were matched with a screen and fitted bench-seat along the wall. A flowing stencil design above white woodwork surrounded the whole area, successfully tying the large space together. The atmosphere was one of affluence and comfort, without the element of display which swamped so many contemporary commercial interiors. There was little doubt here in the critics' minds. *The Amateur Photographer* thought the Regent Street showrooms one of the most striking commercial establishments in London; 'even if the Eastman goods were not so good as they are, they would surely sell in such surroundings'; for taste and simplicity, as *The Photogram* remarked, are 'much more effective than ostentatious elaboration'.[11]

More exhibitions

Another member of the Linked Ring had been attracted by Walton's performance at the exhibitions. As the Regent Street shop was preparing to open, in April 1898 Walton was involved in producing a stand for J. B. B. Wellington's partnership, Wellington & Ward, at the Royal Photographic Society's exhibition at the Crystal Palace. Tantalising details are given in *The British Journal of Photography*.[12] Its view of the exhibition shows just enough to see that the corner of Walton's stand had an extended vertical with a large, flat cap in the manner of Mackmurdo and Voysey. It described the stand as 'a simple, graceful structure, light in form, delicate and harmonious in white and green colouring'. Walton was exploiting the skills of his company with the 'somewhat medieval-looking lamp' hung over the entrance – a device he would repeat many times, particularly on his Kodak shopfronts. Inside, canvas was combined with Japanese matting as a background to framed examples of Wellington & Ward's photographic papers. Walton had often used Japanese matting before as a wall covering, but here it added to the

89. The interior of the Regent Street Kodak showroom.

90. Elegant logo designed for Wellington & Ward.

91. One of Walton's many designs for publicity material for Wellington & Ward. He did graphic work for several other photographic clients also.

lightness and insubstantiality of the building, suggesting an interest by Walton in Japanese structures as well as materials. There is no mention of pattern in the descriptions and the plainness and simplicity of the stand was evidently effective. The *B.J.P.* was extravagant with its praise: 'a marked success'; ' decidedly one of the features of the Exhibition'; 'indescribably pleasing'. Other reviewers concurred. *Photograms of 1898* described it as 'a model of its kind, and a thing one longed to set up at the end of a lawn as an ideal summer house', reminding us that this was in fact Walton's first attempt at a free-standing building structure.[13]

In the autumn of 1898, the High Executioners again asked Walton to decorate the Salon. This year it was 'robed in cool greens, restful browns, creamy whites' repeating the successful combination of the Wellington & Ward stand. Gathered hangings were used to divide the pictures into groups. The wooden shelf had disappeared. Critics agreed that this sixth Exhibition of the Photographic Salon was the best of the series.[14] Opinion, however, could be fickle. *The British Journal of Photography* which in the previous year had been smitten by Walton's 'refined and reposeful' design, this year quite unabashed, made the following remarks:

> Gone, too, are the white wood ledges, the stencilled designs and brown canvas hangings of only a year ago. These things served the purpose of attracting just so much ridicule to the Salon as would force it into notoriety, and, having served that purpose, have been wisely dropped ... Still the Salon has not yet fallen into the commonplace ... it is hung with undoubted skill against a suitable green background, the light upper drapings of last year being retained, and the effect, from whichever point of view the walls are looked at, is always harmonious and well balanced ... Mr George Walton ... has certainly scored a success.[15]

The greater acclaim of the second Salon decorated by Walton, at least so far as contemporary criticism went, resulted from the 'new mood' Walton created: 'it cannot be said, as some said last year, that the decorations met one, as it were, at the doorway, and clamoured so for notice that there was no thought left for the pictures'.[16] Possibly Walton had responded to such criticism, making his decorations less assertive. The few photographs which remain do not indicate any vast change, and though this may be mainly due to the lack of colour, one would suspect that growing familiarity with the idea of 'artistic decorations' would anyway have made the 1898 Salon less of a surprise – or shock – to the uninitiated. There seems to be no reason why brown should have been any more startling than green, though some obviously found the chalk flower motifs of 1897 distracting. Present day observers might feel there was little at the Salons to provoke such a storm, but it must be remembered that earlier exhibitions were often dismal and overcrowded events. Records of contemporary art exhibitions show that in most cases little wall space was left to decorate anyway – the exhibits were so many and so close together as to render any decorative scheme ineffective.

By the opening of his second Salon in October 1898, Walton had been in London for over a year. George Davison had had the opportunity to scrutinise him closely. He was impressed. Walton's work had made an enormous impact on the photographic scene, inaugurating 'a new era in photographic matters, in which the art decorator seems destined to play an important part.'[17] Walton had become 'decorator-in-chief to photographers'.[18] His decorative work and arrangement of exhibitions attracted the greatest attention; yet Davison could see that Walton's sensitivity to the needs of a situation went further than this, embracing atmosphere, function and economics. At the Eastman Exhibition, display was required, at the Salon, a more sober scheme. Walton's use of canvas and cheesecloth at the

92. An exhibition of Warneuke's photographs in the Royal Glasgow Institute in 1898, decorated by Walton.

Salon, where costs were severely restricted, was economical. His irregular groupings of exhibits not only improved the appearance of the exhibition as a whole, but also eased viewing for the visitor. Walton had shown flexibility in different types of work: shopfront, board room, exhibition space. He had set the Kodak venture off on the right foot, winning it the sort of artistic celebrity which gratified Davison. Davison was not simply impressed, he was conquered.

At first the Salon had gained the credit for discovering Walton,[19] but the showrooms and Eastman Exhibition gained publicity in so much wider circles that soon this was forgotten. By the end of 1898, the catchword was 'Kodakoration, the decorative work of George Walton': the names of George Walton and the Eastman Company had become inextricably linked.[20] The company was planning a showroom in Brussels – the first of a steady stream of new branches to be opened on the continent. The continued patronage of Walton was a foregone conclusion.

Yet despite the publicity earned by the Kodakorations, it seems that, in the company, it was Davison alone who championed him. George Eastman, the company's American founder was 'no artist, nor' (according to Davison's son), 'had he any other interest except his camera business, nor even in the scientific side of that. He was a grim, rather dull man and my father never got on well with him ... Nor did he like it when Walton was brought in to design the chief Kodak shops.' But somehow Davison 'conjured the money out of Eastman and then had the vision to spend it like water on endowing the creations of Walton'.[21]

Shopfronts and Hoardings

The Regent Street showroom had been cool, relaxed, spacious, refined. At 59 Montagne de la Cour, Brussels, Walton had to deal with a more restricted space. What mattered most here was to keep the interior as light and clear as possible, so that the customer would not feel confined. Walton's response to the problem was ingenious. He based his design on an eighteenth-century arrangement of bow front, oval fan-light and glazing grid (quite probably on the authentic eighteenth-century premises in Doncaster on which he had worked not long before), making the best possible use of the light coming from the front of the shop within the interior.[22] Light entered through the glazed frieze above the window display, through glass panels in the doors, and even through the backs of the display cabinets themselves. Inside, the woodwork was white, the furnishings were sparse, and a gentle frieze pattern linked with the colour scheme of the carpet and the coloured touches in the glass. At Brussels, Walton achieved a new sophistication to which his elegant long-backed chairs made an undoubted contribution.

The chief difference in conception between the Brussels front and its eighteenth-century forbear, is in the strong division made between the upper and lower part of the glazing. From the first glimpse we have of Walton's shopfront designs – Warneuke's gallery of 1892 – we can see he was aware that the upper reaches of the front were too high to be useful for display, 'generally garnished with various goods which can, by no chance, be carefully examined, and are only seen by a wearisome craning of the neck. These little heeded wares effectually intercept the light which would be so valuable in the shop itself'.[23] At Warneuke's, Walton had simply masked the surplus window with his oriental screen, but here at Brussels he realised its potential without upsetting the overall proportions. There were some shops in London where the same thoughtful distinction had been made (Walton may at times have lingered outside Deighton & Dunthorne's in Vigo Street) but few architects had made such a decisive division.[24]

The grid of glazing bars did not seriously disturb the viewing of small scale objects like cameras. In addition,

93. The Kodak showroom at 59, Montagne de la Cour, Brussels, opened 1899; Walton's first showroom abroad.

94. Interior of the Brussels showroom, with Walton's elegant 'Brussels' chairs: see pl. 137.

95. Shopfront sketched by James McNeill Whistler for his own business, the Company of the Butterfly, at 2 Hinde Street, Manchester Square, London, *c.* 1897.

96. The York office of Walton & Co., opened in 1898.

there were romantic associations with the diminutive shopfronts of the past which were enjoying something of a revival. Norman Shaw and his associates absorbed their elements into the 'Queen Anne' style; Whistler made them subjects of his paintings. Architectural critics clung to them in reaction to the popular plate glass and iron construction, regarding with distaste the London shopkeeper who 'insisted that the shopfront should be extended to its utmost possible size. The stallboard was lowered, the fascia raised, the side and any intermediate piers of masonry reduced, or cut entirely away; until the glass spread its unsubstantial area from the pavement to near the sills of the first floor windows, at the sacrifice of all apparent stability'.[25] Against this background, Walton's imaginative development of the old-style front with glazing bars was appreciated: the 'charming bowed effect' which he contrived, while (economically) using only flat glass, was particularly applauded.[26] And at the same time the Brussels front – 'Queen Anne' without the 'Queen Anne' trimmings – was somehow distinctly modern.

While he was designing the Brussels shop in 1899, Walton and his prospering company in Glasgow were planning the development of their own new premises. Comparison with the Kodak work is natural. On 27th May 1899 the company bought a piece of land with buildings at 35-7 Buccleuch Street for £900.[27] Over the year, they borrowed a thousand pounds more than they needed for the purchase. They were planning major building work, gutting the two small houses on the site in order to erect a large new four-storey workshop block, fronted with a showroom extension at street level. Fortunately, the plans survive, although the building itself has been irreversibly altered. Fred Rowntree made the drawings (as Edward Spencer would have done for the Kodak shops), but Walton was undeniably the force behind the design proposals.[28]

The original houses on the site had been set well back from the building line. Fronting the new main

block, and to a great extent masking it from street level, a single-storey showroom and office were built. With no less than three eighteenth-century-style bows it continued Walton's permutation of the much-admired style of a hundred years before. Steps to the front entrance were embellished with wrought-iron railings and heart-shaped finials, forming an up-to-date centrepiece to the symmetrical façade. Walton & Co.'s branch office, opened in York in the previous year, had a similar character on a much more modest scale.[29] Its simpler front

97. Walton & Co.'s new workshops at Buccleuch Street, Glasgow, 1899. For the floor plan see pl. 121.

reminds us again of the old Chelsea shopfronts of Whistler's paintings, which Walton may have had in mind.

Behind the Buccleuch Street showroom, the workshops formed an integral block. In the same way as the Brussels front, windows were extended as much as possible to light the interior. Once more, small-paned glazing was used to reduce the scale, giving a more domestic atmosphere. The strong horizontals of the main block which contained the windows, and the double cornice of the fascia board bring to mind Mackmurdo; the chimneys, Voysey.

Walton's spreading reputation in the photographic world had attracted several more commissions for exhibition stands – one in 1898, two in 1899 and three in 1900. For Warneuke in 1898 he created a cool and sohisticated display.[30] At the Artists' Guild Exhibition at the Royal Albert Hall in 1899 he produced a stand for the Syndicate of Pictorial Portraiture (whose trade-name was 'Kalmia') and another for *The Amateur Photographer*, a journal which had for long been a champion of Walton's designs.[31] The Kalmia stand consisted of a light, framed

98 and 99. Two stands arranged by Walton at the Artists' Guild exhibition, 1899. *Above*: the 'Kalmia' stand. *Below*: *The Amateur Photographer's* display.

screen, again with square-capped terminals. The lower portion was plain – possibly panelled with Japanese matting – and the main display area decorated with floral stencillings. *The Amateur Photographer's* stand was decorated in reverse, so to speak, with a plain backing to the pictures and a long panel of stencilled decorations beneath. The stencil patterns are close in character to the sort of designs Mackintosh had been developing since 1897, by this time an essential element of the Glasgow Style. Walton's work had developed along the same lines, in a softer, less abstract style, but there was undoubtedly an interchange of ideas.

The Amateur Photographer's display was draped in a similar way to the Salons', but was extremely simple: economy was apparently an important factor. Walton draped the walls with cheesecloth and ordinary sacking, the cheapest material obtainable. This evidently delighted the clients as they claimed in their own article on the exhibition: 'no more excellent groundwork could be found upon which to hang pictures of whatsoever kind'.[32] The colours used for the lower stencilling were light drab, green and pink, the decorative lettering stencilled in green on grey. A cream-coloured hanging (used to disguise the unfortunately-positioned pilaster) was of a coarse-textured cloth tied with a purple sash. Walton's use of cheap, easily-accessible materials shows his habitual ingenuity and flexibility of approach in exhibition work.

Three further displays at the R.P.S. Exhibition of 1900 were again fairly simple affairs. A 'very dainty corner' for Wellington & Ward;[33] a 'very neatly got-up table stand' for Kodak Ltd; and 'a most tastefully arranged background' for Elliott & Son. *The Amateur Photographer* felt that 'if any one thing more than another can convince of Mr George Walton's ability and taste as a decorator, it would be the comparison of some of the adjacent shows with those of Kodak Ltd, Elliott, and Wellington & Ward, for all of whom Mr Walton has acted, and beside which some of the

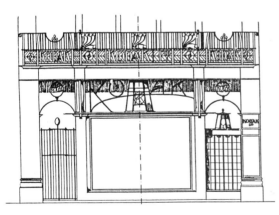

100. The Kodak showroom at 40 West Strand, *c.* 1901.
101. Elevation of the Strand shopfront.

neighbouring exhibits with backgrounds of blazing colour and absence of consistent scheme partake somewhat of barbarian tawdriness, or the trumpery adornments of a cheap café'.[34] Elliott & Son also employed the designer Charles E. Dawson, who produced some excellent graphic work, as well as fine showrooms for the Jaeger company.[35] J. B. B. Wellington and

Walton had by this time become close friends.

As if Walton had, for the moment, had enough of the Georgian grid, at Kodak's Strand branch in 1901 he tried something completely different. Retaining the separation of upper and lower divisions he made use of a large flat area of plate glass to balance the ambitious articulation of the rest of the shopfront. The use of frieze windows to light the interior was taken a step further as Walton recessed the glass in a skilful arrangement. 'Quaint lamps of wonderful design are hung over the window case and in the recess formed over the main transome. This throws a protected and admirably shaded light directly onto the goods. The result is as successful as it deserves to be and the idea is worthy of frequent imitation'.[36] The shopfront at 40 West Strand shows Walton experimenting with positive and negative values and displays a deep interest in structure. It remains one of his most striking and inventive shopfronts.

The hoarding was ingenious too. The grouping of the figures and the arrangement of the panel as a whole is very successful, in style suggesting the influence of the successful poster duo, Walton's friends the 'Beggarstaff Brothers' (William Nicholson and James

102. Walton's hoarding outside 40 West Strand during reconstruction.

Pryde). Furthermore the upper portion of the hoarding was cut out and backed with a tinted canvas screen so it could be illuminated at night. The publicity value of this highly original design was obvious: 'To many the Kodak girl of the hoarding which Mr Walton constructed at the Regent Street Kodak branch ... will still be remembered ... The Strand hoarding is a still more notable instance of how a builder's hoarding, usually such a disfigurement, may be made beautiful and interesting in a decorative way and eminently valuable as an advertisement in advance'.[37] It is unfortunate that such bold graphic ventures were largely restricted

to hoardings. Only at the Moscow and Alexandria branches were attempts made to introduce a figure on the final façade.[38] It is difficult to relate the dynamic pictorial adventures of Walton's hoardings to the advertising designs he produced for Wellington & Ward over the same years.[39] Walton's figure drawing could be very variable; yet the hoardings demonstrate that scale and colour greatly increased his confidence, transforming the weak and nervous lines of his black-and-white adverts to convincing compositions of some power.

Corporate Kodak style

By the opening of the Brussels showroom of 1899, Walton's exploits for the Kodak company had settled into a steady pattern under which he was producing two or three showroom designs for the company every year, many of them abroad, plus occasional designs for exhibition and advertising material. Walton himself mentions work at 'Glasgow, Dublin, London, Brussels,

103. Kodak's branch on the Petrovka, Moscow. Walton's designs were interpreted on site.
104. One of the more successful of Walton's advertisements for Wellington & Ward, for their regular slot in *The British Journal of Photography.*

Milan, Vienna and Moscow'[40] – a new cosmopolitan focus; but he was not expected to travel. Walton designed everything 'from A to Z' – 'from the foundations of the threshold, to the very last turn of the screw'. The discerning German architect and critic Hermann Muthesius greeted the showrooms with delight. His long article on the Kodak work, published in 1903, reveals the logistical difficulties presented by this ambitious programme. Walton's designs for the showrooms abroad were transferred via blueprints to the contractors on site – an operation carried out with varying success. Unfortunately, due to the lack of supervision, 'not everything happened according to the desire of the artist'. At a number of showrooms (Berlin and Alexandria are examples) the Kodak company even allowed subcontractors to emulate Walton's style: 'a process one has to digest'. At times Walton also may have regarded the results with some dismay.[41]

All the showrooms where Walton worked were new premises for the company and the interiors were totally redesigned, with the sole exception of 115-17 Oxford Street, London, which had been set up before Walton was taken on and only needed redecoration to bring it into line (the stencilled hangings from the Eastman Exhibition were re-used to good effect); for by this time also, Walton had developed a recognisable style for the showroom interiors.

Almost always there were stencilled friezes. These varied from the more dominating patterns of the earliest showrooms, to the delicate designs found at 59 Brompton Road, London, at the Brussels shop, at 72-4 Buchanan Street, Glasgow, and at 89 Grafton Street, Dublin which tended to use more of the plain background of the plaster and were closer in character to the work now recognised as coming from Glasgow.[42] Most of the stronger designs were combined with simple, white panelling, and the lighter designs with the richer colouring of natural wood.

The stained glass detailing of cupboards, internal windows and exterior glazing was usually derived from plant forms, but was sometimes more formal in concept. Patterns for carpets and runners were geometrical (not always co-ordinating clearly with stencil designs).

All the new showrooms had special fitted cabinets for storage and display. Often these had stained glass panels with copper details in the doors, relating to designs at Elm Bank, and similar to some of Mackintosh's designs of the same years, but without the carved details. For Brussels and Clerkenwell Road (pls 94, 85-6), Walton created entirely new chair designs, but more often earlier designs were employed. Most common was Walton's black cane-backed chair with tapering legs, used so frequently that it became almost a trade mark of the showrooms (pl. 63).

The metalwork was always inventive. Sometimes it enlivened the shopfront in decorative railings, hanging lanterns or curving wrought-iron signboards. Inside beaten metal panels appeared around the fireplace, and decorative metalwork bands separated individually wired bulbs for the lighting – an arrangement so similar in concept to Ashbee's light fittings at Cheyne Walk that the relationship can hardly be coincidental. Walton produced wonderful spotlighting contrivances to light the wall displays – special metalwork hoods shaped to throw light only onto the work.

Though there was great variety within the elements of the interiors, there was a similarity in the proportions of the cabinets, the cornice shelves, the panelling (sometimes filled with fabric, sometimes painted white, sometimes simply waxed to bring out the natural colour of the wood), a kinship in the colour schemes and in the patterns of stencils and stained glass, and the repeated use of certain chairs and carpet designs, which gave the showrooms an identity without any feeling of uniformity.

105. 59 Brompton Road, London, *c.* 1900, with many features characteristic of Walton's Kodak interiors.

Walton was peculiarly successful in harmonising the elements of the Kodak interiors, an achievement which the commercial aspect of the job had not prevented. This is difficult to appreciate in monochrome, as some critics pointed out. The success of the Strand front 'depends largely on a colour scheme which the camera fails to reproduce; but those who have not the opportunity to see this for themselves, may be assured that the grey-yellow of the wax-polished oak frame, the mellow white of the ivory – or is it celluloid? – the black of the ironwork and the carefully chosen purple blues and greys of the leaded glass, unite in most agreeable harmony'.[43] Contemporary visitors were struck by the subtlety of Walton's colouring. It wasn't just a matter of mixing paint, it was a result of the acute sensitivity to the surfaces, textures and colours of materials which

106. Kodak style at home in Glasgow: the interior of the showroom at 72-4 Buchanan Street in 1900.

he had developed in the early years of his decorating business in Glasgow, the painterly approach he had absorbed through his 'training' with the Glasgow Boys.

What added to the distinction and novelty of the showrooms in London and abroad was the particular Glasgow flavour of the designs. The combination of tilework, copper and glass in the fireplaces; a particular fluidity about the curving lines of patterning; an elongation in the woodwork and characteristic extension of the cornice shelf; certain repeated colour combinations of greens, rose, purple and grey – these constituted foreign elements to a public more familiar with the London avant garde.

As with the tea-room interiors, Walton had adapted his domestic style very little. He had discovered that there was no need. The quiet, comfortable atmosphere of the showrooms was appealing yet unpressured, disarming in its easing of the transition from home to store, congenial to sales. It was Davison who had had the vision to recognise the value of Walton's approach. His vision had not gone unnoticed: other photographic firms followed the example.

The contrast with conventional thinking had helped. Many neighbouring establishments worked on the principle that the more goods they pressed on the customer the more he would buy; the more showy and uniform their branches, the more he would buy from their store. As Muthesius looked back on the Kodak work, with his broad view of both continental and British shop premises, he marked out the importance of Walton's efforts in bringing 'art' first to the tea room and then to the store. In his view, Glasgow was where it all started and Walton, with his elegant, non-sensationalist approach, was the source of a new movement in shop design.

The years of the turning century coincided with the peak of Walton's Kodak work. The Brussels, Brompton Road and Strand showrooms (of 1899, 1900 and 1901) epitomise his achievements – the development of an appropriate and successful house style for a dynamic new company – just as the two preceeding years, 1897 and 1898, had demonstrated his prowess in the exhibition field. The exhibitions had been a gift. They gave the opportunity to work on a larger scale than before. He had more freedom and more control. He was not restricted by collaboration, by the views or furnishings of a single client, nor by the need for the schemes to be permanently lived with. In the same way the hoardings and exhibition stands had encouraged experiment. He could be bold and he could be imaginative. In all, the emphasis of the photographic work had been quite different – different from tea-room work, different from domestic commissions: the viewpoint was new.

They had been eventful years, in the north establishing the reputation of his newly-organised company, in the south providing new opportunities and experience. Amongst all this Walton had gained something else: practical training and increased confidence in architectural work. He had proved to himself and to others that he was capable in quite another field.

VI   J. B. B. WELLINGTON AND THE LEYS

In 1898 the photographic materials company Welling-ton & Ward had approached Walton for the design of their display at the annual exhibition of the Royal Photographic Society. Walton's relationship with the firm had continued with the series of advertisements he designed for use in *The British Journal of Photography* and a further exhibition stand in 1900 (unremarkable works easily forgotten in the hectic productivity of one of the most fruitful periods of Walton's working life). Yet Walton's connection with this company from the spring of 1898 is the first evidence of a significant encounter, a relationship not so much with a company as with a man.

107. J. B. B. Wellington.

James Brooker Blakemoor Wellington, born in 1858, had trained initially as an architectural draughtsman. Soon these architectural beginnings were cast aside. From the time of his employment as factory manager at the Eastman Company's newly-erected works at Harrow between 1890 and 1893, photography, instead, became Wellington's great enthusiasm and the medium through which he would work out his artistic concerns. It was Wellington who was excited by the artistic possibilities of his company's displays, not his partner H. H. Ward, a gifted engineer who was 'only interested in mechanical things and spent most of his time in the works'.[1]

Though not a founder of the Linked Ring, Wellington was elected within a few months of its inception in 1892. The work he exhibited, like Davison's, expressed mood and atmosphere in preference to factual realism. At the end of his contract with Eastman's, Wellington

moved briefly to Elliott & Son of Barnet, Hertfordshire before setting up his own company close by in 1895 for the manufacture of photographic papers with his brother-in-law Ward.[2] With the introduction of snapshot photography in the second half of the nineteenth century, photography was becoming big business. Even Walton could not leave the delights of the camera to Annan: he found his 'small Kodak camera, a most useful little instrument which I carry about with me to photograph my work when I see it finished'.[3]

By 1900 the partnership was prospering. Wellington's increasing affluence coincided happily with Walton's newly-acquired credibility as a potential architect. For, though Wellington had abandoned his architectural career in favour of photography, he had never surrendered every architect's dream – the building of his own house. Wellington probably asked Walton to design a house for his plot in Elstree in 1900 when Walton was at the peak of his work for Kodak. Walton's quiet manner, his ability to wed imagination with efficiency, had inspired confidence. For Walton it was an opening almost as startling as one he had been offered before – the commission from Miss Cranston which had launched his career.

Walton had styled himself 'Artist' on arrival in London. Discarding his association with a decorator's business, he aspired to a higher calling. The transient nature of the artist-decorator's productions was something Whistler as well as Walton would have had to accept. But Whistler had his paintings, while Walton could hardly hope for his interiors and cafés, his shops and advertisements to claim a permanent place in the annals of art. Much of his recent work in London had been particularly ephemeral, a point brutally underlined by a comment on the 1897 Salon in *The British Journal of Photography*:

> The canvas hangings, the whitened shelving, and the flower pots will presently be stowed away in the lumber room ... the picture frames can always be duplicated at so much a foot ... Photography is not to be taken in and done for by the upholsterer and cabinet-maker, and weighed and estimated according to the excellence of the products of those useful tradespeople ... the ornamental accessories are swept aside as more or less necessary but temporary accidentals.[4]

Reference to the impermanence of his art, Walton had no doubt long since learned to swallow, but the term 'useful tradespeople' would surely have stuck in his throat.

He might not ever be a painter but the possibility of an architectural career was becoming markedly more accessible. It was not entirely outlandish that Wellington should think of entrusting Walton with the design of his house. Walton might have presented his credentials thus.

Apprenticeship & Training: Close collaboration with architects and builders on a wide variety of domestic and commercial projects; responsibility for estimating and keeping to contracts, dealing with clients, etc.

Related Experience: Managing directorship of company of interior decorators whose competency includes plumbing, gas fitting, electrical & building work as well as all aspects of fixed and moveable interior fittings.

Recent architectural works: 171-3 Regent Street, 41-3 Clerkenwell Road, London, 59 Montagne de la Cour, Brussels (re-fronting and re-fitting including major structural alterations to some of the interiors). In partnership with Fred Rowntree, FRSA: 5 Blythswood Square, Glasgow (exhibition gallery extension), 35-7 Buccleuch Street, Glasgow (complete design of showroom and workshop building). In hand: re-fitting and re-fronting of 72-4 Buchanan Street, Glasgow and 59 Brompton Road, London.

Set out like this, it could seem most persuasive. However, this unexpected commission is more likely to have resulted from Wellington's vision and daring than Walton's salesmanship. For, to Walton, the architectural profession still seemed far out of reach. As recently as January 1900 he had told the architects of Glasgow:

An architect in the highest sense of the word should have qualified himself for the profession by the study of ancient architecture, ... should have seen, sketched and measured the best examples at home and abroad. His studies should of necessity have been very wide for ... while devoting himself more especially to church architecture, domestic architecture and the architecture of public buildings, he cannot neglect colour decorations, metal work, and all the various subjects which are comprehended in the design and execution of a work of artistic and architectural merit. These studies will, however, be of little use to him unless he has also acquired sufficient practical knowledge to advise his employer as to the probable cost of the proposed work and to keep within such limits in carrying out the work which he has designed. The practical knowledge which an architect must possess includes a thorough acquaintance with the materials which he intends to use, such as to their strength and durability, and as to their method of application to the work. Now a decorator professes to attempt the mastery of one little item in these many qualifications. [You can therefore realize that I come before you with considerable degree of diffidence – deleted] ... you will realize how humble I feel.[5]

Perhaps he could not see it then, but, in much of the practical training he felt essential for an architect,

Walton could hardly have been better qualified.

From another point of view, transition to architecture was not such an unnatural thought. If he was an artist/decorator, an artist/designer, why could he not be an artist/architect? The Arts and Crafts architects' reaction against professionalism held within it a dilettantism which opened up so many possibilities. Walton's son recalled their way of thought: 'They regarded themselves as able to do it all – not out of conceit, but they didn't know it was separate. They were ... totally combined, they were Arts and Crafts Movement in the sense they thought it was all their business and they were entitled to have a go'; again, 'My father was an artist who practiced architecture along with furniture design and anything else he chose to do, because ... it was natural to them to do these things'.[6]

Despite the raging arguments currently surrounding the question of professional registration, Walton and Wellington were still living in the days before architecture became closed to all but the products of exclusive training centres and nationally recognised exams. If Walton could design and put up a building to conform with building regulations, he was entitled to call himself an architect. His long experience as a supervising designer – controlling skills which he did not himself practice – made it relatively easy for him to move to architectural work. He was not so much changing his line of business, as expanding it. Moreover many of the principles with which he operated as a designer, principles drawn from the ideals of Ruskin, Morris and Arts and Crafts Guildsmen, were as much ideals of architecture as of design.

However natural this move was within the ideology of the Arts and Crafts, Walton was unusual. While many architects and artists had turned more or less seriously to design, there were few, strikingly few, who had moved in the other direction. But then Walton's circumstances were particular: his upbringing among artists, his lack of opportunity for professional training, and his background in the enterprising atmosphere of Glasgow. In running his business, Walton had never been one to turn down the varying opportunities offered. Wellington's proposition was certainly not something to be refused. If he could manage the new responsibilities, there would be distinct benefits. Architecture offered, at last, the complete control of the interior, freedom from the vagaries of the building, or the architect, with whom he happened to be working. It offered more. In handling the exterior, his feeling for structure and mass would have an entirely new outlet.

The Leys

The Leys, Barnet Lane, Elstree, was, like its architect, quite individual. The front was symmetrical, almost to the point of severity were it not for the homely

108. A sketch by Walton of The Leys, built in 1901.

emphasis of the enormous hipped roof; the back quite different – high chimneys and the set back hall gave the building a soaring quality. Wellington would have wanted a homely building. He spent much of his time at home with family and friends. Though it is a substantial house, there is nothing pretentious about it. The vernacular materials and detailing of the exterior suit the country atmosphere of its environment. The house was set within large grounds and particular attention was given to the layout of the gardens, which were much used. Walton was still being asked to add details to the garden twenty-three years later. Wellington and his wife would live happily at The Leys for thirty-eight years until Wellington's death in 1939. It was a house to live in.[7]

Walton had had over ten years' experience of different internal arrangements and at The Leys he put it to good use. The plan was symmetrical, compact; it was apparently simple, yet cleverly practical.

The plan was dominated by a triple-height hall,

which played the parts of billiards room and extra living area. It may have been most immediately influenced by memories of Penty & Penty's hall at Elm Bank (pl. 74), but both were part of a well established tradition. Since the Gothicist A. W. N. Pugin initiated a revival of the mediaeval Great Hall in the 1830s, and Norman Shaw and others extended its use in the 1870s, the Arts and Crafts architects had taken pains to convert it to a domestic scale. Of Walton's generation, Baillie Scott in particular had successfully introduced a suggestion of the Great Hall within the confines of the smaller private house, trading size for a clutch of romantic accoutrements – exposed timbering, minstrels' gallery, and dominating fireplace.[8] Hermann Muthesius would later criticise the revival of the Great Hall for its backward-looking romanticism, a position of rationality with which it is difficult to argue: 'The hall serves no real purpose. There is little opportunity to use its great capacity for it lies immediately inside the front door and is therefore in the wrong position in the ground plan to be used as a banqueting hall or ballroom. All that remains, therefore is to look upon it as an imposing area, the sole purpose of which is to create an aesthetic impression ... It exists simply for the sake of its beauty'.[9] This was also its merit. In the artistic climate of the 1890s, the romanticism of the 'mediaeval' (popularised now for the upper middle classes by Morris & Co. and Liberty's) was highly desirable. If there were inconveniences, a great many were prepared to live with them.

110. The entrance hall of The Leys.

109. The hall of a country house in Bedford by M. H. Baillie Scott.

While retaining the hall in an axial position, Walton avoided the problems associated with placing it too close to the front door. Instead, there was a preliminary entrance hall from which the dining room and drawing room opened, so that, at least on the ground floor, passing through the hall was an option rather than a

necessity. It could now become the 'delightful sitting room, particularly in the summer' which that early apologist for the Great Hall, Sir Gilbert Scott, had envisaged.[10] But the main hall at The Leys was still important as a circulation area for it contained the stairs. Muthesius was doubtful that the English liked a staircase in the hall: it gave 'a rather public air which detracts from its more intimate effect'.[11] Walton had an answer for this too. Expanding his use of extended balusters to form a deliberate screen, he skilfully made the staircase at The Leys in but not of the hall. Instead of pressing it on the visitor at the moment of his arrival, Walton had found other means to maximise its virtues. For as the visitor passed up the stairs, the hall could be viewed from every angle – all the upstairs rooms opened onto an encircling gallery which looked down upon the space below.

The plan was formal and symmetrical, but eminently practical. The dining room was immediately adjacent to the serving room and kitchens, while the drawing room, morning room and library were placed on the opposite, and therefore quieter, side of the house. The matching turret-like forms which give such character to the back of the building (pl. 113), contained the separated servants' stairs essential to the smooth running of the Victorian home. The ingle of the main

111. The fireplace in the entrance hall of The Leys.

hall was cunningly formed between the curve of a stair turret and the balancing curve of a partition. Far from being an encumbrance, this doubled as a screen to the doorway from the service rooms. Upstairs, the central master bedroom shared the bay of the entrance. Fitted out as an attractive window-seat, it made the most of the view to the garden.

112. Floor plans for The Leys as drawn for the first volume of Muthesius' *Das Englische Haus* of 1904.

The symmetry of the plan was reflected on the front. Here, the first architect brought to mind is Voysey: there is the same steepness of roof, the same division into horizontal bands, the windows tucked under the eaves line, the use of roughcast and decorative timbering. The likeness of Walton's entrance bay to Ernest Newton's at Redcourt, Haslemere has already been pointed out,[12] but flat-topped, two-storey bays were also a favourite with Voysey, at houses like Broadleys on Lake Windermere. Walton's bay differs from those at Broadleys in its decorative use of vernacular materials (tiles laid neatly in herringbone patterns confined within bands of timber) – a concentration of detail which subtly emphasises the entrance.[13]

Yet The Leys' façade is surprisingly regular for a building of the Arts and Crafts tradition and distinctly more symmetrical than Voysey's manner of building. The urgency of Walton's concern for balance is revealed in his use of a 'blind' window to one of the upstairs rooms, representing the point at which his desire for symmetry could no longer be reconciled with his intentions for the interior (a clear indication of his lack of experience). Symmetry had really been out of fashion all along with the mainstream Arts and Crafts, apart from Philip Webb. Much of the heritage of the last few decades of avant garde architectural development had been against it: the Gothic revival, Old English, even the exponents of the 'Queen Anne' style had inclined more to picturesque arrangement of features than overt regularity. (Ashbee was a case in point.) The haphazard, the informal had been the spirit of the times amongst the artistically minded, who generally spurned Classicism. Now, even amongst the Arts and Crafts, it is true there were other influences creeping in. Norman Shaw himself, father of Arts and Crafts architects, after the patchwork of Cragside and Leyswood, had adopted a Wren-like regularity, around 1890, at 170 Queen's Gate and Bryanston. Though Shaw himself took no more than a fatherly interest in the Art Work-

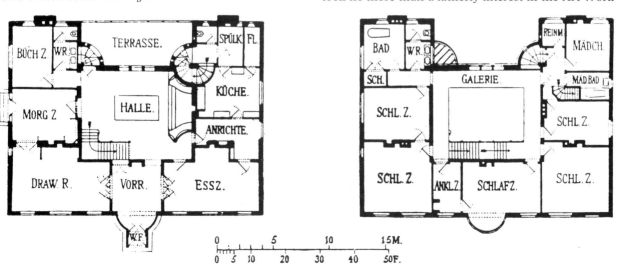

ers' Guild, it had been his pupils who set it up, and his influence still held sway.[14] During the early 1890s, a revival of late seventeenth-century English Classicism was under way, led by architects of Shaw's office, Ernest Newton and Mervyn Macartney. The Palladian window had been absorbed into the Arts and Crafts repertoire early on – a feature Bodley had incorporated in his house at Malvern Link several decades before. In the 1890s Lethaby had employed it at Avon Tyrrell (1891) and again at The Hurst (1893), Sutton Coldfield. Newton took it up at Redcourt in 1895, soon to espouse a style much more explicitly related to brick architecture of the time of Wren. By the end of the 1890s the new converts were making their presence felt. Classically inspired façades were becoming popular even amongst the progressive.[15]

All this goes to explain how Walton's house could combine the picturesque manner of Voysey, the Arts and Crafts love of vernacular materials and techniques, with the almost Classical regularity of its façade. Several of Walton's shopfronts had been decidedly Georgian in flavour. It is clear Walton had been touched by the new Classical spirit in domestic architecture as well. Confirmation is found at the rear, where Walton's own version of the Palladian window is used to light the hall. Here another theme is introduced: the proportions of this window are distinctly personal. Elongated and Scottish, it prompts memories of Walton's Glasgow Style. Walton's northern contemporaries were currently pillaging traditional Scots architecture as part of their romantic return to the vernacular within their own national heritage. Following out this Arts and Crafts ideal had led to the revival of the tower-house turret, to which the cylindrical forms of the spiral stairs flanking The Leys' hall must inevitably be linked. By contrast with the broad horizontal planes of the front, the verticality of the rear, its romantic austerity, disclose Walton's Scottish origins.

Illustrations of the front of The Leys abound; Muthesius applauded the strength of character shown

113. The rear view of The Leys.

at the rear. None have illustrated the side of The Leys, for very good reason: it is at this point that a chink in Walton's hammer-bright armour is revealed. The sides of the building fail to make a satisfactory link between the horizontal façade and the vertical rear. So great is the difference in concept, in fact, between the front and the rear façades that it would take an exceptional architect indeed to bridge the gap. Walton, bursting with architectural ideas, should have waited for further buildings on which to share them out.

Inside, the interiors of The Leys were less 'Scottish' than one might expect (especially considering the strongly Glasgow style of some of the current Kodak showrooms); and less reliant on decorative features and less romantic than Baillie Scott.[16]

In the hall, Walton's splendid fireplace commands the room from the traditionally raised sitting area overlooking the billiards table. The fireplace is one of Walton's finest designs – the strong forms of his firedogs contrast superbly with the flat fields of tile and metal. Yet, contained below a rail placed at mantle height, it does not attract supreme attention as Baillie Scott's so often do, nor is it a focus like his for decorative detail. The light fitting (which goes some way further than Baillie Scott's or anything Mackintosh had produced by this date) – a masterpiece of the metalworker's art – is a perfect foil to the grand architectural space in which it hangs. The fireplace and lights are almost the only decorative adjuncts of the room: save for one thin band of stencilling at gallery height, the walls are entirely plain. Walton's restraint in his choice of ornament reinforces the strength and simplicity of his design, which could not have been maintained if it was carelessly overlaid with detail.

The most dramatic feature of the room, next to the light fitting, is the staircase balustrade, carried straight up to gallery level and topped by the square, flat caps of Mackmurdo derivation. It relates to the balustrade at Ledcameroch (pl. 71), but there the device had provided mainly decorative interest. Here it functions architecturally as a division in the room. There is little doubt that part of Walton's inspiration came from Voysey's hall at Norney (pl. 116), which has other links with The Leys; possibly also from Mackintosh's new School of Art opened in Glasgow in December 1899, for such extended balustrades were becoming more common. Norney was illustrated in *The Studio* in October 1900, just as Walton would have been engaged in designing The Leys.[17] Their friendship would have given other opportunities for Walton's acquaintance with Voysey's designs. If the idea had not originated with Walton, his development of it marks out his own originality. Walton's balusters form a screen, designed to separate the staircase along one side of the room. The Norney stair has two runs which mean the

114. The fireplace in the sitting area which overlooked the billiards table in The Leys' hall.

115. *Below*: The Leys hall, designed for use as a billiards room.

balusters have less functional significance.

Whether deliberately or not, Walton's stair-screen has also caught something of the flavour of a Japanese interior with its geometrically divided wall divisions through which light can penetrate. A recently-illustrated interior comes to mind: Mortimer Menpes' house, where the repeatedly used narrow-spaced, vertical wooden bars had been authentically installed by Japanese craftsmen.[18]

The hall is lit from the long Palladian window positioned above first floor level, so that large areas of fenestration are unnecessary below. Walton had formed strong opinions, which he now endeavoured to put into practice, about the placement and proportion of windows :

> The want of comfort in a house when the window spaces are too large is most unpleasant – and the rooms are almost impossible to make interesting. You get glinting lights on ceilings, glaring lights on wall spaces and no feeling of rest – I do not believe however in being without light but I like to be quite certain whether one is inside of a house or out.[19]

The windows on the exterior of The Leys have been carefully considered in relation to their impact on the interior. The effect at which Walton aimed, which to all appearances he achieved, was an atmosphere of repose intended to augment comfortable living.

At second floor level in The Leys hall, a small semicircular balcony juts from the wall, looking down to the space below. A somewhat contrived remnant of the mediaeval minstrels' gallery (a favourite with Baillie Scott), it did in fact contain an organ, periodically played by Mrs Wellington. It is finished with cutout, circular holes (not the heart-shaped cutouts of Voysey and Baillie Scott) and links up well with the clean forms and repeated semicircular motifs of the rest of the room. The source is not far to seek. Voysey's hall at Norney

116. Voysey's hall at Norney, near Shackleford.

has a similar curve cantilevered from the balustrade of the first floor. Though there are so many links with Norney, The Leys hall is too magnificent to be classified as plagiarism, indeed it is a greater achievement. Voysey complicates his space by too much articulation of form, losing the effect of 'repose' after which they were both striving.

Leaving for the moment Walton's magical hall, it is evident that throughout the house he gave special attention to form and proportion. The ceiling of the entrance hall is groin-vaulted, rather like John Belcher's at Pangbourne, which Walton might have seen, and that of the library partly coved.[20] The doorways are frequently topped with the currently fashionable round arch, bisected by Walton's own stylishly prominent Glasgow mouldings.

In the dining room the woodwork was white, the panels filled with matting, and the room furnished with great simplicity. In the morning room (one of the pleasantest interiors at The Leys), the woodwork was again white, with French windows overlooking a lawn to the side of the house, and a wall settle next to the fireplace; the panelling, characteristic cornice and tapering, capped verticals give an unmistakably Glasgow air to the room. The fireplace of the drawing room was surrounded by a mosaic of small black and white tiles laid in geometrical patterns. The quiet decorative effect of the completely flat surround was quite different from the elaborate copper and glass inlay and organic curves Walton used so often. Flat fireplace surrounds had always been included in Walton's repertoire, and there were copper and glass panels now and again at The Leys, but here was a further instance of the simple surface triumphing over elaboration. This was the emphasis at The Leys.

Surviving photographs of the early interiors show that plain wall surfaces were the norm.[21] Often the woodwork was white, pattern confined to the carpets. The hall of The Leys in particular is a dynamic architectural space which Walton has chosen not to overcharge with fussy detail. On the outside too, he delighted in the new possibilities of formal arrangement. The vernacular detail of rainwater pipe heads, cast with the names of architect and client, currently in vogue, are charming but do not intrude.[22] Neither the bold forms of the gables to the rear, nor the direct statement of the front, require any ornamentation. The few decorative features Walton chose to include sensitively complement the architecture.

Walton's long experience of interiors had brought him to his mature understanding of the relationship between decoration and form: 'Now the proportion of a column or the curve of the back of a chair is as much part of the decoration of a room as an elaborate fresco or the colouring of a plain surface. We must ... consider

117. The dining room at
The Leys.

colour and form in relation to each other'. He had long since known that, 'the first thing to consider is the proportion of bare spaces rather than the proportion of ornamentation for the effect of ornamentation greatly depends on the value of the bare spaces surrounding it'.[23] Walton was presented with new possibilities at The Leys. With the responsibility of an entire building came a new dimension for Walton to explore. His response was to give form a new level of precedence over surface decoration.

Initially, the plainness of the interiors seems sudden, but in his domestic work, Walton had been been moving in this direction for some time. Even though the rooms of Elm Bank and Ledcameroch had been full of pattern, pattern had in general become less dominant. From the vigorous wallpapers of Walton's earliest interiors (pl. 25), to the sparser and lighter patterns of the Elm Bank drawing room (pl. 79), this line of development can be seen, even if it meanders on the way. Walton had been moving gradually when opportunity arose towards a greater simplification.

Yet the hall of The Leys contrasts with some of Walton's other interiors of this date. How different is his hall at Ault Wharrie, Dunblane, where almost every surface is either articulated or patterned. It is an imposing room, the glass and stencilwork delightful. The staircase balustrade is related to that of The Leys, but its power is lost amongst the other attractions of the interior. The Dunblane hall contains the last echoes of Walton's collaborative work with Rowntree and of the heavier style of the Pentys' hall. Its parts suggest a date of 1896-8, but, passing to the dining room, the commission's later date is confirmed.[24] Startlingly simple, it

has the same flat-tiled fireplace as The Leys' hall and an almost completely plain frieze. Apart from The Leys, it is the first of his living rooms which (excepting the carpet) is entirely without pattern. It can only be understood in the light of Walton's experiments at Elstree. They gave him a new vision for his interior work elsewhere.

The new simplicity is marked. The Leys might be seen as a watershed, where a new leaner but more sophisticated Walton emerges, yet there is also a subtler line of development, where the experience of The Leys merely provided impulse to an already precipitous change.

Through all these currents Walton never lost his footing, never lost that ability to harmonise and unify

118. The hall at Ault Wharrie, Dunblane, *c.* 1901.

which makes his work so compelling. There was less ornament, but it simply revealed the purity of his ability to co-ordinate. At The Leys, the special qualities of Walton's talent are revealed. He achieved a continuity of expression, so that the legs of the dining room table at one end of the house and the carved woodwork of the morning room at the other, have a kindred spirit. The shapes and forms of furnishings and fitments belong to the unity of the whole in which the occasional decorative details (Walton's individual style of glass and innovative metalwork) function as links. Within this ability the spirit of Glasgow was fully absorbed – an expressiveness and sense of poetry learnt from the Glasgow Boys, their clarity of colour and a surviving Scottishness of form. Though the treatment is more sparing, like the Kodak showrooms The Leys gives evidence of the same co-ordinating hand.

In Walton's work no detail is left unresolved. Materials were selected with care, from the special thin bricks chosen for the ground floor walls, to the fragments of coloured glass in the leaded windows. Much effort was necessary to complete so much original work, but ironmongery and plumbing did not escape Walton's attention. Like the Drumalis door handles, even window latches were individually designed. Where there were commercial items, they were selected with a discerning eye to fit within the broader scheme – the cast iron fireplaces upstairs (perhaps from Coalbrookdale Co., Elsley or Longden's), the Morris settle, the door furniture with tapering handles and heart-shaped keys, the ingenious cupboard latches.[25] As to makers and craftsmen at The Leys, most of the contributors are unknown. One fireplace bears the name of Walton & Co., suggesting that for the interior work at least the greatest accolade should be the company's.

The full expression of Walton's talents required the patience as well as the capital of his client, but despite some inevitable marks of architectural inexperience, the results were worthwhile. The Leys has a serenity in its strong but simple forms and in the exactly fitting nature of the furniture within the architectural space. Vital to the development of Walton's abilities had been his closeness to craftsmen and his experience in interior design. He had become the perfect realisation of the Arts and Crafts vision of the unity of the crafts under the banner of architecture, 'the belief that the various forms of art and handicraft ... shall not stand alone, but in relation to one another and to the Mother Art of Architecture ... It is only in the right harmony of the artistic family that a worthy end can be attained'.[26]

For an architectural novice, The Leys was a feat of

119. The Leys' coach house.

supreme control. At the coach house in its grounds, there is a hint of relaxation. Though quite different from the exhibition buildings Walton produced in the following months for Annan (at Glasgow) and for Kodak (at the Crystal Palace, pl. 169), the coach house has something of the same playfulness. Its mannered tower attracts the eye like one of the picturesque lodges or gatehouses on an eighteenth-century country estate (perhaps the more accessible belvedere at Elm Bank had stuck in Walton's mind). The rest of the coach house is more straightforwardly in the Arts and Crafts tradition of architects like Philip Webb: red brick and roughcast with simple door and window openings, and overhanging eaves. The dormers, breaking through the eaves line, are typical of contemporaries like E. S. Prior or Walter Cave, used by Bedford and Kitson at Brahan, and of course by Voysey. The north-east wing of the coach house has the same double-pitched, mansard roof as the hall, an idiosyncratic form at this time, which would absorb Walton's attention for many years to come. The angled dentils along the string course (also used on the main house but much more noticeable on this smaller scale building), relate to typical detailing of Walton's furniture and interior work.

Walton's picturesque intentions at the coach house are symbolised in his choice of the more romantic heart-shaped cutouts on the stairs and a greater emphasis on decorative glasswork (pl. 126). Fitments are prettily detailed. The fact that this is servant's accommodation is easily forgotten. One of Wellington's marks of character was his concern for his employees, one of Walton's his conscientiousness, his inability to allow anything to roam beyond his artistic control.

VII   THE COMPANY: PROSPERITY AND PASSING

It was not until the main work on The Leys was over and Walton's circumstances were becoming more comfortable that there was time to consider a move to more congenial surroundings. 16 Westbourne Park Road had never been quite right. Walton had persistently pressed Bolton for alterations to the house, but despite their fairly amicable relations, they were unable to come to an agreement. By March 1899, Walton had already talked of leaving: 'He writes wanting to revive the alteration scheme', Bolton grumbled to his wife, 'but that is out of the question on his terms' ... 'I shall be sorry if Walton goes, but he drives too hard a bargain'.[1]

In fact, the situation relapsed for some time and Walton did not move out until September 1901.[2] Between 1899 and 1901 there would have been little opportunity for house-hunting anyway, as he juggled the heavy commitments of his work for Kodak, plans for The Leys and the continuing responsibilities in Glasgow. But his aspirations reflected the buoyancy of his mood. The exhibitions and Kodak work had been well received; J. B. B. Wellington's magnanimity had opened a new career – the fulfilment of his ambitions; and, throughout this time, the company had been gaining in strength and prestige.

The Glasgow Base

In many ways, it was the company which had made all this possible. The financial support Walton received from his salary and bonuses had cushioned him from the risks associated with his move to the south. As he gained new work, the company benefited from producing it and, in turn, its prosperity was channelled back to him. This interdependency strengthened Walton's position and encouraged growth and confidence in the company.

By June 1900, when the company was settling in to its own new building in Buccleuch Street (pl. 97), the directors of George Walton & Co. had every reason to be satisfied.[3] In the previous year they had taken on a showroom in Sauchiehall Street, now Glasgow's most fashionable shopping street and a far more prestigious location than the previous site. This and the new head office and workshops were tangible evidence of success.

The company now had sizable works, good showrooms and an increasing number of employees. The four floors at Buccleuch Street could comfortably accommodate perhaps ten craftsmen each, with administrative workers housed in the office extension. We can put names to only a few of these: John Shedden, by

120. Company style: Walton & Co.'s letterhead, 1897-1901.

now an experienced glassworker; Robert Paterson, draughtsman and designer; and Robert Graham, veteran employee and originator of designs. The painters Stephen Downie and James Wright and the blacksmith Duncan McLean can be added to the roll, as there is little doubt that all the artisans mentioned in the 1899 shareholders list were part of Walton's workforce.[4] (The idea of offering company shares to employees may have been spurred by Ashbee's or Scott Morton's example.) Administrative workers included the company secretary, John Wilson, and three clerks John Masson, John Courtney and William Rankin Cameron.[5]

The proportion of space given to the various workshops on the Buccleuch Street plans are a useful indication of the emphases of the firm's work.[6] Two whole floors were given over to cabinet-making workshops, one to the glassworkers, about two thirds of the main ground floor workshop for the painters' shop and smaller areas for metalworking and upholstery. These divisions reflect the balance of skills apparent in surviving photographs of the firm's interiors, if it is borne in mind that exclusive designs for woven textiles, carpets and table glass were made outside. If there are any surprises in the plans, it is the comparatively small size of the metalworkers' shop which seems hardly adequate for the vast array of work the firm produced – from beaten copper details applied to fireplaces and cupboard doors, through the hoods and firedogs of fireplace designs, to light fittings, shop signs, and even iron gates and railings. It serves as a reminder that some of the

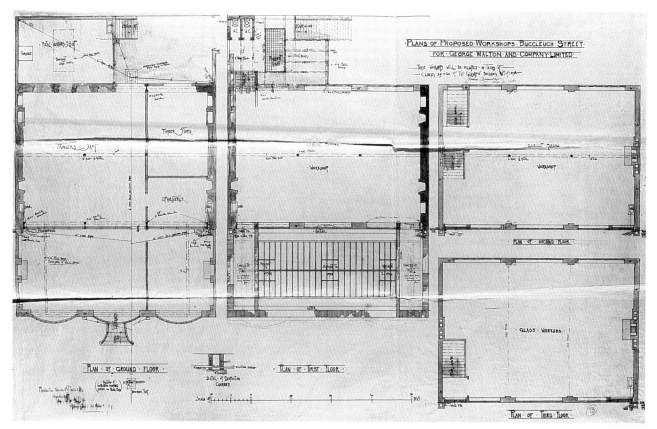

121. Layout of Walton & Co.'s showroom and work-shops at 35-7 Bucccleuch Street, Glasgow.

fireplace parts (cast-iron fittings, grates, brass margins, etc.) were brought in from outside.

Some other areas of work taken on by the firm are not represented in the labelling of workshop areas on the plans. 'Tile Layers and Tile Makers' was part of the business description under which the firm was registered. If Walton indeed produced his own tiles designs (as his sisters had done), they could have been handpainted in a corner of the workshops on blanks bought in from outside. Patterns suitable for longer runs, however, are likely to have been manufactured in Stoke.[7] Other areas of work, such as pictorial mosaic (the 'Eros' panel at Elm Bank for instance which developed skills learnt from stained glass in a different medium), and the fine tile-laying on some floors, fireplace surrounds and hearths, were irregularly commissioned. These and less obvious interior craftwork like parquet flooring, also supplied by the firm, could have been accommodated within the workshops.[8] Though the firm took responsibility for such things as plumbing, gas fitting, electrical and building work,[9] this type of work is likely to have been subcontracted by a standing arrangement with a firm like Hunter & Marshall.

Walton's prospering company ran alongside several similar concerns. J. & W. Guthrie had joined with Andrew Wells in October 1897 and the new partner-ship had a comparable business in the decoration of well-to-do Scottish homes, as well as showrooms in London. While their speciality was stained glass, their catalogue, produced shortly after the amalgamation in March 1898, featured furniture by Mackintosh amongst a host of other productions including eight-eenth-century-style chairs and pictorial mosaic panels. Guthrie & Wells had, like Walton, close links with the Glasgow Boys, and produced work which was both in sympathy with the Arts and Crafts Movement and of a quality which attracted praise even in such discriminating periodicals as *The Studio*: 'Indeed', it pronounced of their work at Buchanan Street, 'it is rare to find a "firm" carrying out work with the same "feeling" that is manifest here'.[10] John Guthrie, who had gained considerable recognition with his brother William at the 1888 Glasgow International Exhibition (where they had collaborated with William Flockhart on reception rooms for Wylie & Lochhead), was a competent stained glass designer in his own right and an early member of the Art Workers' Guild. Andrew Wells, who had worked closely with Cottier on his most sophisticated schemes before joining the Guthrie partnership, brought with him Cottier's wisdom and a reputation which drew several of Cottier's most discerning clients, William Leiper among them. It was, however, chiefly for their employment of the best freelance designers (including a number of Glasgow Boys and such London designers as Christopher Whall and Robert Anning Bell), that they

122. Mosaic panel for an overmantel at the Ferry Inn, Roseneath, by Guthrie & Wells, 1898. Walton experimented with mosaic in his Eros panel (pl. 81).

123. The dining room designed by John Ednie from Wylie & Lochhead's display at the Glasgow International Exhibition of 1901 (see p. 114).

attracted attention in the artistic press; along with applause for the technical expertise and artistic sensitivity of their decorating skills.

William Scott Morton's Edinburgh-based company of decorators and Art furnishers was also on the scene, for it found a considerable portion of its business in Glasgow. Miss Cranston had employed Scott Morton on her early Ingram Street Rooms, where he and Walton may perhaps have met. Although a number of Morton's employees were enrolled as part-time students at Edinburgh's School of Applied Art (where they fell under the influence of the Arts and Crafts sympathiser Rowand Anderson), the output of his firm was largely revivalist in character though with Aesthetic leanings. Scott Morton's Tynecastle canvas, an economic substitute for elaborate plasterwork, spread the influence of his decorative work as far as America. [11]

To Wylie & Lochhead Ltd, one of the main suppliers of high quality furniture in Glasgow, Walton & Co. would hardly have registered as a competitor. Wylie & Lochhead's was an enormous concern – as far back as 1882 it had had 1,700 employees. It produced a vast range of finely crafted articles to fulfil every furnishing need. The company had an eye for artistic innovation and would become one of the chief popularisers of the Glasgow Style, but their interests were far wider, stretching from a business in undertaking to the setting up of one of the City's early omnibus systems. Wylie & Lochhead had a finger in every furniture-making pie and manufacturing was only part of the story. Subcontracting to a network of local furniture-makers, buying in designs from home and abroad, they handled and

retailed huge quantities of stock in every saleable historic style. There were branches in London and Manchester, agents throughout Europe and the Empire. Walton & Co. was tiny in comparison. In contrast to Wylie & Lochhead, the sale of furniture through the showrooms appears to have been a sideline for Walton's firm. It concentrated on the design of interior schemes, operating on a more personal scale, principally to commission. [12]

While Walton & Co. shared the same market – Wylie & Lochhead, Morton's and Guthrie & Wells all had their own contract departments aimed at the more discriminating client – it had a slightly different flavour. For one thing, Walton & Co. never allowed itself to be drawn into the reproduction trade. It specialised instead in its exclusive range of individually-designed products. This was supplemented, where necessary, by a few items secured from progressive suppliers, but increasingly less so as the workshop capacity grew. And while the adverts of its competitors within the furniture trade could all be found on the pages of the trade press, Walton did not choose exposure of this kind. He preferred a more élite position, attracting commissions solely through the discreet means of personal recommendation, viewing in the company showrooms, and the exhibition of his work alongside his artistic, photographic and architectural associates at the Glasgow Institute. Despite the invigorating commercial atmosphere of his Glasgow background, Walton was in no way commercially minded. Career decisions which he later made reflect an ambivalence about trade connections typical of the circles in which he moved both in Glasgow and London. The world he knew best, the world to which he had always belonged, after all, was the world of artists.

In some ways Walton & Co., with its select range of products and its artistic intentions, is better compared to the Arts and Crafts workshops which had sprung up in the south. But here too there are differences which highlight the equivocal nature of Walton's position. Usually run by architects (like Mackmurdo and Ashbee), the workshops of the Arts and Crafts were set up not so much to earn a living as to fulfil a variety of idealistic aims. Ashbee's Guild of Handicraft, which started as a self-supporting educational venture, intending to reproduce 'the best features of the medieval workshops in Italy', had philanthropic as well as artistic intentions.[13] The Century Guild proposed to 'render all branches of art the sphere no longer of the tradesman, but of the artist' and to 'restore building, decoration, glass painting, pottery, wood-carving and metal to their rightful place beside painting and sculpture'.[14] While Walton may have been in sympathy with many of these ideals, if they were not too socialistic, and while his organisation courted the same market (as Ashbee explained, 'Our endeavour will be to make work of such quality as shall satisfy the demand of the professional public rather than of the Trade'), Walton had made no such claims for his own firm.[15] Like the Glasgow Boys, he was not ideologically inclined. His company fulfilled his own aesthetic inclinations, but with no apparent concern to be any more than a profit-making company. Yet his aims were far from mercenary: his ideal was to create what is beautiful.

The company's reputation depended on the unity of Walton's interior schemes and on the quality and individuality of its productions – a reputation built on more than a decade of achievement. The productions themselves combined 'state of the art' techniques with a unique and innovative style, best demonstrated through an overview of the firm's productions.

Walton & Co. stained glass

Walton's company was amongst the pioneers of a new style of domestic stained glass in Glasgow. From the beginning, his windows had emphasised the innate qualities of the medium. He was following the nineteenth-century revolution in stained glass design, a reaction against the heavily painted glass which had gone before. Initiated by Pugin's revival of mediaeval technique and design, the new movement had undergone an important boost when Charles Winston commissioned James Powell & Sons to reproduce the qualities of mediaeval glass for modern stained glass artists in 1849.[16] Walton's early figure-subject pieces – an intriguing mix of Glasgow Boy and Pre-Raphaelite sources – showed him already absorbed by this new approach: the emphasis on painting reduced, the glass

carefully chosen and the leading used, in the Gothic manner, to form the main outlines of the drawing. William Morris, in Ruskinian style, had set himself to show a respect for materials in the stained glass production of his own company. He had explained some of his ideas in a commentary to his firm's exhibits in 1883. He insisted that the distinguishing characteristics of stained glass – the translucency of the material and the strength of the outline – should be expressed: 'Shading is a dulling of the glass; it is therefore inconsistent with the use of a material which is chosen for its brightness … Colour, pure and sweet, is the least you should ask for in a painted window.'[17] These were the criteria under which most progressive glass artists of the 1890s were operating.

Cottier had been chiefly responsible for bringing the new thinking to Glasgow, and his glass work, in a delicate and decorative style, reflected first the work of Morris & Co. and later, the Dutch and Japanese influence probably brought to his studio through his employment of the Dutch artist Matthew Maris.[18] Neither Cottier's characteristically tight arrangement of full-length figures, nor his sometimes rather dominating use of yellow stain were echoed in Walton & Co.'s panels (where the atmosphere is somehow different). Nor did Walton emulate his square, tile-like background patterns with their strongly Aesthetic flavour. This should not obscure, however, the clear connections between Walton's and Cottier's work – the arrangement of the leading, the flowing Aesthetic hair, or the unfurling ribbon-like scrolls of Cottier's windows, which reappear in Walton's in abstracted form.

It is likely that David Gauld's work for Hugh McCulloch of c. 1891 had been crucial to Walton, though the dating of their work is so close that the true priority is unclear. Gauld's 'Music' series for McCulloch entirely dispensed with glass painting over most of the composition, making use instead of pieces of strongly streaked and bubbled glass in the manner of a mosaic. Only in faces, hands and the leaves of trees was there any significant use of painting. This method is not apparent in Walton's figure-study window at Grosvenor Crescent of 1891 (pl. 32), but is paralleled in the Burrell window of 1892 (pl. 30).[19]

In Walton's decorative pieces a precedent is less clear. Only the panels by William Stewart at Ruthven Towers, Auchterarder, to which attention has been drawn elsewhere, are comparable to the mosaic style Walton was using at Dundonald Road or Thornton Lodge in 1891.[20] Though Stewart's window, dated c. 1888, is much more complex, both the Ruthven windows and Walton's use only textured and coloured glass with the pattern of the leading to create a pictorial design. Walton's monochromatic butterfly window at Dundonald Road (pl. 23) in fact relies solely on the

124. Glass from the door into the hall at Elm Bank, York, with characteristic use of jewel-like beads of glass.

were definitely on the wane, any attempt to breach the sewn-up ecclesiastical market was abandoned, and the efforts of the firm turned wholly to the development of a style of glazing sympathetic to Walton's interiors. 1896 saw much use by Walton of individual plant motifs in his wall stencils and fabrics: the result in stained glass was the series of windows at William Rowntree's store. Walton's concurrent involvement with James Couper & Sons' 'Clutha' glass is likely to have reinforced his understanding of the distinctive qualities of the material at this stage. The careful selection of texture in each piece of glass in the Rowntree panels, the juxtaposition of different types of glass and

patterning of the leaded lines, which makes it more diagrammatic. This and a similar design at Thornton Lodge were the startling introduction to his career in decorative domestic glass.

Each window was individually designed, drawn up to full scale at an easel (*cf.* pl. 152), and hand-made in the workshops. In the earliest pieces, according to family tradition, Hannah drew the faces: her superior drawing and her understanding of the material made her the ideal partner. To begin with, there were many experiments, with different techniques and styles of work. In William Burrell's window (pls 30, 32) the painted details are sadly faded, perhaps the result of inexperience. The decorative panels of the Drumalis hall (pl. 34) show exploratory use of an overlay technique where parts of the design are double-glazed for richer effect. But whatever the technique or style, each piece of glass was selected with care, and its particular qualities exploited to the full within the composition.

Decorative panels, with mostly plant but sometimes abstract patterns, became essential to Walton's interior schemes, used increasingly on internal windows, roof lights and the panels of doors and carcase furniture. By 1895 figure-subject windows at Walton & Co.

126. An apparently effortless exercise: in the unostentatious doorway of The Leys' coach house, 1901, the chauffeur could enjoy one of Walton & Co.'s most stunning panels.

the striking colours make these simple pieces some of the strongest and most individual work of the firm. These elements, with a marked emphasis on plain glass as a background (no doubt an influence of Japanese art), and the introduction of copper pieces *c.* 1893, established a pattern for decorative panels which became an essential feature of the Glasgow Style.

Walton's glass of this type had reached maturity both in style and technique by 1897 with the work at Ledcameroch, but the full impact in Glasgow may not have been apparent until the completion of work on Miss Cranston's new Argyle Street interiors at the end of 1899.[21] During the last weeks of October, when this work was reaching its final stages, preparations must also have been in progress for the opening of the Glasgow Kodak shop in Buchanan Street (pl. 106), and the Buccleuch Street workshops (pl. 97) were nearing completion. For the company, the new year and the new

125. One of Walton's panels for Fred Rowntree's bay windows in the store extension at William Rowntree's, 33-9 Westborough, Scarborough. The simplified flower motif was a favourite with Walton: see also pl. 60.

127. Chap-book style design by Walton from the back of a publicity booklet for Miss Cranston's tea rooms, *c.* 1898.

128. Entrance of Miss Cranston's tea rooms at 114 Argyle Street: with characteristic detailing and eighteenth-century references almost certainly to Walton's design.

century would open in style.

Many of Glasgow's artistic set would have long been aware of the company's exquisite productions, but for the ordinary citizen of Glasgow, the 'striking unfamiliarity'[22] of the Argyle Street tea rooms compelled attention – and some of the company's finest work (in stained glass, stencils, wall-framing and fireplaces) was on display. The glazing at Argyle Street includes some of the most effective panels in Walton's Glasgow style: pieces of copper and plain and coloured glass intricately combined, with inset rounded glass beads or 'jewels', in dynamic and decorative compositions (pl. 132).

Most of the stained glass discovered in the Argyle Street building is immediately recognisable as Walton's in style and *The Glasgow Advertiser & Property Circular's* assertion that while Walton & Co. were responsible for the painting and decorating, Kemp, Benson & Co. were contractors for stained glass is not easy to comprehend.[23] Whether they are mentioned because this company had a larger responsibility for glass over-

129. A corner of the Luncheon Room at Argyle Street, decorated by Walton during 1899. The furniture is by Mackintosh.

all (on the ground, third and attic floors) while Walton's was only in the doors, or whether Walton's designs, for some reason, were made up by this firm, has yet to be fully understood.[24] Walton & Co. were listed as glass stainers from early 1891, their windows at Drumalis, Grosvenor Crescent and Devonshire Gardens[25] were signed with the company's name, and their glass craftsman John Shedden demonstrated his skills at the Glasgow Arts and Crafts Exhibition of 1895 (pp. 38-9). It is possible, however, that until 1899, when a whole floor was constructed for the glassworkers at Buccleuch Street, some of the company's glasswork was subcontracted when necessary to alternative makers.

Stencil Decorations

As with stained glass, some of the company's most characteristic and technically mature stencilwork can be seen at Argyle Street. Walton's method, which used stains with resists, revealing much of the background plaster (explained in great detail in a lecture he gave in 1900), gives his designs a recognisable quality accentuated by the subtle grading of tones and careful linking of the colours with the room-scheme as a whole.[26]

Scotland had its own line of sophisticated decorators reaching back through Cottier to the work of Robert Adam in the eighteenth century, and beyond.[27] An emphasis on colour and the co-ordination of wall and ceiling decorations was part of Walton's heritage. Stencilling in particular in the nineteenth century was part of the Scottish scene, paralleled in England by its widespread use in the churches of Gothic revival architects: the attractive interiors of Bodley & Garner come to mind. Walton's reliance on stencilwork, supplemented by hand painting, which gave him great flexibility, facilitated the full co-ordination of his interiors, and linked him to the Scottish tradition.

The patterns used over the years of the firm were enormously varied, from the simple repetition of a single motif to more sophisticated, confidently flowing, all-over designs. The decoration on the walls of the

130. Lavish stencilling applied to the woodwork of an unidentified billiards room, c. 1899-1900. In the foreground is a characteristic Walton carpet.

131. Drawing for a design closely related to the stencil pattern in the luncheon room at Argyle St (pl. 129).

luncheon room at Argyle Street shows Walton at his most lyrical, with springy tendrils and flowing lines in a pattern of roses, stems and leaves in an alternating repeat . Despite the flowing character of the stems, there is an underlying control, which, as symmetry or other structural order, is evident in all Walton's patterns. This was also typical of the work being produced by Walton's contemporaries in the south: typical of the work of the Silver Studio,[28] for instance, as it was typical of the designs of the architects Henry Wilson and M. H. Baillie Scott, and as it had been of the earlier pattern-making of Mackmurdo and Herbert Horne in the Century Guild. Not least, it was typical of Voysey's work and the knowledge of a friendship between the two designers puts the strong influence of Voysey (in motifs as well as arrangements) into context. Behind both Walton's and Voysey's work was the master of pattern, William Morris, and in the Argyle Street Luncheon Room frieze – one of Walton's most characteristically 'Glasgow' patterns – this common source is still surprisingly clear. The grapes and vine leaves, and the branching rose of the Luncheon Room frieze reflect

both Morris's subject matter and his method of arrangement, as can be demonstrated by comparison with Morris's 'Vine' wallpaper of 1873 and his 'Rose' fabric of a decade later. Though the origin is evident, Walton's pattern is quite distinct from Morris's, transformed by a series of overlaid influences. The conventionalisations of Voysey and Wilson, the stylised distortion of Beardsley, Mackintosh's sinuous and organic graphic style, combine with Walton's own sensitive colouring and instinctive decorative sense to give his work its individuality of style – a style which had become widely recognised as Scottish by the time the century drew to a close.

The stencilling of Walton & Co. could be applied with reserve or fluency to suit the occasion, on plaster or ceiling beams, wood framing or doors. The touches of stencilling on the ceiling straps and beams of the Argyle Street smoking room were part of the company's style of decoration, which extended from the major points of focus to the remotest details of a room.

Most of the company's stencil designs were used over again in different interiors, sometimes in alternative colourways or with minor modifications. Like the firm's furniture, the designs were not necessarily exclusive to each commission, and were often used on a

number of separate jobs for quite different clients, for a year or so following the time of their conception.

Fireplaces and metalwork

Walton & Co.'s fireplaces tended to be more unique. Each commission merited its own original design (sometimes closely based on an earlier idea, but rarely in an identical form), reflecting the traditional dominance of the fireplace in interior schemes. After early experiments with tiled surrounds, the company began to add more elaborate metalwork parts. These more sophisticated fireplaces, from 1896, are difficult to match amongst contemporary work. Often the hoods were formed of polished iron, or in hammered copper or brass, with ornamented backplates of cast iron. Surrounds could be tiled, or were sometimes plastered, with the plaster surface incised and coloured to form a decoration. Sometimes pierced metal formed a pattern, or mother-of-pearl was inset, but the firedogs were frequently the most dominant part of the design. The company's fireplaces combined the metalworking skills which W. A. S. Benson or Longden & Co. could command, with an idiosyncrasy of decoration, and what can only be described as a superb architectural confidence in handling form (pls 72, 77, 105).

132. Copper and glass door panel from the luncheon room at the Argyle Street tea rooms (see pl. 129).

Walton's fireplace at The Leys' billiards room (pl. 114) shows his multi-dimensional capabilities, that of the Glasgow Kodak shop (pl. 106) the company's tiling skills, while, on the Argyle Street billiards room fireplace surround, the company's inimitable craftwork is displayed.[29] Walton's decorative combinations of beaten copper and glass, used extensively at Argyle

133. Detail from the 28 Kensington Court fireplace.

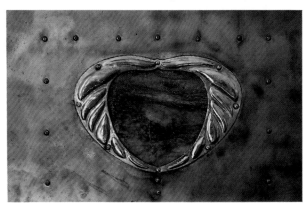

134. A classic example of Walton & Co.'s integrated craftsmanship: leaded copper and glass panels augment the drama of the fireplace in the billiards room at Miss Cranston's Argyle Street tea rooms.

Street, were a particular feature of the company's work, applied to windows, fireplaces, overmantels and as details added to stencilled friezes, wood panelling and furniture, a feature widely influential in Glasgow. There were few parallels initially in the work of other designers, most of whom were satisfied to use more precious substances in the conventional area of jewellery or silverware.

Walton would have had no difficulty in finding capable metalworkers in Glasgow. The many small smiths' shops operating in the backstreets in the 1890s alongside Duncan McLean's, reflecting the traditional importance of metalworking skills in Glasgow's industrial economy, were balanced at the other end of the scale by the enormous shipyards for which Clydeside is famous.[30]

Not all parts of the company's fireplaces could be made in the workshops and the company undoubtedly

135. The fireplace from the dining room, Elm Bank, York (pl. 80), monogrammed for Sidney Leetham, 1898.

bought in grates and other commercially produced components in the early days from Glasgow manufacturers. Later, Walton is known to have selected items such as margins in brass from the catalogues of Ellerwater & Co. or Longden's (who employed Voysey as a designer) – companies frequently chosen for the quality of their products by other Arts and Crafts designers.

Walton's interest in metalwork, which began in the early 1890s, had never been limited to the fireplace. The wrought-iron gates for Thornton Lodge and the signboard for Warneuke's gallery (pl. 29) may have been amongst the earliest metalwork designs, but wrought-iron candlesticks and brass electroliers were in production by 1896. The cast-iron fireplace at The Leys, though marked with the company's name, was certainly beyond its in-house capabilities, but the repoussé work of the signboard at John Rowntree's (pl. 51) required only workbench space, pitch to support the metal, and the hammer in the craftsman's hand.[31]

Fixtures and fittings

It has already become evident that one of the strongest characteristics of the company's interiors was the integration of individual artifacts into a unity in the room. Besides the careful planning of the overall colour scheme, the main technique used to this end was a consistent attention to 'architectural' elements. This was not an innovation. The architectural framework had been a conventional focus of attention in interiors of both the Scottish and English tradition. It is difficult to realise today, in the age of the cheaply-built suburban house, just how important these elements had become in the Victorian room, as a cursory glance at some of the more memorable interiors of the preceding decades would clarify, from the Burgesian fantasy of the Bute Tower dining room at Cardiff Castle, to the intimate detailing of Shaw's library at Cragside or the unrepeatable splendour of Whistler's Peacock Room.[32]

A preoccupation with fixtures – chiefly wood panelling or wall-framing, but also ceiling mouldings or beams – had always featured in the company's interiors, as the East Park drawing room or the hall at Drumalis have testified. Though not always the most immediately striking feature of a room, the subtle influence of these elements was pervasive. It had been the proportions of the panelling (tall and narrow with simple flat stiles), the extension of cornices, caps and horizontal surfaces (often with a cyma recta moulding) which had made the style of the Kodak showrooms immediately recognisable.

The materials were important. In general the lighter native woods, oak or walnut, were preferred to mahogany. Usually these were polished with wax, sometimes fumed or stained, never French polished. Pine and deal could be used for chimney pieces (stained or painted), but the choice was not arbitrary, as Walton was careful to explain:

I have spoken of the variety of colour to be had in using woods in their natural state. Oak is negative in colour and pine is negative in colour when treated as already described [waxed]. In the richer coloured woods we have Mahogany – full and rich in reds, crimsons and

136. Simplicity with sophistication: wall-framing in an unidentified interior – to all appearances occupied by a photographer.

browns. Walnut – in purples, pinks and greys. Satin-wood – in its rich yellows and orange tones, and end-less variety of more fanciful woods such as Tulip, Greenheart, etc., only to be had in small pieces and are more difficult to procure. Take walnut as ... the basis of a most delightful scheme in purple and grey with touches of rose colours and silver; satinwood again the basis of a yellow scheme – the walls canary colour and ivory white; mahogany with browns, crimsons and gold.[33]

These notes bring out Walton's acute and wide-ranging sensitivity to colour within the interior, a feature which had figured so prominently in Alexander Thomson's interiors of a few decades before.[34] Such conscientious planning contributed significantly to the impact of Walton's rooms.

From the period of the Rowntree collaboration of 1895-6, Walton's interest in architectural form increased, followed by a desire to incorporate the company's growing craft skills more widely. To this end panels in doors might be carefully modelled to receive specially-shaped leaded windows; plaster mouldings might be contrived to extend the possibilities of stencilling; cupboards fitted into the fireplace surround embellished with inset leaded glass; beaten copper or polished leather used to cover a door (with repoussé bosses affixed). The fireplace was a particular focus for integrated craft skills, often demanding the co-operation of cabinet-makers, tile-layers, metalworkers, joiners, and plasterers as well as painters and decorators. All this depended on the supervised co-operation of a close-working team.

Argyle Street shows how powerfully these methods could combine. In the luncheon room the lower half of the walls was panelled with alternating bands of wood and plaster: 'broad styles stained a dark oak, and with narrow panels showing stencilling on a light ground, surmounted with smaller panels of leaded glass and copper'. This wall-framing was imaginatively extended into the room at intervals to create low screens or 'stalls', set off sympathetically by the repeated uprights of Mackintosh's chairs. The glazing of doors was sensitively co-ordinated throughout, and the bracketed spheres of the stunning billiards room fireplace were repeated at intervals around the room. At one end of the luncheon room was the Eros panel of the Elm Bank drawing room (pl. 81), a 'nutshell' example of Walton's facility at integrating materials: a 'rare combination', *The Studio* proclaimed, of 'green marble and slate, coloured and opalescent glass, crystal, mother-of-pearl, and touches of clear silver'. The critic in *The Studio* could not suppress his enthusiasm for the Argyle Street rooms: 'If communities could be formed in ideal towns or hamlets, founded on the best principles of the new art, the effect on individual and national health and temperament would quickly be manifest'.[35]

Furniture

One thing not to be seen at Argyle Street – for Mackintosh had assumed this task – was Walton's furniture. It was an area of work that was pivotal to the firm's output and existence. Without its own style of furniture the company's interiors could never be complete, a point not lost on Walton: his experiments probably began as early as 1892.

As his confidence increased, so Walton's use of country styles for seating furniture (still prominent at Buchanan Street) diminished, replaced by a concentration on his own personal interpretations of earlier styles.

There had been direct references to the early eighteenth century (or to its revival in the 'Queen Anne' of the Aesthetes) in the broken pediment and glazed front

137. The elegant Brussels chair, designed for the Kodak showroom in Brussels (pl. 94) *c.* 1899.

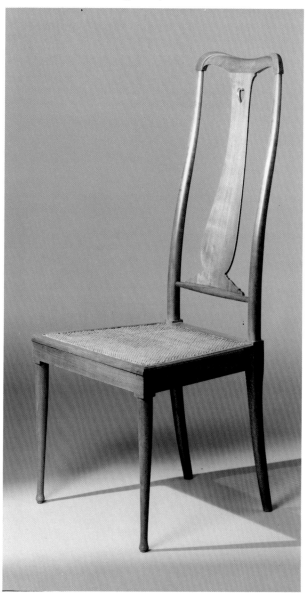

138. A wardrobe with typical company glazing and metalwork.

of Walton's first surviving piece of furniture, the fitted cabinet at Drumalis, set above a simple chest with cut-out handles: indication of his mixed sources of inspiration (pl. 39). Though there is no conclusive evidence to prove it, it is likely Walton had seen a group of exhibits displayed at the Arts and Crafts exhibition of 1890. There were pieces there by W. R. Lethaby, Ernest Gimson, Reginald Blomfield and Ford Madox Brown. With the exception of Brown, these designers (all architects) would join with Mervyn Macartney and Sidney Barnsley to form the short-lived furniture-making outfit known as Kenton & Co. towards the end of that year.[36] Perhaps Walton also visited their show at Barnard's Inn in 1891, for the starting points for his furniture were amongst the exhibits at these two displays: the green-stained chest by Ford Madox Brown with cut-out pulls on the drawers which would not look out of place in a country cottage; a light-weight, cane-seated settee by Reginald Blomfield (which he had a second chance to view at the Arts and Crafts exhibition of 1893); and an oddly-proportioned chair of Chippendale inspiration by Mervyn Macartney, with gently outward-curving lines, the joint of the back's top rail and uprights disguised in a true eighteenth-century manner beneath a flourishing curve. But, unlike Ernest

Gimson and Sidney Barnsley, who would largely reject the lighter proportions of the Aesthetic legacy, concentrating on country styles and the more box-like forms of late seventeenth- and early eighteenth-century case furniture, Walton had a foot in both camps.

Walton's ebonised or enamelled cane chairs (pls 62, 63) combine Aesthetic proportions and finish with eighteenth-century mannerisms of style. They are typical of his refusal to be confined by one set of ideals. He was in good company. Mackmurdo's work for the Century Guild combined Renaissance inspiration with his own idiosyncratic rendering of the Anglo-Japanese; Morris & Co. continued to make country-style chairs and Madox Brown's robust furniture alongside pieces which belong to the eighteenth-century cabinet-making tradition by W. A. S. Benson and George Jack; so with Walton & Co., who produced chairs as different as the flamboyant 'Beechcroft', the sophisticated 'Brussels' or the radical 'Abingwood' (pls 78, 137, 55). There were recognisably personal elements of style – a curving verticality, a strength of outline, elegant but unconventional proportions, fashionable finishes; and recognisable allegiances – eighteenth-century, regional furniture and the Aesthetic style.

139. The 'Abingdon' chair, an upholstered variant of the 'Abingwood', c. 1900.

140. A screen with leather panels handled almost like metalwork, decorated with beads of leaded glass. Photographed at Elm Bank, *c.* 1898.

The fashionable finishes were the black or white enamelling of Godwin (his chairs for Oscar Wilde were described as 'sonnets in ivory') – that is, the finishing of the Aesthetes – overlaid with the influence of the new Arts and Crafts: respectful light wax or polish on oak, walnut, birch or ash, plus the progressive use of stain epitomised in Voysey's green-stained cabinet shown at the Arts and Crafts Exhibition of 1893. These were recognisable features of the company's furniture style by 1896. From the same year Walton & Co.'s integrated craftwork began to be added, particularly to case furniture: hinges of repoussé work in the circular style of the Chinese or in hammered straps, applied decorations of glass, enamels, or copper, and characteristic leaded glazing. Traditional marquetry techniques were also practised in the workshops. Mother-of-pearl, ebony, and ivory were favoured, often worked in the form of a flattened heart. Sometimes leather panels were incorporated, decorated with glass beads or metalwork, like the panels of a screen at Elm Bank.

Despite the radical new lines of much of the company's furniture, their construction always made sense. The techniques of the historic cabinet-maker's craft were the techniques used in the company's workshops. Walton had no qualms about elaborating so long as the structure was sound. The Brussels chair (pl. 137) is a typical Waltonisation of a traditional form, the fiddle-back chair, incorporating time-honoured techniques of construction: the top rail curves down to meet the uprights of the chair back in a way that was common in

141. A glazed cabinet photographed in the Elm Bank drawing room (pl. 79).

142. Mrs George Davison reclining on a Walton settee at Beechcroft.

furniture of the second quarter of the eighteenth century. Once taken by an idea, Walton had no hesitation about changing proportions. The 'Cholmondeley', used in the Clerkenwell board room (pls 86, 87), extends this idea (though it may have come first), the curve of the top rail swelling in an exaggerated curve; but while the outline flouts convention, the structure is declared and the chair retains a relationship with tradition.

Fresh interpretation of historical forms may characterise a good deal of Walton and Co.'s production, but this should not obscure the innovatory aspects of his work. Walton's style could be more widely accepted, was less shocking, than Mackintosh's because it retained a sense of history, however tenuous at times, but there was much that was new. If the design of the morning room desk at Elm Bank (pl. 82) had been inspired by the furniture of a hundred years before, its extended horizontals and applied decorations place it with the most progressive productions of the recent theories of design. That Walton was impressed by the architectural spirit of eighteenth-century case furniture is obvious when looking at the Elm Bank drawing room cabinet (which bears a remarkably close relation to his shopfronts); yet it is stripped of any direct historical

reference and revolutionised by a dramatic reorientation from the vertical to the horizontal. How much more successful is this piece of furniture than the 'architectural' extravagances of the 'Queen Anne' furniture of the previous decade, which somehow seem to try too hard.[37] The key to Walton's success as a furniture designer was his restraint. Many of his most successful pieces are remarkable for their simplicity: simplicity which is classic because Walton was so masterful at handling form. This is what was revealed in the sparingly decorated interiors of The Leys.

The same distinguished simplification was followed in Walton's upholstered furniture. The settee in which Mrs George Davison reclined at Beechcroft has the light and upright quality of a Sheraton settee, keeps the high arms of an earlier style and adds its own Waltonian flavour: an exaggerated verticality with a gentle outward curve to balance the tapering legs of his ebonised chairs. There is no ornament here, simply dynamic yet elegant form. Of course there were mistakes – more often if he tried to work on too large a scale (the early

143. Furniture label of c. 1898-1901.

sideboard or the cabriole-leg cabinet shown at the 1901 International Exhibition demonstrate this point). But such changes in style and proportion are characteristic of the finest furniture productions of Walton's company. He was quite able to produce the best of the joiner's style furniture in the soundest Arts and Crafts manner – the plank-sided settle of the dining room at The Leys, for example (pl. 117). But when it is compared to the Cholmondeley on the adjacent wall there is no doubt where his true originality lay.

Textiles and wall coverings

One of the few areas of production in which Walton had to rely totally on outside contractors was that of textiles. Glasgow was a good place to be. Templeton's, set up in 1839, was a forward-looking manufacturer known for its 'artistic' hangings and carpets. David Barbour, who produced upholstery fabrics by designers such as Lindsay Butterfield, also supplied to Liberty's. Better still was Alexander Morton & Co. with whom Walton had been dealing since 1896, who, as well as carpets, produced chenilles for curtains and woven fabrics for upholstery including the finest double-cloths in wool with cotton or silk.[38] James Morton had shown an early interest in Morris's textile work and when he became involved in the management of his father's firm in 1895 the company moved to the forefront of Arts and Crafts textile production. It is likely that Walton and James Morton had met early on in Glasgow circles and Walton took advantage of the company's sensitivity to artistic designs. Walton's earliest dealings with the Morton company are now obscure and his best known woven textile – the silk and linen tapestry made by Morton's and used at Buchanan Street in 1896 – is the only early design to have survived. (It is likely to have been this design which sold at £2 5s. per yard in

1900.) It was produced in at least two colourways – with rose tints against a purple ground or with rose and green against the background of the natural linen – and was used widely in the company's interiors, probably in different weights, as a covering for walls, as curtains and as an upholstery fabric (pls 62, 73, 79, 151). It was obviously prominent in establishing the style of the more 'feminine' interiors produced by the firm. Its delicate, swaying lines echo perfectly the curving elegance of Walton's chairs.[39]

Much use was made of fabrics as wall-coverings in the company's interiors, and designs were stencilled on canvas or coarse linens as much as on the plaster of walls (pl. 83). Frieze decorations could thus be prepared in the workshops in advance, reducing the amount of work on site. There was the added advantage of a softer-textured surface. Unpatterned wall coverings were frequently employed, particularly within the wall-framing, where Japanese matting or painted cloth was preferred (pl. 136). All the surfaces of the company's interiors were given the greatest attention, so that control not only of colour but of light and reflection was effected: for, if there was one thing Walton hated, it was brash intrusion of uncontrolled light – those 'glinting lights on ceilings, glaring lights on (walls)' which give 'no feeling of rest'.[40]

William Morris had revived the craft of the carpet at his workshops at Merton Abbey, after Pugin's earlier thunderings on the principles of reformed design: patterns should be flat, without perspectival depth, respecting the two-dimensional nature of the medium; geometric rather than naturalistic reconstructions of plants and flowers. These were the type of designs Alexander Morton & Co. now produced to meet the small but growing market of the artistically aware.

For many occasions Walton preferred carpets to be spreads of a single colour with a contrasting border. This must have had a stunning effect in his rooms. Busy, over-patterned carpets were, to the reformed eye of the 1890s, one of the worst follies of mid-Victorian taste, but few were prepared to dispense with pattern altogether. To Walton, it was just another way of simplifying the effect of his interior, increasing the impact of his furniture and inducing a feeling of rest. It strengthened the effect of his colour balancing and the colours he chose were selected to harmonise with his other textile surfaces and painted and polished finishes. Typical combinations were rose-pink and grey, or grey-green and plum. Whistler's paintings may have been an inspiration. The occasional horizontal lines of soft chequering in the background of his portrait paintings suggest the border of a carpet: 'Harmony in Grey and Green: Miss Cicely Alexander' (1873) and 'Symphony in Flesh Colour and Pink: Mrs Leyland' (1873) are examples.[41] Did Whistler have such carpets made to his own design or were they simply decorative conventions of his paintings tempting the inspiration of a Walton (*cf.* pl. 26)? Not only chequering (which Walton used in the drawing room carpet at James Marshall's, pl. 59), but also the colours of these paintings (echoed in his schemes at Elm Bank) seem to have been an influence. James Morton would have been the ideal person to approach for these specially ordered designs.

From the time of his known association with Morton in 1896, Walton began to produce formalised patterns for carpets, based on flowers and foliage. Knowing his fine sense of colour, the lack of surviving examples is one of the great losses to an appreciation of his work. Contemporary photographs show his ability to produce a range of quite different designs (simple circular forms, diagonal stripes with a foliage border, flowing repeats), which are always subtly harmonised with the wider interior scheme.

Walton was not precious about their manufacture. He might develop hand-crafted skills in his workshops where it was essential to his requirements, but mechanical means were not to be spurned. It was a Glaswegian logic: 'This is an age of machinery and keen competition and there is no reason why machinery in certain cases should not be used'. So, while many of his carpets are likely to have been Donegals, hand-knotted in Morton's factory, machine-woven Axminsters were also made to his design.[42]

Clutha glass

Walton's designs for vases, for the 'Clutha' range of James Couper & Sons, were largely unrelated to the activity of interior design. This was unusual. Walton rarely experimented with a medium which had no crucial place in his interior schemes. It is difficult to find an area of craftwork in which he never dabbled at any

time (ceramics, excluding tiles, perhaps; possibly jewellery), but as a general rule he was single-minded in his subservience to the purpose of interior design.

The attraction of glass vessels is nevertheless understandable in view of Walton's intense involvement in window glazing. They added an intriguing third dimension to the flat material with which he was so familiar. The Clutha range, initially designed by Christopher Dresser, used a glass which deliberately imitated the qualities of ancient Roman and Venetian glass. Ruskin's sharp criticism of mid-Victorian cut glass and lead crystal led to a growing interest in earlier techniques, materials and styles, paralleling the revival in stained glass design. 'Art' glass emerged during the later part of the century and Couper's Clutha range was part of this movement.

Dresser was deeply interested in the qualities of craft materials and believed that the flowing quality of glass in its molten state should be expressed in the forms into which it is blown. His designs for the Clutha range included softly curving asymmetrical shapes with elongated necks as well as archaic Pre-Columbian forms transferred from his work in ceramics. The colours were greens, yellows and pinks with contrasting colours swirling around the forms and accentuating the direction of flow within the material as it had formed. Dresser had started working for Couper's in the late 1870s or early 1880s. In 1896 when Walton began to add to the range, Dresser was at the end of his career.[43]

In 1883 Liberty's took on the Clutha range and from then on retailed it for Couper's under their 'Lotus' trademark. In the later 1890s when Walton was producing designs, some pieces were mounted in Liberty's 'Tudric'

144. Glassware designed by Walton for the Clutha range of James Couper & Sons, *c.* 1896.

pewter. Walton is credited with having introduced a richer-textured glass with lustre patches to the Clutha range.[44] His designs follow Dresser's in general style but are simpler and less organic, include more straight-sided forms, and are always symmetrical. Each piece demonstrates a simple formal concept, leaving the glass to take the stage – thick with bubbles, glowing with metallic streaks and lustred patches, untroubled for the most part by the complex curves of some of Dresser's designs. Walton's idea was simple: keep the forms elementary – leave the rest to the glass.

Purpose and practice

There was hardly an aspect of the 1890s interior to which Walton did not apply his fertile imagination with satisfying results. This comprehensive vision typified the company's outlook, and was highly influential in Glasgow. From the start, before the company manufactured anything, Walton's first purpose had been the design of interior schemes – colour schemes, putting things together, designing the components where necessary – so that the lines, the colours, the forms, all related harmoniously together. This, linking him with a strong Scottish tradition of co-ordinated interiors, remained the principal purpose of the company throughout Walton's directorship. The first interiors had not always held together, partly no doubt from inexperience, partly from Walton's inability to lay hands on what he required; but as the company began to make more of the components itself, the overall unity of its schemes became one of the fundamental attractions of its interiors.

Since the earliest days of the company, there had been energetic activity in the various individual craft techniques as a result of the Arts and Crafts renewal – in stained glass and furniture (these had been developed commercially for some time), but now more and more in the areas promoted by the new Technical Studios at the School of Art – in needlework, ceramic decoration (here Walton's sisters had pre-dated the school), metalwork, bookbinding, and by 1894 in mosaics and enamels. These were crafts which could be practised on a small scale and they were quickly developed within small workshops and home-based studios throughout the city.[45] Following Cottier's earlier example, Walton & Co. had been the first of this new generation to fully integrate the new craft emphasis of the Arts and Crafts into the interior scheme.

Walton had gathered inspiration from a variety of sources and through the power of his own creative imagination combined them into a style which Glasgow could begin to call its own. While Walton demonstrated how these elements could be brought together in a homogeneous style, it is significant that the components of his interiors were not an assemblage from

145. Furniture sales: part of Walton's estimate to Sydney Paterson, 1900.

disparate sources. Instead, they all issued from the same pen. This was vital. In this respect also, Walton & Co. fathered the movement in the decorative arts which became the Glasgow Style, a movement whose first achievement was as interior design, in its purest form the imagination of a single designer creating every aspect of the interior himself, a holistic and painterly approach which Mackintosh would develop in extreme form.

The Glasgow public was ready for something new, particularly amongst the professional classes where increasing industrial wealth was fuelling a cultural revival. For those who were ready Walton provided the latest formulation of progressive design with a taste and sensitivity to his clients' needs which produced gratifying results. His artistic impulse did not prevent his desire to provide pleasurable living: he aimed at 'charm, reserve and simplicity', with yet 'some chance of imagination'. His services were comprehensive, his interior schemes total, yet he did not restrict his clients' access:

> Let the house be for the people that occupy it and not a furniture store … Impress upon your client the necessity of using the rooms you design for them. However well designed and however well decorated, a house is always wanting in comfort if rooms are not used and bear some trace of good taste or appreciation of the occupier.[46]

His schemes were not to be drawn up and admired, they were rooms to live in.

The prosperity of the company brought changes. By 1898 business was noticeably expanding – the new developments in York, the rush of work for the Kodak shops, the publicity at home: a new type of job was on the increase. As the firm became more widely known, there was a greater demand for the supply of particular products. Furniture orders grew and increasingly the firm would be invited, by architect or client, to supply one of its specialities for a large architectural job where a number of contractors were involved. Brahan, Crieff Road, Perth, for Rufus Pullar is a case in point, where Walton & Co. supplied 'ornamental glazing' with Stephen Adam of Glasgow and Mr W. Pape of Leeds, alongside numerous separate firms who supplied the remaining components of the interiors between them.[47]

Such a job might have come through a variety of sources: in this case from Pullar's acquaintance with Glasgow developments or from Bedford & Kitson's knowledge of Walton's work in Yorkshire, possibly through the showroom opened in York the same year. One thing led to another. Pullar went on to order furnishing from the showrooms[48] and Walton would co-operate again with Bedford & Kitson at Redhill, Headingley in *c.* 1901, where the company supplied furniture and glazing in rooms which were not to Walton's design.[49] Other work of this type included a sizeable order for furniture from Sydney Paterson of Winecroft, Bickley, Kent. Walton's request for plans and the absence of any fixed furnishings or decorations suggest he did not visit the house, though he took a very personal interest in the designs.[50]

Occasionally stencil decorations were commissioned to fit in with other designers' work. In 1901, Alexander Paterson, a Glaswegian architect (brother of the Glasgow Boy James Paterson), who had married the Waltons' old friend Maggie Hamilton, was building himself a house at Helensburgh, close by Whitelaw Hamilton's Thornton Lodge. Here, the company supplied a fireplace with fitted seat, and stencil decorations for the guest bedroom – but the furniture was not Walton's, and in other parts of the house only the odd fireplace is to his design. Paterson's personal record of work listed the company under 'Minor Contracts': 'grates' were supplied by Walton & Co., and Ellerwater & Co. at a cost of £8 15s. 6d. The company also supplied parquet flooring (to the tune of £23 16s.); Guthrie & Wells supplied the glass and a large number of other contractors were involved.[51]

Despite the haphazard nature of such orders, the company's products sometimes found themselves in sympathetic surroundings, as, for instance at the neighbouring 'White House' in Helensburgh by Baillie Scott (1899-1900), designed for a client who already pos-

146. Walton furnishings in The White House, Helensburgh, designed by Baillie Scott in 1898-9.

sessed some of 'Mr E. A. Walton's [*sic*] beautiful furniture'.[52] (This was Baillie Scott's description when he wrote about the house in 1906. As Scott could not get Walton's name right, it is unlikely Walton had anything to do with the White House himself: Scott and Walton presumably never met.) Yet all these were of the class of commission where Walton was unable to control the environment in which his designs were placed, an arrangement which may have brought his shareholders satisfaction, but which went considerably against the grain.

The jobs were profitable. Sideboards could sell at £35, beds and wardrobes around £30, dining-room tables at 16 guineas, linens (often used extensively) £2 5s per yard. The order for Sydney Paterson amounted to £258 12s 1d (which at 5% commission would add nearly £13 to Walton's salary before his fees for drawings and supervision were considered).[53] These jobs required input from Walton at the beginning, when discussion with clients and provision of sketches was required. Then the system took over: sketches were passed to draughtsmen, then measured drawings to the craftsmen. Where the supply of movable items only was required, there was little need for further involvement, and Walton's attention could pass on.

To facilitate the efficient execution of these orders the company had to be organised. There were difficulties of transportation and timing: more clerks were taken on.

The pressures of commercialism were still to a large extent resisted. The characteristics of the firm's work stayed the same: individual designs in fine materials, finished to a high level of craftsmanship, exclusive to the firm but not necessarily exclusive in themselves. Although orders were mounting, there is little evidence to suggest that such large numbers were sold that the sense of individuality was impaired, though the natural expansion of such a company would have led in this direction. Walton had never been against repeating designs at different locations, but like other Arts and Crafts ventures, his approach was distinct from a firm of 'jobbing' decorators. The company's interior schemes always showed continuation and development of ideas from one commission to the next, never a direct repetition of catalogued styles. Each job had a new combination of elements with fresh designs added to familiar ones. Stained glass panels and fireplaces were rarely repeated in an identical form and where stencils and furniture were reproduced it was often in new colourways or material and with different detailing. The proportion of innovation was maintained.

Walton & Co. and the Glasgow Style

As the company's reputation spread more widely in the later 1890s, the new art movement was blossoming on home ground.[54] Herbert MacNair abandoned his architectural career in 1895 to concentrate on design. His furniture had attracted interest through the fifth Arts and Crafts exhibition of 1896 and in *The Studio*, and was influential amongst the young designers at home.[55] The flowing lines of his graphic work, produced in association with the Macdonalds and Mackintosh, were introduced as strikingly carved mouldings or

147. A smoker's cabinet by Herbert MacNair, *c.* 1896.

applied metalwork on his furniture, an important element of what was becoming an increasingly recognisable style. Repoussé work in brass, tin, copper and lead was issuing from the studio of Margaret and Frances Macdonald in Hope Street from 1896: mirror and picture frames, sconces and clock faces in a style which again incorporated the distictive images of their graphic work.[56] Talwin Morris contributed copper door fittings, stencilled fabrics and, through his work for the Glasgow publishers Blackie & Sons, a series of book bindings in an individual linear style derived from Beardsley and his association with 'The Four'. For his colours he favoured green and heliotrope and his studio walls, described by Gleeson White in 1897, were 'dark olive

green, with devices in softened white, heightened here and there with touches of emerald green or pure vermilion'.[57] Sir Hugh Smiley might have recognised the combination. They were the colours of his hall at Drumalis, a colour range noticeably prominent in a group of works by the Glasgow Boys George Henry, E. A. Hornel, and David Gauld produced around 1889 (including Hornel's 'The Brook' bought by MacNair with his Art Union Prize money in 1891).

There was a multitude of other original artists at work: the Gilmour sisters in West George Street produced metalwork embellished with Celtic patterning; Jessie King, an associate of 'The Four', developed skills in book illustration.[58] A new generation of Art School students began to develop the style – Anne Macbeth in embroidery[59] and De Courcy Lewthwaite Dewar and Ann Harvey in metalwork and enamelling. There were many more peripheral artists who contributed to the style. Oscar Paterson was producing highly original glass from his workshop at The Glass Stainers' Company set up with Harry Thomson in 1893.[60] A significant proportion of his output was in pictorial domestic panels of Pre-Raphaelite subjects, in a personal style distinct both from Walton's glass and that which came from the Mackintosh circle, but nevertheless sharing aspects of technique. Mackintosh's furniture production was still small, but the table and linen cupboard shown in *The Studio* towards the end of 1897 already showed his strength of character.[61]

The prestige of Walton's company could not have been threatened at this stage. Mackintosh was an architect: he could hardly be described as a competitor (designing a few domestic commissions, the Buchanan Street murals and the interiors of his own buildings and home) to a company which had considerable workshop capacity, a swelling workload and a field of operation far beyond the city boundaries. If this was to change, it would be at the end of 1899 when the Argyle Street tea rooms and the new School of Art were ready to open, and Mackintosh's reputation was growing. It was the last time Miss Cranston engaged Walton on her city centre tea rooms before her patronage passed on. Yet, despite appearances, the threat to the company was insubstantial. Mackintosh's dynamic concepts were ideal for a restaurant, his uncompromising angles less comfortable for a home. His domestic interior commissions were never numerous. He was a generator of images rather than comfort and his style needed subtle adjustment if it was to sell in the store.

While Mackintosh's work had successfully complemented Walton's at the tea rooms, this had disguised substantial differences in direction. Comparison of Walton's high-backed chair in the Buchanan Street luncheon room (pl. 62) with Mackintosh's high-backed chair for Argyle Street, of Walton's elegance of line and delicacy of form with Mackintosh's sculptural strength, makes some of the difference clear. Mackintosh had no compunction about discarding historic precedent either in concept or construction. Walton's imaginative forms grew in harmony with his respect for the formal and technical traditions of his craft.

This is not to deny cross-fertilisation between the two designers. Both were affected by their collaboration at Buchanan Street. Mackintosh's admiration for the Abingwood can be seen in his adoption of the pierced heart on his heavy, plank-constructed furniture at Argyle Street, in his continuation of the chair back below seat level and in the encircling curve of the arms of his ladderback. Walton's use of sharper curves particularly in some of the leaded glass at Argyle Street, but also in the stencil designs is a clear link with the plant forms surrounding Mackintosh's large figures in the mural panels at Buchanan Street. Beyond the tea rooms, the similarities between Mackintosh's Board Room fireplace at the School of Art of 1899 and Walton's much earlier one at William Rowntree's (pl. 58) suggest a relationship beween the two designs. And the pastel colouring and delicate floral detailing which hostile critics often attribute to Margaret Macdonald's 'feminine' influence on Mackintosh had always been central to Walton's style.

Mackintosh's less naturalistic approach, his greater abstraction of form, led him to distortions which Walton's respect for craftsmanship could not allow. The lengths to which Mackintosh took his ideas in furniture had unfortunate effects on the construction. Howarth's examination of surviving furniture from Buchanan Street in the 1950s led him to comment: 'in fifty years [Walton's designs] required neither repairs nor modification. Mackintosh's chairs, on the other hand rarely survived for long without attention from the cabinet-makers'.[62] Or, as *The Cabinet Maker* authoritatively declared of a Mackintosh high-backed chair: 'Not that it looks as if it would stand the impact of even the smallest and most harmless pebble'.[63] Walton could manipulate and extend with fluidity of expression, but his distortions were within the repertoire of the cabinet-maker's art: he shared the Arts and Crafts respect for materials and techniques. Though Mackintosh had attended the Technical Studios at the School of Art, he was less interested in soundness than in style. He benefited from visual plundering of the Arts and Crafts, but many of its deeper purposes left him cold.

Mackintosh's interiors and furniture have a sculptural beauty which removes them from reality. This is implicit in the practical nature of his interiors: his furniture was better for looking at than sitting on and in Mackintosh's rooms the client always seems out of place. His achievements were not, like Walton's, in creating interiors for living.

148. Detail of a panel of beaten copper decorated with leaded glass in a rose motif. Designed as an overmantel for 28 Kensington Court, London.

By the end of the century, what had sometimes met with derision in Glasgow at the outset had gathered itself a small but growing market. It was the combined style of Walton and Mackintosh at the very visible tea rooms and the new work coming out of the School of Art which particularly caught the imagination of the Glasgow public. The colours and forms of the Macdonalds' work were softening. The MacNairs (Herbert married Frances Macdonald) had left for Liverpool, and Mackintosh was beginning to take centre stage with the forthright forms of his furniture at Argyle Street and his radical decorative scheme at the new School of Art.[64] The forming style drew from Walton's work the emphasis on integrated craftwork, the soft pastel shades and swirling lines of his stencilling, his simple decorative style for domestic glass. The rose and leaf motif he had borrowed from Morris was now the Glasgow rose; the rose pink, green and purple stain he had used at John Rowntree's were the principal colours of the Glasgow palette. Behind it all was the inspiration of Walton's co-ordinating hand.

Walton's contribution had not gone unnoticed. At the beginning of the new year, in February 1900, the Glasgow Architectural Society invited him to lecture at the rooms of the Philosopical Society at Bath Street: a gratifying moment.[65] An audience of fifty gathered to hear of his 'Personal Experiences in Decorative Work', in which he conscientiously attempted to explain his approach to interior design and the methods he had come to adopt. It was a an indication of the general recognition Walton and his company had achieved. Six years later, when the company had closed and Walton himself had long since left the scene, his importance was not forgotten by contemporaries. As a writer in *The Studio* remarked:

It is not easy to imagine what would be the position of modern decorative art in Glasgow today, apart from the group of tea-houses controlled by Miss Cranston, for it is a remarkable fact that while George Walton was yet a bank accountant, he accepted a decorative commission connected with a new smoking-room for one of these, and when he abandoned finance to carry out this, his first commission, decorative art may be said to have entered on the new phase at Glasgow.[66]

But despite the strength of Walton's influence, in the end the new movement owed more to the stronger, more abstract forms and linear patterning of the Mackintosh circle. Walton's furniture and interior schemes had always been highly individual – perhaps 'idiosyncratic' describes them better – full of variety; he was always open to new visual stimuli, changing, like his father, moving on. Now, already, his work was following a new road, altering direction under the influence of his new circumstances in London.

Behind the chief players over the last few years, had been a growing throng of lesser artists, using and interpreting their images and adding their own. By the beginning of the new century, the components of the new style had formed and were ripe for a wider public.

When the doors were opened at the great Glasgow International Exhibition on 2 May 1901, Wylie & Lochhead were poised for a new offensive on the market. Largely unfamiliar to the southerner, their ambitious display of interior work in the New Style was

149. This menu card of 1901 suggests that Walton may have been responsible for the unrecorded interior work, on Miss Cranston's exhibition Tea House, though he is not known to have done any other work for her business after 1899.

guaranteed to attract wide attention. The Wylie & Lochhead Pavilion presented a set of rooms carefully co-ordinated, with dominating shades of purple, pink, green and grey, touches of yellow, and strongly vertical lines.[67] Their designers, George Logan, E. A. Taylor and John Ednie were given individual responsibility for the rooms, which nevertheless formed a coherent suite (pl. 123). It was a *tour de force* which brought credit to the company (if not to the designers whose names were withheld). The rooms had the new angularity of Mackintosh's Argyle Street furniture combined with Walton's butterfly and rose motifs, his sensitively integrated craftwork and his carefully co-ordinated carpets. A new high-backed version of Walton's Abingwood featured prominently in George Logan's library. Wylie & Lochhead's machine-woven bedroom wall-covering (in fact the work of an English designer) appears rather rigid when compared to Walton's silk and linen tapestry of the Buchanan Street Tea Rooms. This and the predominantly geometric lines of the room schemes, show that, broadly, in the Wylie & Lochhead pavilion Walton's eloquence of line had not been transferred.

In general contrast, other shows at the Exhibition appeared in motley array. A few of the more progressive English designers lifted the tone. W. A. S. Benson, in league with a number of other firms, had organised an appealing display, with Jeffrey & Co. wallpapers, James Powell & Sons glazing, and Pilkington's tiles alongside his own light fittings and metalwork, the artifacts loosely sympathetic, but in no way attempting a co-ordinated style. Heal's also had a stand, their beautifully inlaid and carefully proportioned furniture expressing the English manner of design: good and solid, high on quality, but less conscientiously harmonised than the Glasgow Style.[68]

Walton's own exhibit, put somewhat in the shade by Wylie & Lochhead's extravagant display, still formed a striking and sophisticated show. His 'little house', arranged 'with tact and taste', incorporated several of his favourite devices – the white-painted glazing grid, a lunette-shaped window over the door and the extended Glasgow cornice: on view inside, the whole array of the firm's productions.[69] The display at the Glasgow International Exhibition of 1901 presented the company at its peak: a prosperous firm of interior decorators, suppliers of fashionable, hand-made, quality goods for the discriminating home-owner and business-person alike, and – most impressive of all – essentially a one-man show. The strengths of Walton's company would have been clear to the perceptive viewer of his display at the Glasgow Exhibition. His stand offered a style more personal than Wylie & Lochhead's, more integrated than Guthrie & Wells' (whose work was exhibited close by) or than the Benson cooperative's, and – partly because of the size of his company – it could provide more exclusive artifacts and more individual treatment.

In the early years of the 1900s, Glasgow's new style was in full swing and had unquestionably penetrated the Glasgow home. Most noticeably, the city became 'a very Tokio for tea rooms', many of them 'distinctly ar-

150. Walton & Co.'s 'little house' at the Glasgow International Exhibition of 1901.
151. The bedroom exhibit at one end of Walton's exhibition display, with lavish use of his silk and linen tapestry. The lampshades are covered in watered silk.

tistic'.[70] Mackintosh's Ingram Street and later Willow tea rooms for Miss Cranston were rightly at the centre of attention. But Walton was elsewhere.

The passing of the company

Walton's attitude to the new style has not been recorded. When he first arrived in London in 1897, those of Arts and Crafts circles alert to the Glasgow scene would certainly have heard of the 'Spook School' style and its mixed reception. This contemporary comment on the Salon of 1897 may well have represented Walton's views:

> I believe Mr George Walton's work would be regarded as distinct in much of its character from that of most who may be said to constitute the Glasgow school, ... he has sought to be individual rather than subject to the influence of a cult.[71]

However uncomfortable he might have felt about his association with Glasgow, Walton's energy and efforts were soon directed elsewhere.

How the powerful promotional capacities of Wylie & Lochhead affected Walton's company is unclear. Did it steal his customers or simply expand the market accruing benefit to both? Walton & Co.'s display at the International Exhibition had attracted wide publicity: but the company's subsequent course becomes obscure, with surprising speed. There are a few jobs known here and there. Some of the familiar interior work continued, with the company making up work for Walton's London schemes perhaps till the end of 1902. There was Finnart House to decorate in Weybridge in that year, and in the north the company's directors were keeping them busy: when the two brothers James and Robert Dick, who had been involved in the company since 1899, both married in the early years of the new century, their houses were done out grandly in company style.[72]

Sometimes old clients would return. John Rowntree's approached the company in 1902, wanting an eye-catching display for their café front in time for the Coronation celebrations. But perhaps Walton was not so pleased, in the company's later years, when he heard that Walton & Co. were making up the billiards room and dining room curtains, and embroidered bed-hangings for Miss Cranston's Hous'hill – to Mackintosh's design.[73]

By 1902, Walton's position in London was becoming increasingly comfortable. It is not difficult to imagine that his attention to the company's interests had begun to stray. The Leys and the Kodak work of the last few years had been particularly demanding; his name was becoming known in the best London circles and he was entering what appeared to be a brilliant career in the south. As long as Walton maintained his managerial role at the company, two months' residence in Glasgow was obligatory. What might be an ideal arrangement for a recent ex-patriate, could understandably become a trial to the settled – especially one with a heavy programme. He had agreed to act as managing director for five years when the company went public. That agreement had run out in September 1901. He had not been ready to leave at that stage, and stayed on as director, though the role he took may have been less active. But sixteen months later the situation looked different: Walton resigned from his duties on 17th January 1903.[74]

There were other possible reasons for his flagging interest. Over the last five years, the company had imperceptibly become less of an artist's studio and more of a business. For a designer whose interests lay in fine attention to detail as the components of his interiors came together, a larger company was not necessarily attractive and his remote location could hardly offer satisfaction. He already had less need for the company's skills as he had become familiar with local suppliers. Then there were his new associates in London. Had he become more aware of the differences between a decorating company and a Guild? Was he embarassed at his connection with what was now less and less his Glasgow Style?

Twenty-nine months after Walton's resignation, at an Extraordinary General Meeting of the company on 30th June 1905, the decision was made to wind up George Walton & Co. voluntarily.[75] What had gone wrong? Had Walton left a sinking ship or was the company simply not able to operate without him?

Walton had brought the company a good deal of work from the time he left Glasgow, which it could no longer rely on from 1903. Local competition was rising and there was a need to keep abreast of developments. With the loss of Walton, the company needed strong direction both in management and design, which may not have been available.

Walton had been dependent upon his craftsmen for the execution of his work, but had he shared with them responsibility for design? Through all the years of the firm, Walton's employees rarely received individual credit for their contributions. Had this been why Robert Paterson, the company's most promising designer, left in 1901 to set up on his own? Walton admitted the importance of learning from his craftsmen, but what had they learned from him? The wording of Walton's contract sets the tone: 'The Vendor [Walton] ... shall do the entire designing required in the business'; and

even when he was part time 'in all matters regarding the carrying out of the artistic work his decisions shall be final'.[76] Walton wrote in 1900:

> It is the greatest benefit to a designer or decorator if he has the opportunity of training his own craftsmen so that they understand the meaning and spirit of his work. A clever craftsman if once taught to work with artistic feeling in one thing will be able to apply it to all the work entrusted to his care.[77]

Whatever Walton conveyed in the way of artistic feeling, he does not appear to have transferred his skills in design. The comment of a craftsman, cited by Howarth, comes to mind: 'Walton always remained dignified and aloof, insisting that his designs be executed with mechanical precision'.[78] Had he nurtured designers in his workshop – or had Whistler's attitude prevailed: 'Why on the earth should the workmen think for themselves?'.[79]

In 1902 and 1903 the company was still expanding its workshop and showroom capacity.[80] There is no evidence to suggest that it folded under financial difficulties and the overall market for its products was expanding at the time.[81] William Gray had been in charge when Walton left for London and was still a director, though Robert Dick was Chairman when the company was wound up.[82] John Buchanan Dick, a relative, and director from 1901, had been active in the firm's interests, selling furniture to Liberty's on his trips to London in the last few years.[83] Annan was still involved. Robert Graham, who had designed the 'Lily and Rose' wallpaper way back in 1890, was now 'some sort of business manager', so may have gained promotion after Walton's resignation in 1903. Whether he had any business skills was another matter. Edward Walton recalled: 'I think my mother implied he'd made a muddle of some aspect of my father's business (but GHW was no business man himself!).'[84]

Whoever was to blame, there is no doubt that to a large extent the company had always been a one-man show and a lack of direction after Walton left was inevitable. Despite the surge of optimism in 1898 with the opening of a branch in York, it had closed down three years later: the links with Yorkshire had not been well maintained.[85] The company should already have learnt that motivation mattered. In 1905, whatever the immediate cause of the company's demise, it is clear that in practice it had been unable to make the adjustment to operating without its founder and central source of design.

VIII   HOLLAND STREET, 1901-1905

Back in September 1901 the Walton family had finally moved from 16 Westbourne Park Road to take up residence at 44 Holland Street in the more favoured area of Holland Park.[1] Walton's career had suffered no setback from the move to the more competitive capital. As he settled in to his new residence he could look back on the last few years with satisfaction. His exhibition work had caught the attention of the photographic press, and from then on he had become increasingly conspicuous in the pages of the national art and architectural magazines. His work at Ledcameroch appeared in *Academy Architecture* in 1898 and in *The Building News* the following year, where he also scored a double page spread with the Regent Street showroom; there had been a copiously illustrated article in one of the continental journals in 1900 – and, most gratifying of all, he had at last attracted the coveted attention of *The Studio* on not one but two occasions: generous coverage on Elm Bank in February 1901 and a flatteringly prominent position in its wide-ranging survey, *Modern British Domestic Architecture and Decoration* in the sum-

mer.[2] Not least, with completion of The Leys, he had made a successful assault on the ramparts of the architectural profession. In 1901 he was just thirty-four years of age, with a promising future.

New practice, new outlook

By this time Walton had begun to enter a settled pattern of practice in London in the field of interior alterations and decoration for an ever-widening group of admiring clients. Yet despite his increasing prominence, it is clear that much of his private work of this period has never emerged from its domestic seclusion. Just as the company's early jobs of 1890-95 had to be coaxed from obscurity, similarly many of Walton's commissions of the opening years of the twentieth century are not readily open to view. Walton kept a ledger of designs of this period (probably recorded retrospectively from around 1905), where the naming of the pieces usually relates either to the name of the client or to the geographical location of the work: hence the 'Davison Clock Case', the 'Elm Bank Cabinet Desk', and the 'Clerkenwell Table'. But there were many others: the 'Bowen Toilet Table', the 'Mount Street Sideboard Cabinet', the 'Judd Stool', the 'Court Bathroom Mirror', the 'Lancelot Sofa' and the 'Nevill Screen' – to name but a few.[3] There is sufficient evidence in this ledger alone (with its implicit reference to dozens of separate commissions) to suggest a thriving practice – even if the impressive interiors at Alma House, Finnart House and The Phillippines (*sic*), created at this time, had never been revealed in contemporary journals. The ledger, which is a record mainly of furniture work, but includes a few fireplaces and light fittings, emphasises the fertile energy Walton applied to this area of design, touching the whole range of furniture types from bathroom mirror to garden seat, elegant sideboard to revolving office chair, from grand piano to upholstered fireplace fender.

The ledger contains many of Walton's earlier designs for furniture: important pieces like the 'Abingwood' and its partner the 'Abingdon', his various versions of the Sheraton chair, and the furniture from the Kodak showrooms – the 'Brussels long-back chair', the 'Cholmondeley', and the 'Clerkenwell' chair and display cabinet. On sifting through about one hundred and thirty separate designs it is clear that the promise shown in his early pieces at John Rowntree's has been fulfilled. Though amongst these pages there are drawings which should be quickly passed over (faulty in concept, more often betrayed by poor drawing), there

152. Walton with his daughter Marguerite in the studio at Holland Street. On the easel is a design for stained glass, behind it the Eros panel (pl. 81).

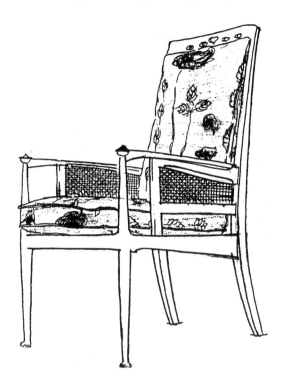

153. This somewhat disappointing drawing of one of Walton's most elegant chairs, the 'Lovat', is typical of the linear style of his Design Ledger.

are other designs which show such elegance of line, subtlety of proportion, and mastery of form that they mark Walton out as one of the leading furniture designers of his period. The 'Brussels' sideboard is a prime example. Walton's personal combination of sources can be distinguished – the horizontal emphasis of Mackmurdo, with a late eighteenth-century lightness of build, but combined so eloquently with the new understanding of materials and Walton's own expressively curving line that this sideboard is now an entirely individual statement. It still has a loose kinship with Hepplewhite and Sheraton furniture, particularly with the Scottish sideboards of that period with their distinctive 'stage top' (the shallow upper cabinet with its sliding doors),[4] but comparison with the later revivalist productions of Morris & Co. (their 'Hepplewhite' sideboard for instance), or with the productions of fellow Arts and Crafts eighteenth-century enthusiasts like Charles Spooner or Mervyn Macartney, shows just how original and modern is Walton's manner of design.

One thing noticeable overall about the designs in the ledger is Walton's method of selection. The only date which appears in the entire collection is 1 February 1905 in a reference to a cabinet sent to Mr Flausch.[5] A number of the designs, like the Abingwood, were in production as early as 1896 and several are likely to have originated at a much later date – the design for the fireplace of Wern Fawr's hall, for example, can only

reasonably be dated to 1910-11 when the room was built. Yet the criteria used for the selection of the earlier designs clearly reflects a later standpoint, for it systematically excludes many of the most recognisably 'Glasgow Style' elements of his earlier work. Where are the copper and glass details, where the leaded glass panels in cabinet doors, and the repoussé hinges? Once this is noticed, other points begin to emerge. There are a number of Classical references, like the wreath, and the egg pendant on a light fitting. There are unfamiliar details like leaves cut in plaster on a moulded arch over the 'Court' fireplace, and small ornamental medallions on the 'Lancelot' furniture. Even the mouldings have been trimmed of their cyma recta curves to leave clean horizontal projections. A new formality of expression can be discerned.

Interiors 1901-5

The more accessible commissions – Finnart House in Weybridge, The Phillippines at Brasted Chart in Kent, Alma House, Cheltenham and Walton's exhibition interior for A. S. Ball – make it possible to explore how these changes in Walton's approach to furniture design relate to the development of his interiors as a whole over the period 1901-5, when he was living at Holland Street. What more appropriate introduction than to take a look at Walton's own house soon after his move to Kensington towards the end of 1901?[6]

154. Walton's corner at the Arts and Crafts Exhibition of 1903, including the Brussels sideboard, the frequently exhibited Eros mosaic, Lovat chairs, a grand display of his new glassware, and the Davison clockcase.

155. Holland Street style: George and Kate's drawing room at 44 Holland Street, London, *c.* 1901.

What is most striking in the photographs of Holland Street is the plainness of the walls. There is no evidence of any stencilling in the house and the only pattern applied to wall surfaces was in the 'Little Drawing Room' where Walton's silk and linen tapestry was fixed in panels to the lower half of the wall. The furnishing was light and elegant – Walton's Sheraton-style chair from Elm Bank finished in white enamel, with a series of related designs including a caned settee. The drawing room fireplace was quite severe: flat and tiled with upright firedogs. Verticality was stressed: in the Brussels long-back chair, in the 'Holland' cabinet on its finely tapered legs, and in the high-backed settees (his upholstered settee was used as well as the new caned versions). This was accentuated by the lack of horizontal wall divisions in a high-ceilinged room, by the tall fenestration, and by the slender standard bay trees grown in pots. The Leys and the Dunblane dining room had indicated changes which these rooms at Holland Street confirm.

Yet the dining room at Finnart House, a few years

later, for the sugar refiner, John Lyle, was quite different.[7] It was surprisingly elaborate, particularly round the fireplace where three different patterns compete for attention around a dramatic beaten-metal hood. This vigour was mitigated by the size of the room, the restraint in furnishing and the undemanding pattern on

156. The dining room at Finnart House, Weybridge, *c.* 1902-3.

157. Drawing room of The Phillippines, Brasted Chart, Kent, *c.* 1902-5.

the large area of carpeting, so that the room as a whole remained calm. But, just as the Dunblane hall (pl. 118) had contained the last echoes of the heavier hand of the Pentys, the fireplace recess in the Finnart House dining room was the last time Walton laid stress on the organic richness of the company's craftwork, and on the rough directness, the ostentatious hand-making, of the Arts and Crafts.

The Phillippines in Brasted Chart, where Walton decorated the drawing room, is different in character and contains clearer indications of the future.[8] There is no want of pattern, but the new formality of the ledger designs is more apparent. The mannered use of the Classical dentil, first apparent at Ledcameroch, is repeated below the wooden moulding of the cornice shelf which is decorated with a narrow, gilded, broken line; the patterned fabric filling the wall panels and the carpet design are geometric rather than floral in origin; the tassels on the upholstery, the swags on the pilaster, the smoother, more ordered forms of the metalwork with its wreath motif, and the light fitting with tassels and egg pendant all contribute to the room's more formal

air, despite the movement in its plant-patterned frieze.

Alma House, decorated throughout by Walton for Colonel G. A. Peake probably around 1904-5, represents one of the most complete of Walton's schemes of this period, much of which has survived in the form of furniture sketch, contemporary photograph or actual remains.[9] Alma House is one of the high points of Walton's career in interior decoration and one of the last sets of rooms to use the range of skills Walton had learnt to command and combine in the company's workshops. His understanding and handling of these crafts is at its greatest maturity, but his approach to design has changed. Most startling is his new glasswork – plainer, more conventionalised in design, containing a new element of humour.

Walton used leaded glass panels extensively on the ground floor at Alma House, but only in the hallway is there any significant use of colour – a deep blue, twisted band arches across the entrance. Elsewhere Walton achieves his effects by line and clear glazing, some use of textured and rippled glass with the palest of colours and a little opaque white glass. This is more like his earliest butterfly panels at Dundonald Road (pl. 23).[10] The flower and foliage themes of his Glasgow glass have been replaced by simple abstract shapes or classical

forms. There is no use of copper, there is less emphasis on pieces chosen for their rich individual qualities of texture or colour. One window has simple wreaths above plain panels where the glass beads, used so frequently in his earlier pieces, have run or dripped from their places (pl. 161). A dramatic wreath bound with twisting lines in the music room is executed only in the diagrammatic form of the lead lines (pl. 233). In another set of windows in the conservatory, the pattern represents drops of condensation running down the glass (pl. 164). This glass is no longer Glasgow glass, but something surprising and new. The economy of Walton's earlier glass is present, but it has been transformed by a new restraint of colour and fresh vocabulary of form.

Walton's new mode of expression has worked its way consistently round the house. The metalwork and light fittings look more formal and less hand-crafted; instead of copper and glass insets on woodwork there are fine bands of inlaid chequering. The furniture, upholstered in leather, has simple elegant lines: there is nothing countrified, no sign of plank-construction. The fitted sideboard in the dining room (which demonstrates Walton's special talent for integrating furniture into

158. A corner of the music room at Alma House, with its fine light fitting (pl. 167). Through leaded glass doors (pl. 233) is a glimpse of the conservatory.

159. The dining room at Alma House, *c.* 1904-5: note the fitted sideboard at the rear and the extended 'Nevill' table.

160. *Above left*: The dining room doors at Alma House.
161. *Above*: Windows in a back room at Alma House.
162. *Left*: Part of the hallway glazing, Alma House

the framework of the room) is freshly considered, more geometric and angular in form than earlier cabinets.

Walton's exhibition interior for A. S. Ball, sent to Germany in 1905, is even more cool and classical than Alma House.[11] Walton unified this sophisticated interior by the consistent repetition of a simple shape, the long rectangle. Almost all the ornament is geometrical. Where they are not panelled, the walls are plain. The light fitting, which forms the one dramatic focal point, is based again on the wreath and pendant. But while the light fitting is impressive, the 'Lancelot' seats are disappointing: intended to be dignified, instead they are dull.

163. The conservatory at Alma House.

164. 'Drips' on the glass of the conservatory.

In the earlier years of his Holland Street practice, in a house in Kelvin Drive, Glasgow, for one of the company directors James Dick, Walton had used dark ceiling beams for a wood-panelled dining room.[12] But it was unusual at this time. Walton's ceilings were becoming increasingly plain, without stencilled details or

165. An interior in Walton's new style: the room for A. S. Ball exhibited in Berlin in 1905.

mouldings, though he occasionally used coved or vaulted ceilings plainly finished, as in the drawing room of the same house. The rooms at Kelvin Drive also have the exaggerated cornice shelf which Walton had used consistently in the later 1890s, and white-painted, fitted cupboards with the plainest leaded decoration on the glazing. This pattern of woodwork was retained from Walton's Glasgow days and used at Alma House, at Holland Street and at Finnart House in this period. A remnant of his more organic phase also survived in the continued use of expressive curves particularly in furniture: the bench seat in the Alma House conservatory is a good example. These familiar elements give continuity to his work and a faint, yet recognisable, Glasgow flavour.

Whether this change of style came from a change in Walton's outlook, or resulted from the demands of a new category of client, is indicated in the interiors where he is likely to have had more control. The simple, restrained rooms of his own house in Holland Street, the unpatterned walls at The Leys and at Ball's gallery show clearly that his own preferred manner was now plain, light interiors and Classical form. (The type of client he was gaining in London – businessmen and professionals – had in fact stayed much the same.)

New Surroundings

Walton's move to London had set him in a different environment. He was no longer in the centre of a busy, industrial city, where commerce reigned supreme, he was in the cultural heart of the British Empire, where the established figures of the art world based their practices and held forth on the principles of art and design, and where the splendid architectural heritage of the centuries could be studied on the streets.

When he first arrived in London in August 1897, Walton and his family would naturally have found themselves mixing with Annan's acquaintances of the photographic world, and Edward's circle of friends. Edward was then renting the studio at Ashbee's house in Cheyne Walk, shortly to move in to his own newly-built studio home at no. 73, designed by Ashbee himself. Edward had become intimately associated with Whistler, as a neighbour, admirer and friend, urging his involvement in such projects as the new International Society of Sculptors, Painters and Gravers for which he hoped to secure Whistler as president. Several other Glasgow artists settled for shorter or longer periods in the south: James Guthrie, John Lavery and George Henry – like Edward, looking for a wider market for their work, attracted to Whistler's coterie and the society of like-minded artists of the New English Art Club who lived nearby. There were other friends of the old days. Fred Rowntree followed Walton to London in 1899, after a distressing break-up of the partnership with Malcolm Stark, and settled in Hammersmith, soon to be joined by Arthur Penty, in 1902, who left his father's practice in York in the hands of his brother.[13]

By the time Walton moved into Holland Street in 1901, his own circle of London friends had grown. Familiar now with photographers and the artists of Chelsea, enjoying the society of Princess Louise, patron of the Arts and Crafts, whom he had met several years before, he had begun to find associates amongst the ranks of the progressive architects and designers of the Art Workers' Guild. When he was elected to membership in 1901, Voysey and Ashbee might have shaken his hand, and Walter Crane taken him home to tea. For Crane, the respected designer, one of the founders of the Guild, was living at the other end of Holland Street, at number 13. Despite Crane's seniority, they became close friends, frequently exchanging visits (and to Marguerite's delight Crane was prevailed upon to decorate the nursery).

Walton's reputation in London was augmented by the increasing interest taken in his work in the art press. His interiors and furniture began to appear alongside the work of successful architects like Ernest Newton, Leonard Stokes, and E. J. May.[14] In the rooms of the Art Workers' Guild at Queen Square, he could rub

166. Walton's 'Ex libris' label (the Latin unfortunately mis-spelled) from the Holland Street years, showing the Artist's and Architect's tools of trade, is indicative of his new outlook. In fact Walton hardly ever read.

shoulders with these and many other long-standing members, such as Mervyn Macartney, Gerald Horsley, Reginald Blomfield and Charles Spooner. Walton was younger than any of these, yet most of them were not quite old enough to seem of another generation. Standing in his recently-acquired architectural shoes, still squeaky and new, thinking of his hoped-for architectural practice, Walton would have looked naturally to these men for models, and it was amongst such architects that the sympathy with English Classicism, which Walton had shown at The Leys, found encouragement. If Voysey's tendency was against the new movement, he was heavily outnumbered.[15]

When Lewis Day visited the Glasgow exhibition in 1901, he thought Walton's exhibit gave a 'very favourable impression of what the newer generation of decorators are doing in Glasgow'.[16] This was not always the tone in which Glasgow work was received in the south. The early work of the 'Spook School' had not found universal acceptance with the English critic; and though in general, over the years, the reaction in England never adopted the irrational tone it had in Glasgow, there were always some who felt the need for personal attack. *The Cabinet Maker*, for instance, in 1903, abandoned its usually dignified stance in the face of a Mackintosh high-backed chair: 'There are many who ... are always glad to take an opportunity of flinging a stone at the vagaries of the new style. Here, I think, is their chance and the more stones that are flung at this class of work the better'.[17] Gleeson White had represented the more open attitude of many in his sympathetic reviews in *The Studio* of 1897 (in which he had been careful to distinguish Walton's work from the

Mackintosh circle's); but still there were those inclined to treat the 'Glasgow School' with some reserve. If Hermann Muthesius' memories of 'ridicule' and 'open objection' (in which he particularly implicated Crane) were not entirely accurate in their detail, they certainly reflected an unevenness in reception, to which Walton, who 'sought to be individual rather than subject to the influence of a cult', is likely to have been sensitive – aware of the risk of being tarred with the same brush.[18]

Yet, even when distinguished from 'the cult', Walton's style of work had not always been considered entirely defensible by southerners. When Lutyens visited the Buchanan Street Tea Rooms, he had thought the tone of the décor, the green- and purple-handled knives 'a wee bit vulgar ... all just a little outré, a thing we must avoid'.[19] This is likely to have been the attitude of the less sympathetic among Walton's new acquaintances to the work he had been doing in Glasgow, but for whatever reason, by the time Walton had settled in Holland Street, his style had undergone a change. In the same volume in which Mackintosh's work was censured, *The Cabinet Maker's* critical eye swept past Walton's exhibit at the Arts and Crafts Exhibition of 1903 (pl. 154), pausing only to pronounce it 'above reproach'.[20]

There were other developments which are likely to have encouraged Walton in his move away from the more organic forms of his earlier style, indeed from anything 'outré'. The continental reception of recent British achievements in design had been overwhelming, but not always what their champions would desire. When some of the fruits of the continental reaction were purchased at the Paris International Exhibition of 1900 and 'returned' as a gift to the Victoria and Albert Museum, they were regarded with dismay. Crane, again (this time in his capacity as chairman of the Council of the Royal College of Art), was forward in condemnation. It was the 'concealment of structural form by the lines of the design and the character of the wood carving' which so offended against concepts of 'truth to materials' and honesty in construction.[21] Voysey recognised the source of inspiration, and expressed the general disgust of his associates at the result, when he wrote in *The Magazine of Art* in 1904 'the condition which has made L'Art Nouveau possible is distinctly healthy, but at the same time the manifestation of it is distinctly unhealthy and revolting'.[22] Criticisms levelled at the work of Mackintosh and the Glasgow Style had related themes and to many minds they could be grouped together. Hence 'Scotto-Continental New Art' became a current description.[23]

Members of the Art Workers' Guild were generally united against the horrors of Art Nouveau – perhaps partly because there were others who had welcomed what might with 'improvement' be quite a saleable line.

A hybridised version of Scottish and English components with traces of continental Art Nouveau had emerged from the furniture workshops of such firms as Timms & Webb and William Birch of High Wycombe (some of the better pieces by the hand of their designer E. G. Punnett). Bought avidly on the continent, they had gained wide popularity as the 'Quaint' style of furniture at home. G. M. Ellwood produced work in a similar vein for J. S. Henry and Leonard Wyburd for Liberty & Co. In a number of these pieces there are clear marks of Scottish, and more particularly Walton influence – of the 'Abingwood' and 'Abingdon' (in the characteristic stance, the curve of the arms and the trapezoid seat, pls 55, 139) and of his elegant cabinet-work. Cheaper and cruder, sometimes double-seated, versions of the Abingwood appeared from time to time from less reputable sources. However flattering, these 'distortions' of his style were almost certainly an embarrassment to Walton as he met with his new colleagues at the Guild's club rooms, as he shared the society of Walter Crane. The general popularity and lowering of tone associated with Art Nouveau in England, had undoubtedly fuelled Arts and Crafts hostility – quite in line with their usual scorn of the trade .

Despite these suggestions to the contrary, it is unlikely that the commonly held dislike of 'Scotto-Continental New Art' did any more than speed Walton in a direction in which he was naturally moving. Walton may not have been an idealist, but he was certainly a man of integrity. The broken pediment of his early Drumalis cabinet (pl. 39), and the furnishing of his tapestry room at Buchanan Street (pl. 62), among his earliest recorded interior work, followed by the Classical dentils on his fireplace at Ledcameroch (pl. 73) and the regularity of The Leys (pl. 108), show that Walton's sympathies with historic and Classical forms had run parallel with other aspects of his work throughout his career. The general wind in the air towards a new interest in Classicism, the effect of his new environment, would have been enough on their own.

And Walton's experiences in Glasgow had had thoroughly positive results. At the company, in his role of designer-supervisor, not maker, he had gained understanding of a diversity of skills and techniques and, freed from any association with a particular craft, had developed an unusual breadth of vision, a style of work in which all the components were realised as a whole. Walton's approach to the interior, his painterly, unifying skill, made his rooms in whatever manner markedly more coherent than those of most of his English contemporaries. How many of those architects whom he passed in the corridor of the Art Workers' Guild were really designers of interiors?

At the time it was only an outsider who could fully understand the difference between Walton and the

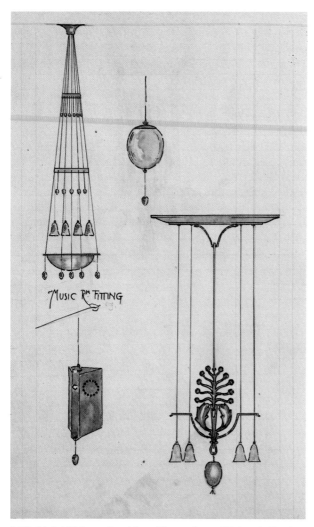

167. Light fittings for Alma House from Walton's Design Ledger: this attention to every detail of his interiors resulted in a remarkable unity of expression.

English: the German architect Hermann Muthesius saw that from the efforts of Morris in the individual crafts:

> England has forborne to draw the ultimate conclusion that must consist in regarding the interior with all its contents as an autonomous work of art. A complete room has never yet been exhibited at an Arts and Crafts movement exhibition in London. The movement is still content to trot out little boxes, embroidery, designs for wallpapers and materials, metalwork and furniture as before.

In Walton he saw a lyrical and expressive understanding of the room as a unity: he was 'a poet from whose creations a subtle spiritual atmosphere always radiates'.[24]

From his German background it was easier for Muthesius to see. The interiors of the English Arts and Crafts came from the hands of architects, while in Germany it was more normal for the better class of decorator – the *Wohnungskünstler* or 'artist of the home' – to

be drawn from among the ranks of artists.[25] For this reason Muthesius' expectation of harmony in colour and overall form was too advanced for the designers of most English interiors: their interests (and often their talents) lay elsewhere. Their intentions, in any case, were rather different. Architects in England had not on the whole concerned themselves with furnishing the interior in the nineteenth century. Of more recent years, Godwin and Burges had been exceptions to the general rule. The majority applied themselves simply to the framework of the room, concentrating for the most part on the fireplace, plasterwork and mouldings: for traditionally the client would furnish the room. English reserve had perhaps encouraged the architect to withdraw from the interior: not to leave it without a quiet distinction, but to give the client more room. This approach required great sensitivity, which in many cases was expressed. It did, however, make it all too easy for the less conscientious to leave behind them bland and characterless settings for the client to resolve. Others, intending to show their respect for the new decorative movement, supplied unco-ordinated showrooms of individual works of craft.

In Muthesius' view, the southern Arts and Crafts architects who did provide furniture for their interiors (chief amongst them Voysey), sought an 'extreme plainness in which imagination is suppressed'. This he saw as an abdication of the architect's responsibility to provide a complete environment. Muthesius set Walton, in a northern group with Baillie Scott and Mackintosh, apart from the mainstream of English Arts and Crafts as the group who best understood 'the idea of the interior as a work of art'.[26]

Muthesius' perceptive understanding of the differences between Walton and the 'London camp' does much to explain the attraction of Walton's more recent work to all but the strictest adherents to 'truth and honesty'. Those who saw plainness and the more rigid forms encouraged by this concept as its only interpretation might be offended, but among those who left room for movement and 'poetic' qualities of line and colour, and who were 'not afraid of historical echoes', Walton's work was fully appreciated.

However much Walton was in sympathy with the more reserved outlook of the English, he was never much attracted to ideas – and was never bound by the strictures of such a commitment. For the Glasgow Boys, 'Art' had been the essential goal. As Annan explained: 'If a picture has any real merit, it should touch a sympathetic chord in the intelligence of the observer, and give him pleasure. If it does so, it has fulfilled its mission, but if it does not, no amount of argument will enable him to realise or enjoy the artistic intention of the producer. The aim of a picture is not to demonstrate any theory or fact, but is to excite a certain sensory pleasure.'[27] Substitute 'interior' for 'picture', and Walton's outlook could not be more clearly expressed. Like the Glasgow Boys and Whistler, Walton's first loyalty was to beauty and decorative qualities – like them, to beauty even at the expense of 'truth' – which, in such 'poetic' pieces as the Cholmondeley, ultimately laid him open to the charge of Art Nouveau tendencies.

Questions of independence, pressures of practice

As these currents of change swept around him, it is understandable if the interiors of Walton's Holland Street years were not entirely homogeneous. Yet why did the plainness of his own rooms and of The Leys contrast so strongly with The Phillippines' juxtaposition of pattern (a tendency which has been recognised before)? And how can the use of pattern be accounted for anyway in one who saw himself as a follower of Whistler? In Walton's own words, Whistler's exhibitions had 'brought a gaiety into all decoration' by the 'use of white paint and simple light colours on walls'.[28]

It was the plainness of Whistler's walls as much as his colours which made such an impact. Yet, at the time, these interior effects were not widely sought after. Exhibitions do not have to be lived with, and the interiors of Whistler's decorating partner Godwin were rarely quite without pattern: they combined sophisticated use of colour with patterned fabric hangings and wallpapers of his own design.[29] However effective had been the influence of the Aesthetic movement in improving decoration and bringing Art into the drawing room, it had not done away with pattern. With the rise in taste, the market for Morris-style patterns had simply increased in relation to their earlier 'unreformed' counterparts. Frankly, people wanted pattern – more, they expected it from a decorator.

Walton's interiors had always been lighter and simpler than the bulk of work emanating from the decorating profession. As a progressive designer of his time, he was not unusual in his reaction against Victorian clutter. Morris, despite his busy pattern-making, had himself expressed an interest in plainer surfaces and there was a general move in this direction under way. Voysey, amongst others (architects, not decorators) had produced some quite plain interiors from the early 1890s when he and Walton had met. But as a decorator, Walton's ideas had to suit his clients needs. His clients of the Edwardian years, like the collectors of Glasgow School paintings, were drawn from the professional and business classes, many from among the new industrial rich, those with a taste for the modern. These clients often had a great deal of money. Some, no doubt, gave Walton a free hand; others wanted their interiors to impress. Hence Walton's despairing cry:

> The client sometimes calls out for richness and ornament in every corner of his house with the impression

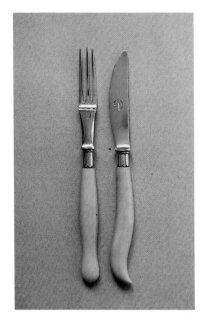

168. Bone-handled knife and fork from a set of cutlery for George Davison, a client for whom Walton designed almost everything.

that ornament or richness is everything. It reminds one of the child that desired to live entirely on candy ... The difference is that the child lived to know better but the client only believes that he is right, and lives on with no chance of imagination because you have been the cause of dulling that sense in the desire for better things by being so lavish in your design instead of putting before him work which is not only beautiful in detail but possesses the greatest charm reserve and simplicity.[30]

In addition to difficulties with the clients, many of Walton's earlier interiors had been designed in collaboration with others, who had different ideas and sources of inspiration. Some, like Rowntree, were chosen and genuinely contributed to the formation of his style and approach; but had others, like the Pentys at the Elm Bank hall, influenced him beyond his better judgement down the road to elaboration?

In the early years in London before Walton's practice became fully self-supporting, Walton was financially dependent on his company, and its success was dependent on his ability to produce interiors which would be pleasing to a wide range of clients. While some of his rooms of 1896 (at Glen Bank and John Rowntree's) had been quite plain, the decorations of the hall at Elm Bank and of the Clerkenwell showrooms had been surprisingly vigorous. Had there been the pressure, at these points, to fulfil what was expected of a decorating business; did he feel his practice as an interior decorator would be threatened if he produced only plain walls; or was this simply the only way he could make his voice heard in an architectural space outside his control?

There was, alongside the influence of Whistler, an ambivalence in Walton's thinking like that of Morris, who admitted: 'I have spent, I know, a vast amount of time designing furniture and wall-papers, carpets and curtains; but after all I am inclined to think that sort of thing is mostly rubbish, and I would prefer for my part to live with the plainest whitewashed walls and wooden chairs and tables.[31] There is every reason to think Walton enjoyed designing pattern, even if at the same time he saw plain walls as an ideal. The general flow in his work was towards plainer walls, but he was never dogmatic. Pattern was part of his thinking – as the tapestry covered walls of his 'Little Drawing Room' at Holland Street declare. It provided variety, like his wall-framing, or like the tradition of panelling 'men's' rooms which he happily pursued.

There is another issue to be considered in the context of his changing Holland Street style. While Walton remained a director of the firm, the terms of his employment obliged him, as a norm, to use the company's workshops for executing his designs. If there had been any parallel pressure to use hand-crafted decorative details, to keep workshop capacity full, it was removed in 1903: now he would no longer be restricted by the workshop style he had created himself. The ease with which he dropped the company style suggests his outlook had already changed. His lessening interest in hand-crafted details may in fact have contributed to his loss of interest in the firm.

Continental connections

Alongside the interior commissions were other non-domestic activities. There was work on the last of the showrooms and on some advertising material for Kodak; and a magnificent stand in the buttressed, Voysey manner for their display at the American Exhibition at the Crystal Palace in 1902.[32] (The later Kodak shops at Milan and Vienna confirm the trend in Walton's thinking towards plainer, cooler, less craft-orientated interiors.) An office for Walter Judd Ltd,

Advertising Contractors, extended the dominion of Walton's enlightened shopfronts towards the City; and a photographic studio was decorated – most likely for Lyddell Sawyer or Henry Van der Weyde, members of 'The Linked Ring'.[33] But, on the whole, commercial commissions became less numerous, while at the same time the influence of the Kodak shops helped to broaden Walton's activities in other directions: his work had begun to attract attention on the continent.

The ideas of Morris and Ruskin had inspired the countries of Central Europe in a vigorous revival of their applied arts which was well under way by the end of the 1890s. Invitations to Arts and Crafts designers to exhibit their work from 1898 had been preceded by invitations to the Glasgow Boys to display their paintings, first in Munich at the Glaspalast in 1890 (where seventeen of them showed, including Walton's brother Edward) and later in 1898 at the first exhibition of the Vienna Secession. Mackintosh's invitation to design a room at the eighth exhibition of the Vienna Secession in 1900, followed an established path of contact.

Walton's first commission abroad had been the Brussels showroom for Kodak of 1899 (pls 43-4), followed by others for Milan and Vienna completed during 1902-3. The showrooms must have been partly responsible for the sudden surge of foreign interest in Walton's work, chiefly between 1902 and 1905, but at least joint honour should go to Hermann Muthesius.

Muthesius had arrived in London with his wife Anna in October 1896, to work as technical and cultural attaché to the German Embassy, a position he held until his return to Germany in 1903. By early 1897 he was already planning a book on what had become his consuming passion, the English house.[34] English design held a fascination for the Germans, and Muthesius began to explore the new movement in architecture and design with great energy. He developed a special sym-

169. Walton's stand for Kodak at the American exhibition at the Crystal Palace, London, of 1902.

pathy with the work of the Glasgow movement and his friendship with the Mackintoshes and the Newberys is now well known. Ashbee also figured prominently in his writings, and the Muthesius' social circle included Walter Crane. A relationship with Walton, therefore, should not be ruled out. Muthesius gave particular attention to his work. In 1899 he wrote an extended article on Walton in the magazine *Dekorative Kunst* accompanied by no less than twenty illustrations. In 1901, in his article on the Glasgow International Exhibition, he laid particular emphasis on Walton's contribution and in 1903 produced a second lavishly illustrated account in *Dekorative Kunst*, this time on the Kodak shops.[35]

It may also have been Muthesius who put Walton in contact with the architect Professor Alfred Grenander in 1905, as he is known to have done with Mackintosh. Grenander was organising an exhibition of modern interiors in conjunction with the industrial art company A. S. Ball of Berlin (where one of the Kodak showrooms was set). Walton furnished a room in company with that celebrated designer of the Viennese Secession, Josef Olbrich, and with the lesser known Paul Ludwig Troost, Professor Billing, and C. Westman, as well as with Mackintosh and Grenander himself. Walton's furniture was more traditional in form certainly than Mackintosh's at that date and was perceived as such by the Germans, who described his furniture as 'based more on older styles'.[36] The increasingly geometric manner Mackintosh adopted had been far more influential.

The A. S. Ball exhibition in 1905 (pl. 165) was one of Walton's last continental commissions – perhaps understandably as his style of work was moving away from the direction of thinking in Central Europe at that time – but before this there are indications of quite a series of jobs. 1902 saw the opening of the Kodak showroom in Vienna and Walton may have designed an interior there at the residence of the branch's new business manager, Henry Frederick Goshawk.[37] Concurrently, he was packing exhibits for a show of British Arts and Crafts which was to take place in the National Museum of Applied Arts in Budapest – the 'South Kensington of Hungary'.[38] The museum director, Jenö Radisics, had made a recent visit to Britain which included a call at the Glasgow International Exhibition, from which many of his exhibits were drawn. He had already organised exhibitions of work by Walter Crane in 1900, and by Aubrey Beardsley, and in 1902 Walton's work featured amongst a Scottish selection alongside that of E. A. Taylor, Ann Macbeth, Kellock Brown, Wylie & Lochhead and Guthrie & Wells, with Robert Anning Bell, Edgar Wood, Alexander Fisher, Arthur Gaskin and others among the English contingent. Out of all these, Walton was chosen to design

170. Catalogue cover by Walton for the 1902 exhibition of Arts and Crafts in Budapest.

their catalogue cover and poster and Walton's hoarding from Kodak's Strand branch found extended use as an advertisement for the exhibition outside the museum – a more elevated destiny than any of his previous hoardings attained.[39] (His 'artistic barricade' from Buchanan Street had ended up 'in front of a railway operation in Gibson St, Hillhead, but as the planks have been put on any-how the ensemble suggests a nightmare of the new poster designer after a supper of lobster and stout'.[40]) Crane had remarked, when visiting their country, on the Hungarians' 'rich and endless imagination in floral decoration'.[41] Their more 'poetic' instinct added to their appreciation of Walton's work which they evidently preferred to Mackintosh's. Inside the Budapest museum, Walton showed furniture and his Eros panel. When, at the close of the exhibition, the museum wished to make a purchase, he was delighted to oblige, and (though he wished it had been a more important item than a chair) offered them 10% discount.[42] A chair of Walton's was also bought around this time by the Trondheim Museum in Norway.[43]

Around 1902-3, Walton was involved in a commission to decorate the house of Carl Bembé in Mainz. Photographs of the interiors show Walton's 'Lovat' chair in the Ladies' Room where Emanuel Seidl of Munich designed the decorations and fittings, which show the influence of the Glasgow Style.[44] The fireplace was the same as the one used by Voysey at The Orchard,

171. Walton's Lovat chair in Carl Bembé's Glasgow-influenced Ladies Room in Munich, designed by Emanuel Seidl, *c.* 1902.

Chorleywood – perhaps one of Voysey's designs available through Longden & Co. – while in the Men's Room, a Walton stencil pattern is used on the frieze and the decorations on the ceiling beams are in his style. Perhaps it was for this commission that Walton designed the 'Mainz', his own version of the barrel chair, a type with which so many Arts and Crafts personalities experimented – Burne-Jones in a tapestry, Baillie Scott at Darmstadt for the Grand Duke of Hesse, later Mackintosh at the Willow and Ingram Street Tea Rooms.[45]

Another European commission is suggested by the suite of furniture in Walton's ledger called the 'Brussels', which includes the long-backed chair of the Brussels showroom (pl. 137). Although clearly intended for

172. The low-backed 'Brussels' chair, designed *c.* 1901, from Walton's Design Ledger.

a domestic situation, it bears an interesting relation to the Kodak work – the elegant proportions of the 'Brussels' sideboard (*cf.* pl. 154) recall the design of his shopfront – strong horizontal lines above a shallow bow. Later, in 1905, Walton found further work at Brussels for Mr Flausch. Possibly for a house called 'Jordaens', this commission is now represented only by two ledger drawings, for a cabinet and settee.[46]

Walton's furniture and interiors were almost as well-illustrated in continental periodicals as they were at home, and there are tangible instances of his influence: Richard Riemerschmidt was responsible for a version of the Abingwood illustrated in *Dekorative Kunst* in 1901; Ludwig Holwein for another, appearing in *Innen-Dekoration* in 1906; and attention has been drawn to a third by Alfred Althaus of Berlin. In the elegant lines of Paul Haustein's suite, illustrated in *Dekorative Kunst* in 1904, there are clear echoes of Walton's Sheraton-style chairs and high-backed upholstered settee. But, on the whole, though many interiors were produced which owe something to Walton's work, his influence was merged within that of the Glasgow Style.[47]

The wider éclat of Mackintosh's work was important for a designer who received little encouragement at home. While Walton must have found the growth of his reputation abroad satisfying, it was probably not something he sought ambitiously. He rarely travelled, so commissions abroad were difficult to supervise. What had always given him satisfaction was to see through the execution of a commission: to take time, to ensure the details were right, that the effect was what he wanted, to be there on the spot. Designing at a distance was a method alien to Walton's way of thinking.

New companies, new experiments

When Walton resigned from his company in January 1903, he needed to settle on alternative sources for making up his work. There are indications that he had used local firms as early as 1898, when pieces began to appear in the design and cost books of William Birch of High Wycombe, a large furniture-making company not far outside London.[48] Though there is some possibility that Birch's firm had copied these designs, it is not improbable that Walton should have been obliged to use a local cabinet-maker on some occasions, when the Glasgow workshop capacity was full.

By 1903 the majority of Walton's commissions had for a long time been coming from clients based in the south, spreading slowly from London out into the home counties and sometimes further afield. Now that his practice was wholly independent of Walton & Co., the irritation of having his work made at such a distance evidently triumphed over any wider loyalties. All four pieces of furniture exhibited by Walton at the Arts and Crafts Exhibition of 1903 (including the Brussels side-

173. Advertisement for the cabinet-maker J. S. Henry.

board) were executed by J. S. Henry & Co. of Old Street, London, so were the furniture and fittings in fumed Austrian oak at Walter Judd's office in the same year, so was the furniture ordered for Mr Flausch in 1905.[49] J. S. Henry was a safe choice. Voysey had used his company on several occasions and might have recommended him. Henry's was popular with designers of the Arts and Crafts and several, including W. A. S. Benson, provided them with designs, so much so that in 1903 when Walton took up with them, some thought 'Mr. Henry's ... showrooms at present constitute a veritable arts and crafts exhibition, in comparison with which that at the New Gallery sinks into insignificance'[50] Their products were retailed by Wylie & Lochhead in Glasgow and when Walton commissioned them to make his pieces for the Arts and Crafts Exhibition he is likely to have had more than a passing knowledge of their work. Henry's remained a useful source. Later, Walton may have found that small specialist cabinet-makers suited his purposes better – he turned to J. Falconer for carving and gilding in 1907, and the unknown T. Smith and R. Gervan (or Gowan) were entered as makers of his furniture at the Arts and Crafts Exhibition of 1910.[51]

In metalwork, there were a number of excellent firms who had strong links with the new movement. Voysey was particularly attached to Elsley & Co., but he also designed for Longden's and the Falkirk Iron Co.; Ashbee designed cast-iron fireplaces for both Falkirk and the Coalbrookdale Co. It is to these firms Walton is likely to have looked for a new source for making up his designs, and though there is no record of his regular practice, a design among his papers for Elsley & Co. suggests he may have used them on other occasions.[52] He is known to have chosen brass fireplace margins from Longden & Co.'s catalogue as well as using their door handles (designed by Voysey) for The Leys.

Arrangements with outside contractors like Alexander Morton & Co., which had been established for some time, remained undisturbed by his break with the firm. But leaving the company stimulated Walton to look again at areas of design which had not formed part of the company's expertise. There are signs of a renewed interest in wallpapers (he produced several rather mediocre designs for Jeffrey & Co., for whom Voysey worked);[53] Comyns & Sons produced some cutlery to his design;[54] and as he lost his connection with his own stained glass workshop, his attention returned to table glass and vases.

The glass designs Walton produced over this period were quite different from the earlier pieces for James Couper and in general reflect his move from the chunkier hand-crafted look of some of his earlier work to the smoother more classical lines of his Holland Street style. Venetian glass was enjoying a vogue in England and James Powell & Sons, a glass-making firm based in London at the 'Whitefriars' Glass Works, were producing table glass in a Venetian style. Philip Webb's table service for William Morris – simple, functional pieces in colourless glass – were also made by James Powell. Harry Powell, who was active in the company from the late 1870s, responded to Ruskin's call for 'reformed' glass by emphasising form as opposed to decoration in the items he designed and displayed at the Arts and Crafts Exhibitions during the 1890s and beyond. Ruskin thought cutting or engraving the surface violated the essential character of the material and because the Venetians had developed alternative methods of ornamentation (hand-manipulated decorations using trailed or threaded glass), principally in response to the fragility of the material they used, they were admired by the designers of the Arts and Crafts. The Holland Street glass, as a whole, brought together these varying influences and added another – one group of designs reflects both the shape and ornament of the new Arts and Crafts silverware.

For James Powell, Walton designed a series of plain, functional drinking glasses with conical or bell-shaped bowls: elegant, sophisticated, classically simple – just what would be expected of his new mood. Other pieces are more experimental and show his strong attraction to Venetian glass, which he may well have sought out at the South Kensington or British Museums, following the footsteps of Walter Crane.[55] He also had some interest in purchasing antique glass, though whether for himself or a client is unclear. A series of sketches in Walton's hand, recording sixteenth- and seventeenth-century German, Spanish and Venetian pieces, makes clear his own source of inspiration.[56] His resulting designs for vases and vessels, sometimes with covers or stoppers, are highly effective – simple forms, often with hollow stems, decorated with coloured spiral trailing

174 and 175. Glass vessel with hollow stem decorated with spiral threading and prunts, *c.* 1902-3, and other simple glass shapes designed by Walton at this period.

and prunts (or blobs of glass): Venetian-inspired but idiosyncratically conceived. When Walton saw some 'imported' Venetian glass blowers demonstrating their skills at the Earl's Court Exhibition of 1904, he set about providing them with wild and imaginative designs. As his son records, 'He couldn't resist a craftsman'.[57]

As Walton had no showroom in London, he had to rely more than ever on the alternative sources of attracting work, those which reflected the image of his practice: recommendation, journal reviews and exhibitions. His stepped-up presence at the Arts and Crafts Exhibition of 1903 (pl. 154), which included a stunning display of his new glass work, shows he was keenly aware of this potential weakness in his new position, though in fact there is no evidence during this period that he had any difficulty obtaining work.

It is possible he approached, or was approached by both Liberty's and Goodyer's, the furniture retailers, as his furniture designs appear occasionally in their sketch books, catalogues or displays, mostly after the closure of his firm.[58] Walton's connection with Liberty's had started indirectly with his work on Couper's Clutha range in 1896, which was retailed through their shop. John Buchanan Dick, in the role of salesman, had brought Walton & Co. furniture to their attention, when he made visits to Liberty's in the later years of the firm, though no evidence records his success. Alexander Morton also sold fabrics and carpets through Liberty's. Walton's connection with the company, though not clearly documented, is certainly plausible: their policy of not naming their designers makes Walton's relationship with them even more difficult to fathom.

In fact, the attractions of Walton's painterly vision had done much to encourage retailers in their promotion of furniture in room settings, carefully co-ordinated with matching frieze, carpet, fabrics and integral woodwork. As Wylie & Lochhead had promoted their new line of furniture in this context at the Glasgow International Exhibition, so it was the vogue for more discerning retailers – Liberty's among them – in the promotion of the new furniture in the south. Many went further and opted for a distinguishably 'Glasgow' style.

Friendships

However busy the days at Holland Street there were always moments for relaxation. Kensington life provided ample entertainment: the parties were grand (and often at home), there were theatricals and fancy dress balls. Nor did Walton's working interests prevent his absenting himself from Holland Street from time to time. There were (besides visits to Glasgow) two primary destinations, first of which was The Leys.

In J. B. B. Wellington, Walton had found not only a sympathetic client but a friend. Like Walton, Wellington was a quiet, reserved and practical man. In the workshop he set up in the coach house, he turned his hand to carpentry and painting, and assembled cameras to his own design. Like Walton, Wellington's interest in artistic matters was wide-ranging, but he was not of a literary frame of mind.[59] Although he had strong views on art and was not short on character, he did not share his opinions readily. His contributions to art photography were acclaimed, but photographic critics experienced the same difficulties in interviewing Wellington as they did with Walton: Wellington was known to be 'wisely enamoured of silence', 'not fond of writing and does not at all believe in writing about art',[60] while Walton's 'natural modesty or diffidence when speaking of his own work makes it difficult upon a brief acquaintance to ascertain the position he would himself claim'.[61] Besides the notes for his lecture, Walton never wrote on art. Wellington was similarly reticent. Nevertheless one critic thought that Wellington's 'chief idea is ... in Art, Beauty comes first and Truth afterwards', an attitude of mind from the same school of thinking as Walton and the Glasgow Boys.[62] Wellington was a man of feeling rather than theory, and like the Glasgow Boys, he avoided the exceptionally picturesque as much as he did that rigid impressionism which spurned the structural discipline of composition. For Wellington's 'casual' domestic studies, he invariably posed his figures deliberately (*cf.* pl. 218), resulting in the strange combination of natural and contrived effects which characterises much of Walton's work.

Working trips to The Leys to supervise remaining decorative details turned into friendly invitations for George, Kate and Marguerite to stay the weekend. Wellington was domestic in his habits, enjoyed his new home and in his unostentatious way was thoroughly hospitable.

Walton's other destination on outings from Holland Street was the Davison household at Molesey-on-Thames.

Davison, or G.D. (as he was always referred to by

family and friends) had risen quickly from humble beginnings to the position in the Exchequer and Audit Office at Somerset House which he left to work for the Eastman Company in 1897.[63] In his spare time, Davison's avid interest in photography as a member of the Camera Club led to his role in the founding of The Linked Ring in 1892. Davison's father had been a skilled shipyard carpenter at Lowestoft harbour, and boating on the North Sea and the River Waveney were among the richest of G.D.'s childhood experiences. When, therefore, in 1892, he was able to move from his first London home in Clapham Junction, at the age of thirty-seven, it was natural for him to seek out the 'real country' and a place by the river. On his £200-£300 p.a. Civil Service salary, he could just afford the move to Clovelly, Arnison Road in Molesey, a short walk from the Thames. Boating again became a way of life: punting, canoeing, sailing, renting a houseboat in the summer; any form of river pleasure went towards satisfying a passion Davison found almost as consuming as photography.

Molesey was, moreover, just the place to invite fellow Links and their wives, for an afternoon's boating by the river before retiring to G.D.'s house for the meeting proper. Annan and Wellington would have joined some of these outings, and, in the early autumn of 1897, we can imagine the newly arrived Walton sitting beside them on the river bank, invited to share his plans for the decoration of the Salon in the autumn.

Almost certainly Walton's visits to Molesey had begun by the time G.D. and family moved to Beechcroft. When G.D. left the Civil Service in 1897 to take his post as assistant manager in the Eastman Photographic Materials Co., his salary more than doubled, prompting this further move to a larger house in a smarter district of Molesey. Like Wellington, Davison's artistic sensibilities were not simply satisfied. Besides his role

in the Photo-Secession and in masterminding the decoration of the Kodak shops, he dabbled in drawing and painting, and was concerned to make his own home as artistically interesting as the Kodak showrooms. Walton was invited to decorate Beechcroft. Among the likely results is the 'Beechcroft' chair (pl. 78).[64] Perhaps his earliest piece of furniture for Davison, it is startlingly unconventional, a foretaste of how fruitful their relationship would be. In the future Davison would stimulate some of Walton's best and most innovative work.

At home, as at work, it was Davison alone who championed him. Susanna Louisa Davison, G.D.'s wife, 'was generally keener on becoming respectable and conventional, on Molesey standards, than on launching into still higher flights such as the new artistic experiments with George Walton'. In fact 'SLD disliked both Walton and his wife ... and she said so in unmeasured terms' – presumably only to the family: George and Kate continued to visit the Davisons socially for many years. If Susanna gave the Waltons a somewhat cold reception, they chose not to notice.[65]

It was from the time of his move to Beechcroft that Davison's fortunes began to rise sharply. In 1898 when Kodak Ltd was formed, George Eastman offered him shares as part of his salary and he had the option to purchase more while they were cheap. By the turn of the century he had become a major shareholder. Eastman's business, particularly the American and Canadian sides, was hugely successful, the profits fuelling the company's European expansion. As the fortunes of the company rose, so did Davison's own personal circumstances. Within a few years he was a remarkably wealthy man.

Behind his orthodox middle-class circumstances, Davison was an unusual and unconventional character. Walton benefited from his outgoing, progressive outlook and they were in each other's society often. The youngest of a large family, Walton found his friends naturally amongst older men: Davison was twelve, Wellington nine, Voysey ten, and Crane twenty-two years older. To all appearances Davison and Walton became close friends, but there were aspects of Davison's temperament which may sometimes have made Walton feel uneasy.

An outing on the river

From 1896 houseboat life in the summer months had become the routine for the Davisons. To those who spent their days in the city's streets, semi-rural Thameside was enormously attractive. Crowds of Londoners thronged to the riverside every weekend. There were punts to hire, dinghies, and canoes. Launches decorated with flags and chinese lanterns were illuminated at night. Molesey became particularly popular with fashionable society. At the elegant hotel on Tagg's

176. George Davison.

Island the better class of visitor could lounge on the verandah within full view of the river. Drifting from the tow-path would come the sounds of talk and laughter and gramophones playing. There were fêtes and pageants, and at the height of the season, Molesey Annual Regatta. Riverside life was colourful, musical, and fun.[66]

As a rule the Davisons rented their houseboats for July and August, until around 1902-3 when G.D. had the bright idea of building his own – to Walton's design.[67] With no possible sort of training for the task, only someone like Walton could have agreed. Walton's career has already demonstrated his ability coolly to take on anything. There can be no doubt that even in an age of non-specialisation for designers, Walton's range of activities was unusual: picture frames, cabinet designs, glass, exhibition interiors and stands, carpets, cutlery, shopfronts, advertising graphics, showrooms, parquet flooring, dress design (a Coronation-Day dress for Princess Louise), light fittings and houses, among the list of his accomplishments.

For the houseboat he would need to have a model, which the 'Alcedo', possibly a houseboat rented by Davison, provided.[68] Walton is likely to have worked closely with boatbuilders to develop his ideas, as the work involved a considerable amount of specialist knowledge, but the results and contemporary comments leave no doubt as to the importance of his contribution. According to *The Studio*, 'houseboats are for the most part both ugly and inconvenient. Attention to

good proportions and harmonious colouring are rarely given, and there can be no doubt that the absence of beauty is a sad fact in connection with the riverside life'.

Clearly Walton had enough to cope with without complicating the matter further with too much innovation. He stuck fairly closely to a standard houseboat plan, but by adding his own judicious touches, created a convenient, attractive and sensitively detailed result.

The houseboat was of generous proportions: lounge or saloon, three bedrooms, WC and kitchen on the lower deck, extra space for guests above. Folding doors opened the main saloon out to the river and the adjoining pontoon sported seats with gaily coloured canopies. An outside stair led to the roof, where, by means of metal framing and pinoleum blinds an extra canopied deck was formed above. Walton made no attempt to disguise the metal construction or give the upper deck the feeling of solidity which contemporary architectural thinking demanded. The upper deck resumes his evident fascination with light-weight structures and semi-solid effects, which had been revealed in the insubstantial screens of some exhibition stands and the pierced balustrades at Ledcameroch and The Leys (pls 71, 115). On a houseboat, he may not have been criticised, but it was an omen of the future, a preliminary to his unconventional use of metal at The White House a few years later (pl. 188).

Davison's name for his houseboat, 'The Log Cabin', is a puzzling choice, on which the later naming of his home, The White House, appears to throw light. Mrs Garfield had told the story of her husband's rise to fame

177. Plan of the Log Cabin houseboat's lower floor.

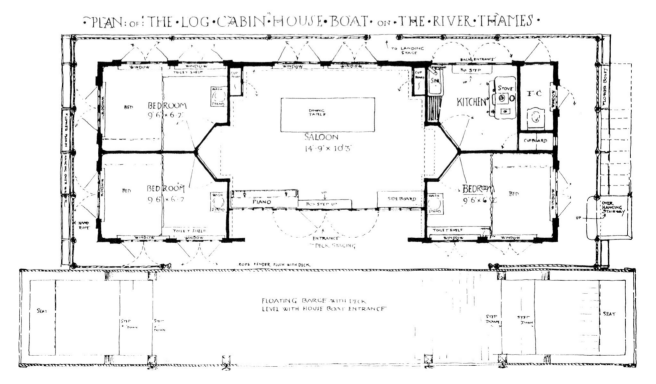

178. George Davison's son Ronald out boating in June 1909, with The Log Cabin houseboat and the later White House by Walton behind. A photogravure by James Craig Annan.

in *Log Cabin to White House*, suggesting a sophisticated joke on Davison's part, an allusion to his own rags to riches story. Weatherboarding facing the exterior of the houseboat gave plausibility to the name, and the theme was followed throughout. A special American Indian motif was designed, then used as part of a hanging light fitting, as a notepaper heading, embroidered on the curtains and woven into the saloon carpet, of which sadly only a description and the haziest of photographs survive. 'The carpet is one of Mr Walton's many triumphs. The general scheme is a silvery drab with a soft velvet effect, the border being an American Indian in his birch-bark canoe in approximately a heliotrope and delicate green colour.' Kate was now more prominent in supporting Walton's concerns as well as producing her own work. The embroidered panels at the Log Cabin were executed by her hand.[69] At the Arts and Crafts Exhibition in 1903 she exhibited a 'child's coat', which she had 'designed, woven and ornamented' herself.

179. Notepaper heading with the American Indian motif used throughout the Log Cabin houseboat.

180. View of the Log Cabin houseboat, showing the embroidered awnings on the pontoons, the striking wickerwork chairs and the lightly screened upper deck.

Walton's careful attention to detail contributed to the total effect of the design. Flower boxes on the upper floor created a summery, open-air atmosphere. His grouped dentil motif, repeated on the white-painted window surrounds of the lower floor, added a touch of class. There was herringbone-patterned inlay on the table top, and there were specially-designed wicker chairs 'of picturesque design and good construction'. Walton had found a new medium to explore. Flanking the entrance, were two remarkable constructions: *The Studio* thought 'The sentry-box beehive chairs standing one on each side of the saloon entrance, are among the most ingeniously constructed items on the houseboat'.

The finished result was stunning. Not only was it large and (harmoniously) colourful, but it had the attraction of the upper floor, the surrounding flower boxes, the fluttering of the curtains in the wind, the stripes and patterns of the pontoon. There was, about the houseboat, a suggestion of showmanship, which had been present at the showrooms too. Yet Davison, who possessed considerable taste and discrimination, and his houseboat, floating elegantly on the Thames, were far from flashy.

Walton's part in realising Davison's dreams meant that by 1903 he had become a necessity to Davison's way of life. At the Arts and Crafts Exhibition of that year Walton showed an entrée dish, a clock, and part of a cutlery set he had designed for Davison. There was no limit to the ways Walton could contribute comfort and sophistication to Davison's increasingly affluent lifestyle. Even at his son Ronald's birthday celebration Walton's skills were required for the design of a dinner card.[70] As far as Davison was concerned, Walton's quiet yet stimulating presence was always appreciated: besides the working visits, he was invited often.

Life at Holland Street was full. If Walton's attempt to follow Bolton and Ashbee's lead in house-letting back-fired – an misguided experiment of the Holland Street years – it was a ripple on otherwise smooth waters.[71] There was no doubt Walton's reputation was established. Commissions came more rapidly than ever. It is understandable if he spent little time planning for the future.

When Whistler died in 1903, Edward Walton's commitment to London was tested: a certain disillusionment was inevitable. James Guthrie encouraged him to return to Scotland, and despite his still new, tailor-made house, Edward was not long in packing his bags. The Glasgow Boys' success in London and abroad had finally had its effect on traditionalists at the Royal Scottish Academy, now ready to welcome those it had previously spurned. Guthrie had returned from his brief stay in London to settle in Edinburgh and was now the Academy's President. Edward's reception among the art establishment was assured.

If George's eye turned to Glasgow now, it might be to consider the fortunes of Robert Paterson or of Mackintosh.[72] The stability of the company might be causing anxiety, but it had ceased to be an intimate concern and was no longer his problem. Otherwise there were no regrets; he had no intention of returning.

Walton's resignation from the company had been well timed. And now he had achieved his independence, where did he stand? He was not quite – yet – an architect like the others, but he was much more the 'Artist' (applying himself all round) he had hoped to be on arriving at Westbourne Park Road.

IX   ARCHITECT ALONE

George Davison had always kept in touch with a fellow civil servant and old school friend, Harry More. Harry had become Crown Agent for the Forestry Commission in Wales and in 1892 settled in Harlech. Summer visits to Harlech by the Davisons began in the early 1900s, as G.D. came to feel more expansive about holidays. It was Ronald, Davison's son, who went at first: 'I visited the More's at Crown Lodge, Harlech and received a family friendship which began when Harry More and G.D. were school boys together at Lowestoft. My ecstatic account of Harlech brought the whole family up to have a look in 1906. They saw and were conquered'.[1] Besides the wonderful scenery, presided over by Harlech Castle, there was the magnificent golf course and, not least, the sea. Harlech had by this time several English families in addition to the Mores, and there was even something of a tourist season at the height of summer. The life of this new, rather anglicised society (not always appreciated by locals) revolved around the Winchelseas. Lord Winchelsea's brother had helped lay out the golf course in 1894. Lady Winchelsea was musical. There were dances, croquet parties, whist drives. The Winchelseas' guests were interesting, many of them artistic.[2] But it was the feeling of now being really in the country which, for Davison, carried the day. Molesey no longer seemed so countrified, indeed 'Beechcroft and the Thames at Tagg's Island began to seem very dull and suburban to all the family'.[3]

Their financial situation had a lot to do with it. Davison had become Managing Director at Kodak in March 1900. His shares had more than flourished and a considerable surplus of resources was piling up. He had always been hospitable. Beechcroft, with its small suburban garden, no longer seemed adequate to entertain the guests.

Davison begins to build

On the 1906 visit, filled with dawning possibilities of a new Harlech life, Davison inevitably met the main personalities of Harlech society, including the Winchelseas, W. Bowen-Jones and Lt-Col. G. Frederick Scott. To these he must have expressed his newly-forming idea of building a house, and have explored with them and Harry More the prospect of acquiring land.[4] The house would be firstly for the family, but then there would be guests.

By the end of his stay at Harlech, a site had been selected for the house, and another idea had been floated with these new acquaintances, if not agreed. Numerous golfers had expressed the need for an up-to-date hotel. Why should they not form a company and develop a hotel themselves? The improved facilities would encourage more visitors, provide accommodation for any overflow of their own guests, and generally add to the attractions of Harlech. Bowen-Jones agreed to go ahead with plans for a road to the site Davison had purchased for Wern Fawr and in the ensuing months there would be further discussion on the question of the hotel.[5]

It would have been interesting to be present at Davison's first meeting with George Walton on his return from Harlech, when he had not one but two architectural projects to propose. Although Walton may have been aware that Beechcroft was losing favour, he was probably unprepared for the extravagant plans Davison would divulge.

It is doubtful that Walton had regretted his decision to resign from George Walton & Co. The transition to 'private practice' had gone smoothly and there had been plenty of work. Nor is there doubt that his relinquishing of 'commercial' connections reflected to some extent a hope for a more professional future. After all, it had not been a bad time for craft workshops. As if to confirm this, by 1905 (even as Walton & Co. was foundering in Glasgow), a number of new workshops had been opened, several by his former associates. Walton's own employee Robert Paterson had started 'The Crafts' in Glasgow in 1905 (in one of Walton & Co.'s former premises) with the stained glass designer Stephen Adam.[6] Edward Spencer (probably laid off several years previously when Walton could no longer justify his employment) now produced his own metalwork for the Artificers' Guild.[7] Spencer had fallen in with Arthur Penty (perhaps introduced by Walton) and they were deliberating together on the virtues of the mediaeval guild system, while running a new venture with Fred Rowntree. In April of the previous year Walton may himself have attended an exhibition of the work of Elmdon & Co., Arthur Penty's and Fred Rowntree's new furniture-making workshops set up with Charles Spooner, an architect of the Art Workers' Guild.[8]

For Walton, however, the prospect of becoming an architect, a professional, held a good deal of attraction. The cutting of his ties with the company so soon after completing The Leys, suggests he was preparing himself, was full of expectation. Yet, since The Leys (now five years ago), there had been no comparable architectural commission and, since the Log Cabin houseboat was completed and the showroom commissions

181. The Waltons' drawing room at 26, Emperor's Gate, London: Walton's candlesticks, the Holland cabinet and two Brussels chairs arranged in a symmetrical composition.

began to peter out around 1903, there had been little with any architectural element at all.

If Walton had had doubts in the intervening years it is likely that the new prosperity which came to him chiefly through interior work (he was just this moment moving into a grander house in Emperor's Gate), enabled him to brush them away. Now it was as if all his hopes and actions had been vindicated.

By January 1907, Walton had completed his first proposals for the hotel. By June the 'Harlech Hotel and Land Development Syndicate Ltd' was established. Then (as far as the hotel was concerned) there was a lull; but plans for Davison's new home in Harlech, Plas Wern Fawr, went on apace.[9]

Even as Walton was forming his first ideas for Wern Fawr, there were more surprises in store. By June 1907, the Log Cabin houseboat had been moved on from Tagg's Island to a mooring adjacent to the Henley Sailing Club Boathouse at Wargrave.[10] Davison had a new interest in this stretch of the river. He was buying a second plot of land at Shiplake, intending Walton to design him a new riverside home in addition to his country retreat.

Plas Wern Fawr

The crystallisation of the Wern Fawr design probably came first. Davison is said to have declared when he first came to Harlech that he wanted his own castle, which, in the absence of any surviving brief, gives some

idea of the sort of house Davison had in mind.[11] Walton obliged. Reflecting on the rugged scenery, the great cliffs and stretches of sand, the dominating and romantic form of Harlech Castle, he produced a house very different from The Leys.

Built of great roughly-hewn blocks of stone, the building is solid and heavy in character. On its precipitous site, the retaining wall of the garden recalls the fortress-like aspect of Harlech Castle – indeed, the turret cylinders are consciously echoed. Yet there is another equally strong ingredient. The forms of the house are not castle-like at all, but distinguishably Georgian. There are the large pediment and dentils. There is a Classical regularity about the windows. Edward Walton recalled the emphasis of his father's interest in the Georgian:

182. Plas Wern Fawr from the south with Harlech castle in silhouette against the sky.

183. The entrance front of Wern Fawr, 1908: a strongly symmetrical façade.

My father had very Georgian ideas about decoration and about the intervals of windows on buildings, regularity, ... He loved Georgian architecture, he loved Bloomsbury as the highest ... achievement of any architecture that he saw. He was very Georgian, very regular ... When he came to England, he became English, loved English order, Georgian terraces, thought very highly of these things.[12]

The revival of interest in English Classicism, which had emerged in the 1880s, had gathered considerable momentum by 1908. To George Walton, whose father was in some ways more Georgian than Victorian, it was not an unnatural sympathy. Neither was it a sudden alteration in taste: there had been historical echoes in his work from the beginning. The strongly Classical reference of the pediment at Wern Fawr, the Palladian atmosphere which hangs about the building, is, however, new to his architecture.

Walton's Georgian forms are always derived rather than copied. The simple statement of the entrance front shows his determination to use Classical form and proportion to his own ends. Yet taken as a whole, the main house at Wern Fawr is not completely successful. The entrance front in its paved stone courtyard has a quiet strength, but the over-emphasised chimneys of the side elevation detract from its simple power. The jutting bay to the rear is daringly conceived and provides panoramic views of the sea, but is not fully integrated in the design. Viewed from the road above, the squareness of the plan makes the building too box-like, almost uninteresting; a criticism which is equally valid of The Leys. All in all there is something about the proportions of the building which is disappointing.

When its critics come down from the road for a closer acquaintance, the building dares them to reconsider. There is a subtlety in the handling of materials and detail which counterbalances the loss of proportion. The sheer quality and craftsmanship of the stonework explains immediately why Walton wanted such flat unarticulated surfaces. The simplicity of the architectural features is set off by a few masterly details and any feeling that the building lacks interest is immediately lost. The rear porch with its bold metal supports is a daring adjunct to a Classically-inspired building, yet in its chaste, its understated, elegance, it is brilliantly successful. The monogrammed leadwork of the

184. The rear porch, showing the bay behind.

185. George Davison at his desk in the library annexe.

rainwater pipes shows Walton's habitual attention to every detail: even functional necessities at Wern Fawr reinforce the conviction that this house is at the apex of building craft.

At Wern Fawr, Walton has taken the semicircle as a springboard for his design. The visitor passes through a semicircular arch to the garden or is greeted by the bow-shaped roof of the entrance porch or by arches above the panelling of the hall. At the rear of the house round-arched windows gracing a small extension give a hint of the Palladian: inside the extension a low-roofed corridor with repeated round arches is strikingly similar in effect to Mackintosh's 'Loggia' in the School of Art extension, not opened until the following year. The high ceilings of the circulation areas of the house give the semicircle a third dimension in the tunnel and groin vaulting which immediately recalls the entrance hall at The Leys.

The semicircle laid flat is a theme of the garden. Here the work Walton completed in 1908 was just the start of a comprehensive scheme. The 'turret' curve of the retaining wall was used to good effect. In line with the garden porch it made a perfect viewing point to the sea. An enclosed garden area was essential for shelter on such an exposed site. On the south side of the house Walton built a walled garden divided into smaller areas by the walls of the terracing. Electric lighting in the garden was part of the brief, so there were built-in shelters to soften the glare and protect the wiring. Walton's insistence that all aspects of the design merited his attention was as essential to his approach to architecture as it was to the harmonising of his interiors.

A view of the dining room is among the few surviving photographs of the 1908 interior scheme at Wern Fawr.[13] The furniture, probably brought from Beechcroft, is of the period 1898-1901. Comparing this

186. The Wern Fawr dining room: furnishing includes Beechcroft and Abingdon chairs and one of Walton's beautiful carpets. This photograph, taken after the extension of 1910, gives a glimpse of the new library beyond the annexe.

187. The White House, Shiplake, built in 1908.

dining room with the interior of Walton's 1901 exhibition stand at Glasgow, where the furniture was first exhibited, shows how much the setting has changed. Like the interiors of The Leys, the walls at Wern Fawr are plain. This time there is not even panelling. Attuned with the architecture is the classic simplicity of the fireplace and light fitting. Pattern remains only on the excellent carpet. Walton's move from a preoccupation with surface pattern to an interest in the form and proportioning of internal space is again confirmed.

At Wern Fawr, Walton had the opportunity to build on a magnificent site. The house is impressive – self-consciously so. His references to the Georgian indicate his intention that Wern Fawr should stand within the country house tradition. Yet in choosing Georgian forms, Walton had not thrown over his Arts and Crafts principles. They had merged. The depth of his Arts and Crafts thinking is revealed in his attention to the functional and his acute sensitivity to materials and site. The beautifully cut and laid Cambrian stone comes from the vicinity. While Wern Fawr is imposing it is also linked with its landscape and with the vernacular buildings nearby.

The White House

As the building work at Harlech in 1908 was nearing completion, Walton was also adding finishing touches to The White House, Davison's riverside home at Shiplake.

The character of The White House could hardly be more different.[14] The White House is almost as much of a contrast to Wern Fawr as Wern Fawr was to the seven-years-earlier Leys. The key to the difference is location. Both Wern Fawr and The White House are close to the water (an essential requirement in Davison's choice of site), but there the similarity ends. Wern Fawr, from its fortress position, speaks authority and strength; the greys of the clouds, the broken rocks, and the choppy sea are answered in the grey and rugged surface of solid stone. By contrast, The White House is glossy, white-painted, reflecting sunlight in a cloudless sky, a transient vision set on a smooth surface of close-clipped lawn like a gleaming riverboat on water (pl. 178). As The Leys belonged to the quiet domestic atmosphere of its rural setting so the characters of Wern Fawr and The White House are determined by their sites.

Lurking behind these contrasts there are inevitably common themes. The Georgian inspiration, and the arrangement of bay placed asymmetrically on a pedimented front, which link the two houses of 1908, are only the most obvious. The curving balconies of The White House are in fact the cylinder of The Leys' porch transformed (pl. 108). The double pitch of The White House roof is the mansard roof of The Leys' rear elevation (pl. 113) given a new dominance. Walton again employs the device of low roof and dormers to reduce the apparent scale, and prominent chimneys to strengthen the elevations of both The White House and Wern Fawr. Inside and out, the favoured semicircular arch, sometimes forming openings, sometimes merely alluded to in relief, is found on all three buildings. References to Voysey at the White House cause no surprise. The chimneys and buttress-shaped balcony supports on the south side of the building are blended so carefully with the overall composition that they are now part of Walton's own idiomatic style.

Unlike The Leys and Wern Fawr, The White House is open and light. With large areas of lawn and a tennis court, open balconies and windows from floor to ceiling, it is a building for the summer. Inside, glass doors, which separate the living and dining areas, can be folded away to give a large, L-shaped space, with the long windows on two sides looking out to the garden and front lawn. In its emphasis on openness, The White House is in a quite different class from other domestic buildings being produced in Britain at the time.

188. *Above*: Looking onto the terrace of the front bay from the hall.
189. *Opposite*: The White House was for summer living.

A question is immediately prompted. Did Walton any longer feel the need, as he had in 1900, 'to be quite certain whether one is inside of a house or out'?[15] The experience of the Log Cabin houseboat and familiarity with the river had worked upon Walton. Links with the houseboat are clear. As the folding doors and pinoleum blinds of the houseboat had opened it out to the river, so a light division of folding glass screens is the only separation between The White House's hall and outside terrace and (above) between its landing and balcony. An allusion to the insubstantial upper floor of the houseboat is strengthened by the use of fine curtaining in the hall – which (in case we miss the point) is furnished with wicker chairs.[16]

Part of Walton's inspiration for The White House may well have come from Ernest Newton's Steephill, Jersey, though there a very different effect is achieved. A pupil of Shaw, Newton was in the vanguard of the domestic revival of Classicism. In 1915-16, Newton and Walton would have offices in the same building. At the time of The White House, both were members of the Art Workers' Guild. Walton would have been familiar with Steephill if he had spent any time with a copy of Muthesius' *Das Englische Haus*, where it was illustrated a few pages from The Leys.[17] Like The White House, Steephill is a white-walled, bow-balconied, shuttered

house, of Georgian influence, but a more solid building: the shutters are dark; the balcony, relegated to the side, is more ornamental than structural (at The White House it is integral). By extending the windows from floor to ceiling, by painting the shutters white and increasing the proportion of balcony within the composition, at The White House the sense of solidity is lost. The smaller size of Walton's house and the reference to country vernacular in the low tiled roof also make his building a less formal, more intimate design.

The White House attempts more complex spatial arrangements than The Leys, not always successfully. On the upper floor behind the entrance bay there is a change of level extending from the top of the stairs to an adjacent bedroom: in effect a mezzanine floor, expressed on the exterior by the level of the balcony. While by this means Walton added interest to interior and exterior alike, its execution lets him down: the hall ceiling is uncomfortably low, particularly in conjunction with the stairs. Despite the apparent deftness of his highly detailed plans, it is clear that Walton still had plenty to learn.[18]

The bay is in fact pivotal to the design as a whole, cleverly bringing together the somewhat diverse array of elements on the entrance front. It is a fascinating design, quite innovatory for a domestic building of its date. The thin, vertical bars of the railings only slightly relieve the cantilevered effect of the flat platforms of balcony and roof. It is the construction of these platforms which provides their strength. The use of curved

channel iron linked with RSJs embedded in the balcony floor and roof, means that that the slim wrought-iron uprights are only as necessary as they seem. The simple bolting of the railings is deliberately exposed – an open declaration of construction which was one of the first principles of Arts and Crafts design – but the cantilevered concrete-and-metal platform of the balcony takes Walton beyond the normal range of Arts and Crafts thinking. The idea of revealed construction (stemming from the Gothic revival), though a line in the Arts and Crafts creed, was in fact not consistently practised. When Walton ingenuously transferred the idea from one material to another, and revealed the constructional possibilities of rolled steel and concrete on the façade of a domestic house, he may have been surprised at the lack of applause.[19] Voysey would have thought such things immoral (though he may not have expressed this to his friend). More traditional architects simply felt exposed metal construction was visually unsatisfactory. Walton might have justified The White House bay by pointing to the white-painted balconies of the Regency period, with their prominent metal railings:[20] the Regency was a style which the house deliberately evoked. It would have been less easy to find a precedent for the reinforced concrete seat he built into the balcony extension. The metal-framed windows were also unconventional. This time Voysey would have approved. He thought them 'less liable to rattling and more economical in upkeep than a timber window';[21] but Voysey filled his frames with small, leaded panes.

At The White House, the panels are large, the metal kept to a minimum: the effect entirely different.

Walton's lack of architectural training made him independent of conventional architectural thinking (to which even Arts and Crafts architects often succumbed). With the experimental approach he had developed in Glasgow, it was possible for him to approach new materials and methods of construction in a less prejudiced way than many of his contemporaries.[22] Though in sympathy with so much Arts and Crafts thinking, he was never a partisan. At The White House his method was a logical realisation of his aesthetic intention. If he conformed to a way of thinking it was only in his lack of inhibition.

And what of Mackintosh, whose formative years were spent in a similar environment? However unconventional and exciting his domestic architecture, Mackintosh produced nothing at all like The White House.[23] His houses, traditional in construction, proof against the Scottish winter, their wood-framed windows with small leaded panes, were quite different. The importance of location at The White House is again underlined. Walton had the opportunity, which eluded Mackintosh, of designing in a more favourable climate, where lightness, openness and insubstantiality are far more appropriate. Walton also had the important previous experience of designing a houseboat on the river, clearly a catalyst in his development of The White House. How Mackintosh would have responded in similar circumstances is, unfortunately, a matter of speculation.

How was The White House received? It was simply ignored. Admittedly, Walton was little known in architectural circles, but with so much recent interest in his work, could The White House really have gone unnoticed – or did the Edwardian press simply not know what to make of it?

The rooms of The White House were emphatically plain: the fireplaces simple, flat compositions in marble or tile in the plainest of surrounds, the walls plastered straight to the ceiling, without dado, picture rail or cornice. RSJs were used over openings, extending the airiness of the sitting and dining areas, and allowing for clean-cut lines. Fitted cupboards were simple both in shape and detail. The 'Thames' sideboard, specially

190. Dinner at the White House: Walton's candelabrum lights the table, behind is his black and white fireplace.

designed for the dining room, was elegant and refined, black-enamelled to be in keeping with the fireplace and chairs.[24] Though little of the furniture was newly-commissioned, these dining-room chairs (familiar from the Kodak showrooms) and the hall table (its inlay relating it to the earlier Beechcroft chair) fit well with the restraint of the interior scheme. In this dining room, the only original White House interior fully recorded, Walton's interest in pattern is only evident in the bold geometric design of the fireplace and the waving lines of the carpet in delicate shades of green.[25] There is none of the characteristic Walton & Co. craftwork (only the light fitting which is more concerned with structure than ornament), and little indication of any Glasgow features of style. Only in the delicate curves of the furniture legs and light fitting and in the outward extension of the sideboard top are there reminders of the style of earlier years. In the Holland Street period it was apparent that Walton's approach to interiors was changing. In the rooms of The White House (amongst the plainest of all his interiors) Walton's decorative instincts are entirely channelled into the formal problems of architectural design and the fine execution of building craft.

For this, the relationship with craftsmen and building workers was vital. Walton probably contracted T. H. Kingerlee & Sons, builders of Oxford, for the first time at The White House and Wern Fawr.[26] The highly detailed instructions on The White House plans indicate that Walton was still unsure of his workmen. Without the close relationship he had built up with builders and craftsmen in Glasgow, he was leaving nothing to chance.

Individuality and quality of craftsmanship is essential to the character of these buildings. The Leys, Wern Fawr and The White House bear the message on their plumbing: 'George Walton/Architect', 'G. D.' or 'J. B. B. W.', and the date emblazoned on the heavy lead waterpipes of the façades. These were individual designs for individual clients with considerable resources, where everything was specially designed, from the plumbing to the floor-coverings, from the silver to the garden.[27] Production was not to be rushed. Each detail must be thought through. The architect must be given space for inspiration. This was part of the clients' expectation. It was not essentially a commercial relationship, and to Walton it was hardly a business. For Davison and Wellington, architect was artist. The client commissioned and approved; the artist's integrity was honoured. The attitude and expectations of his clients helped to form the character of Walton's work.

At Shiplake there was again no skimping on servants' accommodation. The gardener's cottage was as conscientiously detailed and attractively designed as the stable block had been at The Leys, the exterior care-

191. Staircase to the top floor of the gardener's cottage in the grounds of The White House.

fully related to the north, less formal end of The White House. Planning it after an intensively creative year in January 1909, Walton had not run out of ideas.[28] The ground floor was for the gardener, the upstairs to be a studio for Davison. There would have to be separate access. Walton boldly decided to by-pass the inevitable planning problems this would create, making an outside stair the dominating feature of his design. The rather basic external stair of the houseboat may have given him the idea. He made a grand improvement. It is the dramatic curve of this centrally placed staircase which gives the building its identity.

The large areas of lawn were ideal for parties. The Davisons now had their place amongst the glitterati of Henley. Davison was more of a showman than Wellington: The White House more of a showpiece than The Leys. Wellington's house was solid and homely. Davison's houseboat and The White House were lighter, more transitory affairs, more suited to open air parties and summer entertaining than as a permanent home, a fact which would become apparent to Mrs Davison later, when her lifestyle underwent a permanent change.

Interlude

There was an interlude in Walton's work for George Davison during 1909. With the first phase of Wern Fawr completed, and with detailed plans and specifications for the Harlech hotel submitted towards the end of 1908, Walton managed to absent himself from Harlech for a time. He had a new client.

Miss Emily Madelina Du Pre lived at 24 Warwick Avenue in London, but was not often at home. An eccentric lady, a member of the Catholic Apostolic

Church, she was an extensive traveller, with a particular love for the Mediterranean, which she fed with frequent visits to Italy and France. As she travelled, she collected. Her specialities were marbles, timbers and antiques which she brought from as far afield as India and Canada. Wanting a base nearer home, somewhere in which to park her multifarious treasures, she chose the Isle of Wight, atmospherically as well as physically closest to her beloved Italy.[29] How she selected Walton as her architect is less clear.

It must have become obvious fairly early on that Miss Du Pre was not the easiest of clients. With the determination of a lady who could transport teak from the orient and fireplaces from the palaces of Savoy, she had distinct ideas about the design of her house, even if she could not quite settle in her mind what the house should be for. Surviving notes by Walton recording meetings with Miss Du Pre show that in June 1909 she was oscillating between different philanthropic schemes. Walton was asked to produce sketch proposals for a hostel, and almshouses 'for Gentlewomen' with a private dwelling house attached; he subsequently recorded 'conferring with Miss Dupre [*sic*] with regard to making plans for entirely new scheme'. By July her decision on the arrangement of the rooms had emerged and on 15 October the builders, Messrs Wheeler Bros of Ryde, had been chosen and the contract signed. A 'villa' was to be built on the site by 25 February 1910, for which they were to be paid £1,640. The account submitted in November described the final result as 'St John's Hostel'.[30]

Settled as she was on the Isle of Wight as a location,

Miss Du Pre may have found it difficult to expel from her mind the all-pervasive presence of Osborne House, royal holiday home and one of the most popular models for country houses, villas, town halls and hotels alike since it had been built in the 1840s. After all it exuded that Mediterranean atmosphere she longed for herself.[31] Osborne House pervaded the final design, from the twin belvedere towers with their paired round-arched openings, to the balustraded walls and the Italianate gardens.

The house was a strange mixture of ideas. Alongside Osborne House, echoes of Alexander 'Greek' Thomson's Glasgow villa style can be distinguished – similarities, for instance with Thomson's Craig Ailey, Kilcreggan, a few miles down the road from Robert Dick's house at Cove, where Walton had worked.[32] Some of Walton's familiar preoccupations protrude. The garden elevation is taken up with iron-railed balconies in exactly the same way as the south elevation of the airy White House. Yet the front is solid masonry with small window openings. An enormous two-storey, flat-roofed bay dominates the side elevation. Not the pillared bay of 'Greek' Thomson's villa style: in contrast with the adjacent tower, Walton has brought the glazed surface forward to form a smooth-faced cylinder which is almost all window glass from floor to ceiling (had the influence of Mackintosh's conical-roofed bays at the Scotland Street School contributed, or was it the Spooners' eighteenth-century Hall?[33]). The bay itself is an interesting focus: with its cleanly-cut dentils and detailing, and small-paned glazed surfaces, it is disarmingly reminiscent of Walton's cabinets.

192. Side elevation of St John's, Ryde, showing the fully-glazed bay and the belvedere. The lower block showing to the right is a later addition.

At St John's, Walton attempted a more ambitious formal arrangement than in his other projects of the last few years and the resulting building could never have been boring. Should the conjunction of such diverse elements on the St John's elevations simply be passed off as an unresolved experiment, or has the architect indulged in a sophisticated game, playing off surface against surface, form against very different form? Whatever the case, there is no doubt that Walton's habitually sensitive detailing would have compensated for any lack of coherence: a possibility which, sadly, the poor quality of surviving photographs of the original building can do little to confirm.

As far back as 1888, Walton had struck up acquaintance with the architect Charles Edward Mallows, whose name appears on the St John's contract as arbitrator along with that of Andrew Prentice (who worked in Ernest Newton's style).[34] It may have been Mallows who introduced Walton to T. H. Kingerlee's, the builders, and he to whom Walton turned as an expert on garden design for inspiration and advice in his work on the gardens here and at Wern Fawr.

Perhaps, at Ryde, Miss Du Pre's vacillations interrupted Walton's thinking. Though 'St John's' is fascinating as an enigmatic stage in his development, Walton himself appears to have felt somewhat ambivalent about the results. The house was the only one of his buildings not to be included in his list of architectural works set before the RIBA in 1911, when he applied for recognition as an architect.[35]

St David's Hotel

There are signs that Walton took a much-needed break during the summer of 1909 after a visit to Ryde. His sketch books record visits to Teignmouth in Devon, and to Little Shelford.[36] In June he was planning some painted decorations for the frieze panels of the entrance hall at The Leys.[37] In August, in the company of his old friend James Craig Annan (who was often in the south) and his more recent friend Walter Crane, Walton

was dining with the Davisons at The White House, Shiplake.[38]

Walton's life was more deeply enmeshed with Davison's now than it had ever been. It had been Davison as much as Wellington who had launched him on his architectural career, for the Kodak shops introduced Walton to the responsibilities of building design well before Wellington had offered the design of a house. Although it had been primarily Walton's design work which stimulated Davison's patronage, and though Walton approached his work more as an artist than as a businessman, Davison had long been convinced of his efficiency and practical capabilities. It would have been these qualities which gave Davison confidence to propose Walton as the architect of the Harlech hotel back in early 1907, before he had completed any architectural work on The White House or Wern Fawr.

St David's, as the hotel was to be called, was a commercial commission demanding a commercial solution. St David's is Walton the architect at his most 'professional'. The constraints were as great if not greater than they had been at the Kodak showrooms, for he had not only Davison to please but the founding shareholders of the Harlech Hotel and Land Development Syndicate Ltd (who unlike George Eastman were there on the spot); and however great Davison's powers of persuasion, it is more likely his fellow-shareholders saw themselves making an investment, than commissioning a work of art.[39]

Early progress on the project had been slow. The first set of proposals, drawn up in January 1907 (before the company was formed) was radically revised in October 1908, after a gap of more than eighteen months.[40] Then there were further delays. The building was not erected until 1910 to a design close to the 1908 revision.

While the initial design had had four floors (including a basement) on an L-shaped plan, the later version was a simple six-storey block. Originally designed with forty bedrooms and service accommodation for twelve, it later had fifty-seven bedrooms with service accommodation reduced to nine. These changes imply that Walton's first design was more extravagant than the company intended. One problem may have been the site, where foundations would have to be cut directly into solid rock: a lavish ground plan would mean expense. In addition, Walton's 1907 plans were probably rushed off to aid Davison's promotion of the project: subsequent exploration of the site may have proved the original proposals impossible to implement. Though the

193. Dinner guests at The White House, sketched by Walton, including James Craig Annan, Edward Carter (later librarian of the R.I.B.A. and editor of its journal), and Walter Crane.

revised design was several storeys higher, its smaller ground plan may have been more feasible as well as cheaper all told.

Walton's revised plans may represent a less exciting building but they included a number of improvements. The kitchens were relocated in the basement, enabling food to be transferred to the dining room by lifts and removing the problem of noise and smell on the principal floor. The loss of the light well at the south end was made up for by the better lit central section which contained the main stairs and hall. The stairs, like those at The White House, had a well in the centre over a square plan and were flooded with light from the large area of windows carried from floor to ceiling on each of the first three floors. The revised plan also, by removal of a fireplace and the use of a reinforced concrete beam, allowed glass doors to replace a solid wall so that light could now reach the stairwell from the other side of the building through the bay on the west wall. As a result, the central section of the hotel was remarkably well lit for a heavy, stone-built structure.

For two reasons, this arrangement is unlikely to have been reached without the experience of The White House, which would have been nearing completion as Walton drew up the revised plans for St David's at the end of 1908. The White House had grown out of the riverside experience of the Thames Valley and the necessarily light-weight structure of the houseboat. By contrast, the Welsh coast, with its traditional use of heavy masonry (followed by Walton on the exterior), is unlikely to have inspired the same open structure. Secondly, his use of RSJs and reinforced concrete to open up the interiors of The White House had been so successful that any hesitations he may have had could

now be swept aside. Walton used reinforced concrete unstintingly at St David's to simplify structural problems both inside and out. This made the most of the views to the sea, and gave the internal character of the building a cheerfulness which could survive even a dull Harlech day.

On the exterior, Walton successfully minimised the apparent size and height of the building by using his favourite mansard-style roof, in much the same way that Ashbee had reduced the height of his terraced houses on Cheyne Walk. The taller central block again recalls Ashbee's group in its massing – the taller nos 72-3 against the low-roofed nos 74-5.[41] With its prominent chimneys, intimate dormers and overhanging eaves, the effect at St David's is a rustic simplicity, a faintly domestic air: arriving from the station, direct from town the guests, golf clubs in hand, were reassured – despite the size of the hotel – that they had come to the country.

It is inevitable that somewhere Walton's inexperience of large-scale building work should show. The atmosphere was right, the planning successful, but the elevations of St David's lacked resolution.[42] The idea of the central block had started well – expressing the internal arrangement by different treatment on the exterior as at The White House – but what has happened at the top? The fourth floor of the central block looks like an uncomfortably prominent afterthought, as if Walton had not quite managed to fit everything in.

While he was obviously concerned to give good views to the sea, and to open out the internal structure, Walton's intention was not to break down the barrier between inside and out. Responding to the character of the more traditional buildings nearby, St David's stone-built exterior instead preserved the sense

194. St David's Hotel, Harlech, west elevation: the sea front.

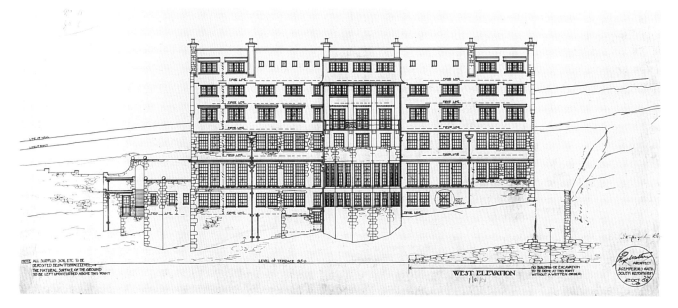

WEST ELEVATION

195. St David's Hotel: the entrance front.

of protection from the elements. Standing at the windows of the bay of St David's, or of Wern Fawr, was not the same experience as looking from the hall windows of The White House. Amidst all the difficulties and problems of the brief, Walton retained his integrity.

All the fixtures and fittings at St David's were to Walton's design or specification: fitted furniture,

196. Notepaper heading for the St David's Hotel.

carpets, tables, chairs and settees were all laid out precisely on the plans; ironmongery and sanitary wares specified from reputable manufacturers.[43] It is unfortunate that a devastating fire in 1922 has made it impossible to examine Walton's response to furnishing from a limited budget. Walton himself was happily unaware of how appropriate this commission was as training for the future.

Wern Fawr extended

Looking from the top of the building site at St David's in the direction of Harlech castle, Davison's land was spread out below. It had been the scene of almost constant activity since the foundations of the main house were laid in 1908. After the building was completed, Walton had turned his attention to the gardens, first the terracing of the walled garden to the south, then on to the landscaping of the lower reaches, then a summer house and garden furniture, and walls to mark the boundary with the road. At exactly what stage Davison

197. George Davison at his organ in the magnificent Wern Fawr music room.

thought of building a hall for musical events is unclear. Had he had always intended to build on from the single-storey annexe at the back of the main house? Or was the original purpose of this passageway-room different from the link it would now become to the music room block? These are questions which now may never be answered.

Harlech life was strongly musical: led by Lady Winchelsea there were numerous events – organ recitals, singing groups and choral services. Music had become increasingly important to Davison and when the idea of a music room emerged it was natural for him, in his typically hospitable fashion, to envisage providing enjoyment for more than his immediate family. The music room would be grand. While, on the adjacent plot, St David's was rising from the ground, new foundations were laid at the site of Wern Fawr. The annexe-passage from the dining room would open into a library, passing to the upper floor of a large new block which would drop sheer to the lower level of the ground to the north. If the hotel had been a restrictive project for Walton, his return to working for Davison alone on the extension to Wern Fawr was like returning to a feast.[44]

The interior was masterful. It was a long room with exposed trusses and stonework above, Italian walnut panelling and fine parquetry flooring below. The emphasis was on materials and craftsmanship. Flatter areas of wood and stone were set off by rich panels of wood carving. Massive electroliers hung from the ceiling, combining, in their design, a simple grid with the richly ornate, and perfectly suiting the space in their weight and proportion.

The round arches and roof beams gave the effect of a long barrel vault. Where the abbreviated 'transepts' met in the centre there was one of Walton's favourite elements, a groin vault – cleverly linking the music room with the landing of the main house and with the vaulted annexe which now led to the library and hall. The 'transepts' contained a fine Orchestrelle on one side and a fireplace on the other. It is as if, in his 'quiet' fireplace phase, Walton had been working up a whole new idiom of decorative design. Two side panels, of interlaced steel rods were set within a bronze surround. The central panel is not unlike Ashbee's hall fireplace at the Magpie and Stump in concept – circular hand-beaten motifs in tile-sized panels – but the irregularities of Ashbee's hand work are gone. The overall effect is more of a machine aesthetic: simple, mechanically-produced metal rods in a geometrical pattern, forming a dramatic pierced screen, from which the hand-beaten panels in their regularity do not detract.

The pierced screen introduces another theme of the music room: a clever play with lighting. Light enters the lower part of the room directly only by the curving bay at one end and the windows flanking the fireplace.

198. The fireplace in the new music room.

Yet the room was not dark. Most of the light came down from windows above, or through the pierced carving of the organ or gallery screens. This obliqueness in the lighting added to the subtlety of the room's atmosphere.

How did these great windowless areas of wall function on the outside? Walton had no doubt had enough of windows at St David's, and, for a Scotsman, handling large areas of plain masonry did not present a problem. Though erected twelve years after Walton's move to London, there is no doubting this building's ancestry. It is an extraordinary adjunct to the main block: its walls of towering masonry with small window openings clearly follow Scottish precedent; great vertical bays break through a series of unmistakably Scottish dormers along the eaves line.

English details are evident too. The bow window at the north end of the building, now carried through four floors, recalls the great bows of eighteenth-century English country houses: Elmdon Hall again comes to mind. Voysey's use of the bow at Broadleys can be compared, though Broadleys as a whole is long and low

199. *Opposite*: Plas Wern Fawr from the tennis courts.
200. The new library, in Walton's Classical mood. Beyond, the arched annexe leads to the main house.

and quite different to the Wern Fawr extension. More like Walton's are the great flat-topped bays George Devey used in his Kent houses Betteshanger and St Alban's Court.

By contrast with the rather stiff results Walton achieved at Wern Fawr and St David's, the music room block is a work of inspiration. Of all Walton's work at Harlech, this was the high point, and this, ironically (after the fire of 1968), the part most completely gone.

Wern Fawr as a whole was enormously improved by the music room extension. If, before, there had been any question about the proportioning of the house, it was suddenly resolved. The new extension relieved the attention previously focused on the main block, breaking its rather contrived symmetry. The new components of the composition are skilfully ranged along the cliff face with a sense of casual improvisation: Devey's favoured arrangement of main house, lower block and tower asymmetrically arranged to suggest the haphazard growth of centuries is paralleled here.

The music room, though it could seat 300, filled only half of the new building. Below were suites of guest rooms and offices. To the south was the new library, visually connected with the annexe by its arched windows and height. The annexe now formed a delightful passageway between the library and dining room. Lined with cabinet-work and a fireplace which gently echoes the more elaborate Glasgow Style, it forms a fitting connection between the Glasgow-furnished dining room and the furnishing of the library – where Walton used the more restrained style he had adopted in his room for A. S. Ball (pl. 165). In the library, an assiduous search for traces of the Glasgow style is barely rewarded. The coffered ceiling relates directly to the Ball interior. The furniture is simpler still. Not even foliate medallions can be found, and like the fireplace in the music room, the furnishing – even the carpet – is regulated and geometric in tone. The outward curve of the chair arms and the tapering elongation of the table legs are a faint reminder of earlier eccentricities, in a room which is now firmly within the English tradition. The 'Castle' suite of furniture, probably designed for one of the new suites below the music room, reflects the same approach.

201. Strong sunlight shows off the beautiful workmanship of the walls of the extension and the main courtyard at Wern Fawr.

Davison reputedly spent between £50,000 and £60,000 on the building of Wern Fawr, and Walton, several years of his life on its design, and on supervising its execution. From 1906-1911 there is remarkably little evidence of other projects. The house at Ryde is the only prominent exception. Wern Fawr was not ostentatiously grand, yet in its execution and detail no expense was spared, and the facilities – central heating, marble bathrooms with hot and cold, gardens lit by electricity (generated from the estate's own power house), a music room with one of the finest automatic organs in the land, offices, garages (centrally heated), stabling, spectacular gardens, even a specially-appointed dark room – were certainly lavish.[45]

The workmen were drawn from several sources. T. H. Kingerlee's (by now a trusted source of building craft) were brought from Oxford, but the Clerk of works, Amos Jenkins was a Harlech man; the carving was executed by Esmond Burton, a sculptor friend of Davison's from Molesey days, yet the gates were made by the local smith. Walton, with his experience of directing craftsmen wove these threads into a fabric broad in vision, rich in detail, where the individuality of the craftsmanship serves his wider aims.

A decade in the workshops of Walton & Co. had sharpened Walton's eye for detail and his talent for integrating a variety of skills and techniques. It had taught Walton how to get the best out of his craftsmen. Wern Fawr, like so many country houses, came about through a particular combination of circumstances – cheap hand labour, the availability of traditional skills, and a leisured pace of work brought about by a good relationship with the client and an abundance of resources – circumstances which had delivered centuries of country house production and which would one day abruptly end. At Wern Fawr Walton synthesised his skills with a new liberality – a liberality which suggests he was aware the opportunity would not arise again.

X UPHEAVALS

It is 1911. Most of the last four years of Walton's life have been concentrated on solving architectural problems. Wern Fawr, The White House, St John's at Ryde, the St David's Hotel, the Wern Fawr music room extension, had one after another crowded his thoughts. His preoccupation with building work meant that he had had little time for anything else.

The small number of other commissions which he took on over this period were in complete contrast to his architectural work. Wellington asked for a decoration over the fireplace in the dining room of The Leys in 1907 or 1908 (pl. 117).[1] Walton's answer was a mediaeval scene hardly advanced in concept from the murals at Elm Bank of a decade before (pl. 80). Two years later he took on a more ambitious assignment at The Phil-lippines where a different theme emerges: his painterly outlook has caught up with the direction he had been taking in design since his Holland Street days.[2] The mediaeval romance of The Leys which still savoured of Rossetti, Morris and the Pre-Raphaelites is now replaced by Grecian dress and and a more classical tone.

The recent revival of mural work had been strongly encouraged by the Art Workers' Guild as part of their effort to overcome the split between the 'fine' and 'applied' arts, but painting was certainly not Walton's forte. The cool greens and silvery greys of his work at The Phillippines are subtly modulated, but to a critical eye, the outcome is flat and unexciting, and his figure drawing poor. The draped figures perhaps recall Puvis de Chavannes, Lord Leighton or Albert Moore. Memories of E. A. Walton's landscapes are stirred in the background. While the mural is a brave attempt to produce something decorative but modern, its size and prominence as a painting ask too much of an amateur, as Walton was in this field. Yet Walton could succeed in a decoration where in a painting he would fail. The even larger project of the hoarding at the Strand, had been

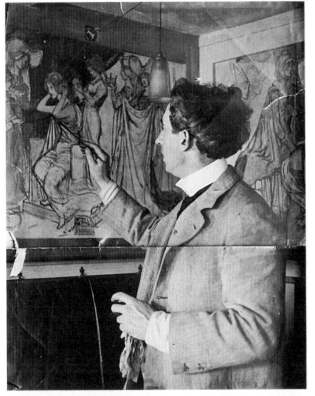

202. George Walton at work on the dining room mural at The Leys, *c*. 1907-8.

203. Painted mural by Walton at The Phillippines, Brasted Chart, Kent, where he had decorated a drawing room several years before (pl. 157).

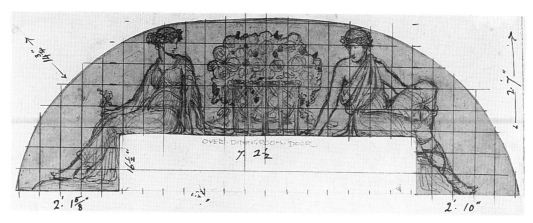

204. Design for a painted mural over the dining room door, in the entrance hall of The Leys.

recognised for its accomplishment: there, in his 'Beggarstaff'-influenced style, he had boldly sketched the outlines, applying the colour with verve and dash (pl. 102).[3]

The same is true of his mural work in the entrance hall of The Leys of 1909.[4] The classical mood of his painting at The Phillippines was again adopted – though now with an emphasis on the current French taste – for the decoration of the awkwardly-shaped frieze panels created by his groined ceiling. The shape of the panels called for decoration rather than painting – so immediately Walton feels at home. No longer overcome by the immensity of the task, Walton gaily filled the awkward spaces with decorative designs.

That Walton could take on such a commission as the mural at The Phillippines reflects the outlook of the Arts and Crafts. Walton's son Edward described their way of thinking:

> They regarded themselves as able to do it all ... They did some things better than others ... My father wouldn't have called himself a great painter or anything like that, but he thought it was normal to paint still life now and again, or draw a portrait ... or design some jewellery or enamelwork, or anything ... if you had your oats and you were loving enough you'd be able to come up with something. That was the expectation: not conceit, but an assumption that it was all one world.[5]

It is clear that between these two commissions Walton was looking for a change, for the Baroque had been momentarily reconsidered in a brief courtship on the Waterer & Dickins shopfront of 1908: an attractive (if out of character) combination of undulating Georgian bays and decorative Baroque detailing.[6]

Rumours of change

In late 1910 or early 1911 Walton the Architect returned for the last time, on the crest of a wave, from his exertions at Harlech to resume his London practice.

The intensive nature of his work for Davison (not only the buildings but their complete furnishing and decoration) had inevitably led to a slowing-up of his London operations. He returned to a city full of large architectural offices vying with each other for the lucrative commissions available in a nation still resolutely celebrating the peak of British imperialism and commercial power – despite threatening signs of decline. There was not much hope of entering this field (and besides, it was probably not what Walton wanted), but the clients with domestic development in mind were equally well catered for by the smaller established architectural practices. In the limited field of shop design, Walton's name was known, but the Shiplake and Ryde houses had had no public response, neither had the St David's Hotel. The attention given to The Leys (besides Muthesius' publication published only in Germany and in German) was chiefly in the context of successful interior design. Wern Fawr alone had been favourably reviewed as a building. It was illustrated in *The Studio Year-Book* of 1910.[7] Undeniably, in the field of domestic architecture, Walton was virtually unknown. Davison's desire to build was for the moment satisfied. In an environment of far more distinguished and better-trained architects, Walton could hardly expect architectural commissions to come in a rush.

To oil the process, Walton applied on 18th March 1911 for institutional recognition at the R.I.B.A.[8] The battle between the 'Artist' architects and the 'Professionals', which had been going on for twenty years and more, was settling out on the side of the professionals, who were calling for statutory registration to restrict the legal use of the term 'architect' to those on a drawn-up register. Walton's application was no doubt partly a response to this threatening development, as in 1911 the Society of Architects (the Professionals) and the R.I.B.A. (containing the elements of dissent) agreed on a truce and compulsory registration seemed imminent.

The Licentiateship scheme, a special category of membership, had been introduced in 1909 to allow R.I.B.A. status to practising architects who had not followed an approved course of education but were nevertheless competent.[9] In 1911, Charles Mallows agreed to propose Walton: perhaps had encouraged him to apply. Walton's application relied on his presentation of a *fait accompli* – and possibly on the intervention of Mallows. All went well, and Walton was duly received as Licentiate Member on 20 July 1911, now at last recognised by a professional body (even if he had entered rather by the back door). Yet there would be no more building commissions for Walton for the better part of a decade, and all his major architectural works were now behind him. Walton, mercifully, was unaware of the irony.

In practice many of his jobs had an architectural component. In the period up to the First World War, Walton's London 'office' relied on commissions for domestic alterations and the occasional shop design. He was already known as a specialist in furnishing and interior decoration and his reputation was spreading in the fields of domestic extension work and garden design.

Typical of this type of job is his work on James Robertson McIsaac's Kensington home. The McIsaacs were of Glasgow origin and, like Walton, had settled in the south. Scots families in London kept in close contact: they had their own preferred meeting places and their own preferred schools. A close relation of the McIsaacs in Glasgow had been a shareholder of Walton & Co., so Walton, living literally round the corner in

206. Ironwork at 50 Victoria Road, London, designed c. 1911-12.

Emperor's Gate (with more accumulated experience and prestige than he ever had in Glasgow) was the natural choice for the realisation of their domestic dreams.[10]

As much as any alteration job on a terraced house could, 50 Victoria Road provided Walton with the opportunity to parade his full accomplishments. Flushed with the success of his recent gates at Harlech, his confidence is demonstrated in the restrained splendour of the ironwork front. Walton's treatment of 'columns' and 'capitals' is a witty burlesque in the Neo-classical idiom – the humour of his Alma House glass rephrased. The tiny paved garden well displays his new architectural abilities and is a masterful example of his talent for tight planning, no doubt developed through the Kodak work, which would prove useful in the future. The beautifully laid tiling of the walls recalls the virtuoso treatment of The Leys' front bay, and probably reflects Walton's knowledge of Mallows' garden craft. The garden creates a series of interconnecting spaces consisting of a glazed Japanese-style pergola, a semicircular garden seat and a separated lower-level terrace. Inside the house, Walton's new dignity of expression is demonstrated in the perfectly simple marble patterning of the fireplace surrounds, the geometric order of the stained glass and the fine proportioning of the panelling.

Knowing that Walton worked elsewhere on the plot, it is hard to imagine the ground floor bay which overhangs the basement at the rear to be by anyone else. This asymmetrically placed bay shows just how well Walton could adapt his newly-acquired architectural ideas to a different scale.

There were a number of other useful jobs in this period, like the fitting out of the Halcyon Club at 13-14 Cork Street.[11] Walton decided that where convenience and comfort were the order of the day, an unpretentious, conservative style would be most appropriate. He developed a suite of furniture to co-ordinate with a fresh version of his Sheraton chair and other furniture in-

205. Pergola in the garden at 50 Victoria Road.

207. Large carved wooden sign for Wellington & Ward.

cluded some of his plainest furnishing to date. Wellington & Ward took over the Reeves shop at 101 High Holborn and Walton fitted out the interior in refined and sophisticated style, creating a huge wood-carved wreath with the 'W & W' insignia for the window display. It opened in early 1914.[12]

It was to be expected, if not relied on, that after thirteen years of almost constant patronage Davison would think of something he needed before long. Sure enough in 1914 he approached Walton again. In the intervening years his life had undergone a change. When Walton returned from Harlech in 1911 there may have already been doubts in his mind about the direction Davison was taking. Rumours of further change may have reached him from Shiplake – rumours of G.D.'s increasingly unconventional guests and lifestyle.

Wherever they were living, the homes of the Davison family had always been full of guests. Walton, who joined the party in the later 1890s, along with Annan and Wellington, quietly mingled in the crowd. He had never been as close to Davison as he had to the other two (sometimes unsure of Davison's ideas, not quite in sympathy with the way he looked at things) but this had not got in the way – most vitally, it had not prevented their fruitful artistic rapport. And besides, dinner at the Davison's often included many with whom Walton felt at home (pl. 193).

For Davison, somewhere along the line, these parties had lost their magic. He had always been a man of very individual ideas. His enthusiasm over George Bernard Shaw's connection with the Camera Club represented his welcome not just of radical artistic affinities but of distinctly left-wing ideas. Davison's early interest in anarchism can perhaps be traced as far back as his fracas with the R.P.S. and the organisation of

The Linked Ring ('a kind of little Bohemian Club' as it was thought of by its founders), an organisation without rules and regulations and with no figure of authority.[13] Freedom of expression and freedom from authority were the concepts which interested him, while a sensitive social conscience allied him with the working class. At the last, it had been this tendency which soured his relationship with Kodak. Back in 1907 he had been asked to resign from his managerial post as a result of his poor management record, though at this stage he was asked to join the Board. Davison was a major shareholder and his Kodak shares paid so well that he was already independent of employment: in effect the forced resignation had simply freed him to follow his developing interests in music, workers' movements and political action. He began to distribute his funds to organisations as various as the Central Labour College and the Omega Workshops.[14] Just how important Davison's decorative interests remained is demonstrated by an earlier incident: his support of the anarchist paper *The Voice of Labour*, started up by by Guy Aldred on his release from prison in 1910, did not last long: 'there was a preposterous argument between [Davison] and Rose Witcop over the subject of interior decorating and Davison went off in a huff'.[15]

Davison remained on the Board until 1912 when his encouragement and financial support of anarchist activities and publications, (not least his 'hatless' involvement in a socialist procession) so outraged the Kodak hierarchy that Eastman wrote: 'While I should not feel at liberty to volunteer any criticism of your attitude on any social question, I do feel that if you are lending aid to an advocate of anarchy you are not a useful or suitable member of our Board of Directors, and I think you ought to resign.'[16]

Opposition to Davison's now more blatant divergence from bourgeois opinions did not come only from outside. Family relationships became increasingly strained. If Eastman felt driven to pushing G.D. out after all these years, Susanna felt the same. As Margaret Morris later explained: 'Quite naturally, his wife did not take kindly to having the gardener in to dinner'.[17] But in 1913 it was Davison who announced his departure.

After the break, Davison went to Liverpool to stay with the photographer Malcolm Arbuthnot with whom he had exhibited at the new London Secession of 1911.[18] The Linked Ring had gradually stagnated and a group of advanced photographers including Annan, Alvin Langdon Coburn, Arbuthnot and Davison had left in 1909 to set up their own separate, but short-lived, exhibiting group. Arbuthnot, an admirer and associate of Shaw, had every sympathy with Davison's ideas and offered his support. Davison was not ungenerous to his wife. She would have The White

House, he Wern Fawr. There would never be any short-age of money either for Susanna or the children. But, however minimal the unpleasantness, such events were upsetting to someone of Walton's disposition and they disturbed what had been part of the pattern of his life for more than a decade. It was only the first of many changes to come.

Initially the situation had its benefits. Wern Fawr had been an ideal retreat from city life, a place to invite friends for those extended Edwardian gatherings, but, unlike The White House, it was remote from the capital where Davison's business life and artistic interests had always centred. Rapidly Davison felt the need for a London base: money being no object, he took on a large house in Holland Park. Walton was invited to convert the interiors to something suiting Davison's tastes and current life style. In the early summer of 1914, T. H. Kingerlee's was approached for an estimate. C. H. Hosken, Kingerlee's cost clerk recalled the work they were asked to carry out: 'the scheme being to pull down internal walls on the ground floor making one large room to be panelled out with Ancona Walnut, the two Bay windows fitted with a special Arabesque or Persian design of Grilles in Walnut – seats for the windows, etc.'[19] This would be the Music Room, where an organ and specially designed harp, both in Ancona walnut, were installed. Various alterations and decorations were made elsewhere in the house and the garden laid out

with paving and seats and shrub boxes made in teak.

The rooms at 32 Holland Park had to be enlarged, for Davison's growing dissatisfaction had been not so much with entertaining as with the type of people he had felt obliged to invite along – those solid (boring), establishment figures uncritical of the *status quo*, not inclined to appreciate Davison's increasingly unsettling ideas. His house at Holland Park would be open to his new friends, amongst whom were the young musicians Eugene Goossens, Cyril Scott, Joseph Holbrooke and Granville Bantock; the editor of *The Anarchist*, George Barrett; Margaret Morris the dancer; the artists J. D. Fergusson and Duncan Grant; and the ubiquitous Bernard Shaw. In the new music room, concerts were organised for 'local residents of several grades of social position' (as C. H. Hosken remarked with eyebrows raised).[20] It was decorated by Walton in a novel man-ner: pierced triangles and diamonds decorated the doors and a pierced screen surmounted the organ console; the hanging light fitting reflected the current Chinese taste and paralleled Mackintosh's adopted source of inspiration at his Chinese Room for Miss Cranston of 1911-12 (while the emphasis on triangles parallels Mackintosh's later work at 78 Derngate, Northampton of 1916). The Chinese figure on the mantelpiece set the tone. There was simple upholstery with loose covers and the harp, which matched the one at Wern Fawr, was topped with a wonderful Welsh dragon.

208. Working in a new style: the music room at 32 Holland Park with its fine Orchestrelle.

This striking room shows Walton's design thinking again moving on, though Davison's appetite for the modern was now probably further advanced than Walton's. He had joined the Contemporary Art Society, set up in 1910 to support the cause of modern art, and was urging the Welsh politician Thomas Jones to 'achieve a post-Impressionist exhibition'. He saw in their work 'an expression of that natural evolutionary & revolutionary spirit which is moving and working everywhere these days, a revolt against the authoritarian mandate (academic or whatnot) *from above* & a reliance on the expression *from within*'.[21]

Walton, by contrast, was well entrenched in the increasingly insular spirit of gentle comradeship and respect for crafts of the Art Workers' Guild, where he was currently on the committee. The sort of artists – and others – Davison was supporting were not altogether to Walton's taste, but he had never been one to comment on personal differences. His reticent manner had, for instance, allowed him to continue to visit the remaining family at The White House from time to time, and also provide for Davison's needs without offending either party – though from continued social intercourse with Davison and his altering circle of friends, Walton drew back.

The Arts and Crafts movement was by this time encountering difficulties. The 1912 exhibition had been a financial disaster and the designers were less able to sell their work. Their devotion to the workshop ideal had inevitably raised the question of relevance in an increasingly industrialised society. This was pointed up by Eric Gill, whose recognition of the achievements of Arts and Crafts designers had to be prefaced by the comment 'accepting their detachment from the common life of our times'. Gill was realistic: 'You can't possibly make good tables and chairs and pots in price competition with industrial mass-production'; inevitably they had made only 'luxurious articles such as only the rich could want'.[22] By its preciousness the Arts and Crafts movement was fast becoming an anachronism; Walton was in the company of many colleagues who were unable or unwilling to adjust and apply themselves realistically to the task of improving design for industry. In Shaw's more jaundiced opinion their apparent encouragement to many 'to make an ugly chest of drawers out of unseasoned wood, stain it green, devote it to the simple life and offer it to our cottages for 36 guineas [was] not to contribute usefully to the welfare of modern man'.[23] Muthesius again was amongst the outsiders who had recognised the backward-looking tendency of the Arts and Crafts, putting his energies instead into setting up the Deutscher Werkbund in 1907 to apply the more lasting of their ideals to his search for quality in design for industrial production.

If Walton found Davison and the plight of the Arts and Crafts movement unsettling, there was worse to come. For Walton, who never took much interest in politics, the war came as a rude surprise. It would become difficult to bury thoughts of the outside even in the warmth and brotherhood of that 'spiritual oasis in the wilderness of modern life' – the Art Workers' Guild.

If he considered the future as he sat on the roof of St Paul's watching for air raids, Walton might well have felt discouraged. Within three months of war, a nephew had already been lost in action. There were the difficulties of the Arts and Crafts to turn over in his mind and his own shortage of work. He was arranging to use an office in 4 Raymond Buildings, Grays Inn Road, where Ernest Newton, Arthur Keen and others were ensconced, no doubt to spread the net wider in his search for work: but was it the right decision? Marguerite had grown up. She was about to marry a doctor, Philip Scott, but it would be one of those disrupted marriages of war times, for after the wedding he must return to the front. She would not see him again until 1919.

The bleakness of circumstances in the first years of the war (despite news of more work through Davison on the London studio of Malcolm Arbuthnot)[24] was devastatingly exacerbated by Kate's unexpected illness and death. The sense of loss Walton would experience in the following years, stretched beyond the loss of his wife. After the war nothing would ever be the same again. And in that altered society, with its changing financial climate, its shortage of servants, the necessarily increasing focus on design for industry, it would become more apparent than ever that the Arts and Crafts movement had somewhere – despite the massive influence it would have on twentieth-century design thinking – lost its way.

The C.C.B.

Some time during 1916, Walton was called to a position on the Central Control Board (Liquor Traffic).[25] Set up by Lloyd George, who was then the Minister of Munitions, the C.C.B. was a desperate attempt to solve the worsening drink problem which surrounded the munitions factories on three principal sites – Gretna (near Carlisle), the Cromarty Firth, and Enfield Lock, outside London. Vast numbers of Irish navvies had been imported to work in the factories and, at the weekends, they spilled out into the surrounding neighbourhoods in their search for entertainment. These unsuspecting, mainly rural, localities had little more to offer than the public house, and the resulting dissipation was jeopardising the urgently necessary production of war weaponry – was, according to Lloyd George, 'doing more damage in the war than all the German submarines put together'.

Compulsory purchase of the breweries and the vast majority of drinking houses began in January 1916.

There was necessarily a gap before the new policies took effect. At the end of that year, at Christmas, in Carlisle, insensible bodies still littered the streets of the town.

While all this may have seemed at first a rather daunting prospect to Walton, it was considerably alleviated by the character of the team in which he was set. In the clubby atmosphere of the Piccadilly office, Walton found fellow Art Workers' Guild member Harry Redfern, once partner of J. J. Stevenson (the Glasgow man and celebrated exponent of 'Queen Anne'), and his old friend C. F. A. Voysey. Working for a Government department may not have been a natural choice for Walton (self-employed since 1888), but it was a contribution to the war effort, promised congenial society and brought an income of sorts, of which by this time he was badly in need. To be honest, the jobs he had found since he finished at Harlech had not provided the level of income to which he had become accustomed: the income which at Holland Street and Emperor's Gate he had consumed – like his father – with such enthusiasm. The war had brought everything to a standstill (everything that is except Davison's project at Holland Park which was still in full swing). New work was plainly not forthcoming.

Walton had been taken on as Assistant Architect to the older and more experienced Harry Redfern. His duties initially involved him in trips to the targeted districts for surveying those properties compulsorily purchased through the powers of the new Act of Parliament. In Carlisle he found the sympathetic support of the architect Basil Oliver (recently elected to the Art Workers' Guild), who had taught alongside Charles Spooner at the Central School of Arts and Crafts, and was currently based in an architect's office in Carlisle. Born in a brewery house himself, his own contribution to the development of the 'reformed' public house would be large.

The scheme of State Management was entered into with gusto but, for the most part (as a result of the urgency) hurried improvisations were the order of the day. Later, in the more extended years of the 'experiment', Harry Redfern would be able to bring into being a whole new order of public houses redesigned from scratch,[26] but in these early years of Walton's employment, their aims were largely achieved by closing down the most dingy and disreputable and by gutting and refurbishing the rest.

The aims of the scheme would be realised on several levels: by limiting the beer and the number of places it could be bought; by providing attractions other than drink – music, games such as bowling or billiards, facilities for writing letters, in one place a 'picture theatre', in all of them 'cheap and good food, so as to discourage the drinking of alcohol apart from with meals';

and by reconstruction and refurbishment of the premises to remove the dark and uncontrollable 'snuggeries' of the past and provide instead 'light air and colour' – which is of course where Walton came in.[27] With more realism than the Temperance movement had shown, the overall aim of the C.C.B. was not to proscribe but to improve public drinking. A change of image – from the glitter of the nineteenth-century 'gin palace' to a more civilised and restrained environment with as many diversions from drink as possible – was their earnest, educationally-minded endeavour.

Though Walton was employed as Assistant Architect, the architectural improvements have always been attributed to Redfern. Walton's main task appears to have been supervision of the furnishing and decoration, while Voysey contributed posters and graphic work and framed decorations for the walls.[28] At the time, of course there was no concern to credit the work of individual designers. If the munitions workers could be returned to their factories on Monday morning in a state of sobriety, the end was achieved.

209. Wheelback chairs and pewter plates in The Globe Tavern, Longtown.

Just how hurried some of these refurbishments were and how much of an adjustment Walton had to make in his approach to the work is demonstrated by the conversion of a disused Post Office in Lowther Street, Carlisle to the Gretna Tavern one of the earliest jobs on which he worked. The Post Office counter became the bar, and the hangar-like sorting room a restaurant. Redfern equipped the kitchen and installed the lavatories, Walton decorated, and the entire job was completed in ten days. Walton learnt quickly that his approach would have to change. To his dismay he found that the sophisticated and elegant colours of his favoured schemes did not transfer from the genteel surroundings of his usual commissions to the vulgar walls of the Post Office – which had come out 'battleship grey'. Nor were they popular with his new class of client: even the sympathetic Oliver could not deny 'its failure was immediate'. Walton was obliged to accept the lamentable necessity of supplying what to his view

210. The sorting room of the Carlisle Post Office converted into a C.C.B. tavern, prepared for the opening by the King and Queen.

must have seemed indeed a debased alternative: the revitalised scheme of 'rosy pink', co-ordinating floral decorations and red artificial leather upholstery was greeted with general approval.[29]

In time, Walton found a middle road. When he had become accustomed to the new rigours of his situation, his schemes were considered (by the right class of observer) a 'marked success'. To Voysey's mind, he made 'many public houses into public palaces'.[30]

To the public bars and refreshment areas, Walton introduced a rough and ready country style. To the rest rooms (for reading and writing) and the bedrooms, he brought a modest element of sophistication. Some smoke and tea rooms combined features of both to give the closest (if pale) reflection of their Cranstonian forbears.

For the furniture, ordering available designs had the advantages both of reliability and speed, not to say cost. Walton adopted the Windsor wheel-back for the greater proportion of his refreshment rooms and bars, giving the same sense of corporate identity with which his black-enamelled chair had endowed the Kodak showrooms. The use of traditional seating in the bar areas was also a wise ploy to avoid total alienation of the clientele, which was in general far from eager to be 'improved'. Walton noted down details of some standard pub furnishings on his travels. The 'Dorset Table' he sighted in 'The Lion and The Lamb' was recorded and reproduced for his pubs in Carlisle.[31]

For tables and benches he often used the plank-constructed, revealed-joint style of the Arts and Crafts, to create interiors of an 'Old Inn' style. The lighter pieces for the writing rooms and bedrooms were necessarily an exercise in simplicity – a refinement of his design ideas and forms to their most basic level of expression. And somehow he often managed to avoid that sense of

'poor relation': there was a delicate elongation, a suggestion of the cabriole leg, fine judgement in the sense of proportion: even the plainest of chairs has a touch of elegance in its detailing or proportion, even the simplest of cupboards a slender distinction of form and an outward-turning leg.

As the Utility furniture engendered by a later period of aggression judiciously resolved the needs of its own time, Walton's efforts for the C.C.B. provided a sensitive solution to the task with which he was faced. There might have been other ways, but this was his solution – not the solution perhaps of a Duncan Grant or a Vanessa Bell who might have brightly painted off-the-shelf furnishings. That was not in his nature. Nor would it have suited his customers – or the sensibilities of the C.C.B.

The frustrations – the hard, often depressing work of the innumerable surveys, the inevitable regurgitation of ideas necessitated by the rushed nature of the job, the limited opportunity to create original designs – were relieved from time to time by the decorative delight of designing a pub sign. Here Walton could venture some freedom of expression and the sometimes humorous results show him still buoyant despite difficulties.

However much they disliked its socialist overtones (the dubiety of nationalisation), none in the future would deny that the scheme was an enormous success. For Walton it had been an adventure of sorts. The design of collapsible canteen tables and picture-house seating – a new, unanticipated experience – may have brought with it some satisfaction. It had been an attempt to do something useful for his country and the common man. Yet from the grand old days of Harlech it was a far cry indeed.

XI OLD FRIENDS

In the offices of the C.C.B. there was a young lady called Dorothy Anne Jeram. Daughter of a Hampshire doctor, she had worked before the war in the theatre as secretary to Granville Barker and Sir Henry Beerbohm Tree, with such writers as John Masefield, Arnold Bennett and George Bernard Shaw. Efficient and conscientious, she endeared herself to all. To the offices of the C.C.B. she brought her lively memories of the indiscretions of the famous and, to her work, her down-to-earth practicality and unflappable common sense.[1] Perhaps Walton's weakness for amateur theatricals put them initially in sympathy, but soon she had again become indispensable. Walton, twenty-three years her senior, recently-widowed, his career plagued by uncertainty, found a new focus for his life in the future. During the final blood-letting months of the Great War, on 20 August 1918, he and Dorothy – or Daphne as she was always called – were married.[2] Voysey was best man.

Although State Management had been intended as a temporary measure to ensure efficient arms production, in the end the scheme ran on for fifty-five years. The advantage for Walton was that he could continue with the C.C.B. while attempting to re-establish his independent practice. It was not an easy task.

The return of Marguerite's husband, Philip Scott, from the war in 1919, must have afforded some relief. The differences between Marguerite, flighty and extravagant, and her new mother-in-law, only two years older, had brought unwanted tensions. Walton had always had a flair for making choices to suit the requirements. So it was with Daphne: her comforting and practical attitude to life would cushion Walton to some extent from the blows which were to come.

For when Walton emerged from the C.C.B. to look for new work, the scene had changed. The extravagance of his opportunities and living, the prosperity which had seemed so permanent, would never return. Though the twenties were, for some, a period of recovery, to many of the designers and architects of Walton's generation they were to bring a growing sense of redundancy.

Starting up again

George Davison, in the end, had not used his house at Holland Park a great deal. Far more of his time in the war years had been spent at Wern Fawr which was undergoing 'transmogrification' as he called it ('a long-standing intention') – altogether a new régime, with no live-in servants, and a training school for children from the London slums. In the war years he had also poured his energies, and several thousand pounds, into renovating a derelict house to aid the political education of the South Wales miners. And at Wern Fawr, then and after, there was always some group or other staying.[3] In 1919 (to the consternation of the county) it was the Margaret Morris dancing school in their flimsy Grecian tunics (cf. pl. 217). J. D. Fergusson came to paint. The young musicians who had come to Holland Park, enjoyed his splendid music room and 'unlimited hospitality'. Alvin Langdon Coburn bought a house near by. There were charity performances in the hall and Davison established a tradition of regular free concerts and Christmas parties open to all. Mr Amos Jenkins, clerk of works on the Wern Fawr building site, had become an installation, manipulating the magic lantern and presiding over the show. Some, it is true, were barely tolerant of their host – that 'elderly idealist' with 'little musical ability', 'slightly hard of hearing', but on the whole his guests were thoroughly appreciative.[4]

Evidently, G.D. had had similar intentions on a smaller scale for the music room at Holland Park; but, by the end of the war, his visits were already becoming rare and by the early 1920s the house was taken over by various of his friends and protégés. Adrian Boult wheeled his bicycle through the front door, Malcolm Arbuthnot (facing eviction by his landlady) took a room, and Eugene Goossens the studio over the mews: it was just what Davison liked to see.[5]

George Davison inspired conflicting views. To those who knew him well he simply 'wanted to use what he had to make as many people who were trying to do something, happy and useful'. To those who disliked his political orientation he was a 'moral menace' making his homes 'a headquarters of any subversive organisation which could enlist his financial aid'.[6]

Davison's intimacy with struggling artists made him only too aware of the adverse climate in which they were operating. He had recognised the uncertainty of Walton's future as early as 1913. As it was, he had bought some land in 1917, up-river (a polite distance from Shiplake), on which to moor his houseboat. By the end of 1918 he had decided that a small cottage would be a useful addition[7] especially as Joan, whom he had brought from Liverpool to help with the adoptees, was expecting a child.

Whatever Walton felt about Davison's activities and personal lifestyle, an architectural commission, however exiguous, was more than welcome. At his C.C.B.

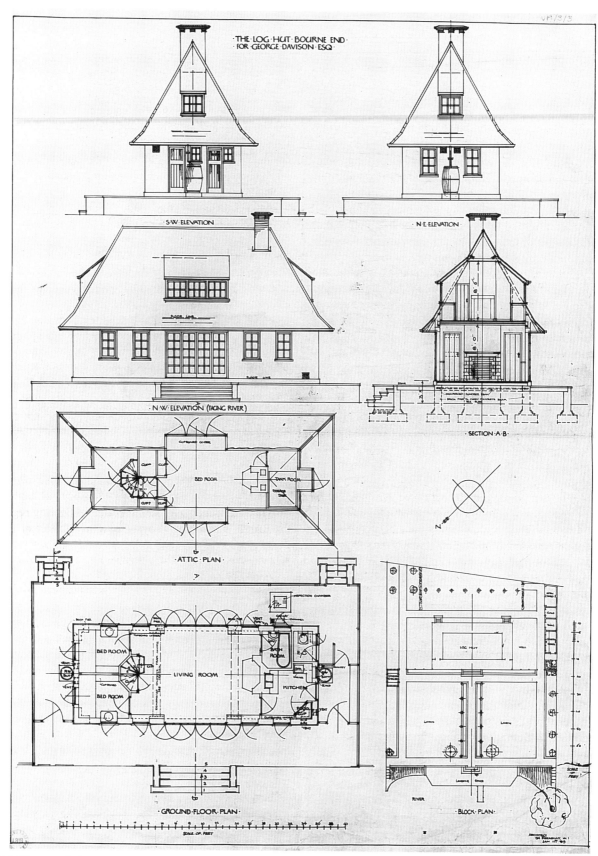

211. Plans and elevations of The Log Hut, built at Spade Oak Reach *c.* 1919 overlooking the river Thames at Bourne End, a mooring point for George Davison's Log Cabin houseboat.

drawing board in January 1919 he drew up plans for a tiny one-bedroomed cottage (with two cabin bunks squeezed in) for Davison's riverside site – his first design for a complete building since 1910.[8]

To a large extent Walton's designs of 1908-10 had constituted a series of experiments – regrouping, shifting proportions, trying different materials for different effects – with some or all of a group of elements: the semicircle, the bay, the pediment, Georgian regularity, the mansard roof, the Palladian window. At the Bourne End cottage he returned to an idiom closer to The Leys. The Log Hut (for through its relation to the Log Cabin, so it was called), paraded none of the classical touches he had used on the Log Cabin, and its steeply pitched roof enclosing the upper floor was in complete contrast to the sleek, flat-roofed character of the houseboat. This dominating roof, with its dormers and its windows tucked under the eaves-line, gives the building a clear affinity to The Leys, though it is more in Voysey's style, as if to mark their closer intimacy at the C.C.B.

From the folding doors of the houseboat across the miniature lawns and formally laid beds, the visitor arrived at an almost identical set of doors into the Log Hut; from there into a room which must have given a sudden sense of *déjà vu*. For the proportions of the Log Hut's downstairs interior exactly matched those of the houseboat saloon – in fact the plan of the Log Hut was an almost exact copy of the Log Cabin's lower deck (pl. 177), with the difference that it incorporated, by a little neat juggling, a spiral stair behind a cupboard door.

The job was quickly completed, and the need to find more work given a renewed urgency with the news that Daphne was pregnant. Work was difficult to find. There was a request from the congregation of St Peter's Church, Glasgow, for whom Walton had completed one of his firm's first commissions thirty years before, for a memorial reredos in the form of a triptych. It was far too big to be done at home so Walton borrowed the studio of a friend in Melbury Road, where the finished painting was later exhibited. Some of his figure drawing in the central panel was rather wooden, but there was bolder work in the side wings faintly recalling his old hoarding style. Connections with Glasgow were weaker these days: the Oxford firm T. H. Kingerlee's made the frame, transported the work and installed the memorial in Glasgow. It was warmly received. The commission was a reminder of earlier days and more sanguine expectations.[9]

In early 1920 there was news of another job, to remodel the garden of the Bank of England at Threadneedle Street, 'which had become a veritable wilderness during the war'.[10] Walton may have gained the commission through Kenneth Grahame the writer, a friend of the family, who was connected with the Bank.[11] Frustratingly, although the builders' contract

212. Parental delight: George and Daphne with baby Edward, 1920.

was signed in March 1920, the project rumbled on for many months with the usual bureaucracy and red tape of such commissions before it came to anything. In the meantime Edward was born. Phoebe Stabler was asked to provide a statue (by the time it was executed, Edward had grown large enough to model for the putto).[12] Walton was to retain an ancient lime tree in the centre, to match the materials of the existing balustrade, to provide appropriate flower boxes. Perhaps over-awed by the dominating formality of the architecture, discouraged by the restrictions of the brief, Walton produced designs which were conscientiously detailed, but conspicuously dull. Had the society of Voysey at the C.C.B. (Voysey so dismayed by the Classical revival) also had its influence?[13] For, through his lasting regard for Ruskin's teaching, Voysey saw in Classicism tendencies as insidious as Art Nouveau. He had written, quite recently, in the tones of Pugin, of the renewed influence of Rome as a revival of 'ancient sin', a 'return to the forms and modes of a corrupt period'. Rustication, for example (a suggestion of which enriched the walls of Wern Fawr), was 'a deliberate attempt to deceive, it being adopted to make walls look more solid than they really were, a direct and immoral effect on the part of the originators'. Symmetry, to which Walton had fallen prey at The Leys, 'will impose its iron law, and lead the architect to cover his library door with books, if the door by proclaiming itself should upset the symmetrical balance of the room' (Walton may have recalled uneasily his 'blind' window at The Leys if he read these words) '... surely that which requires fraud to defend it cannot be morally sound'. These were the thoughts which ate at Voysey in his office at the C.C.B., while he longed for the old popularity of the architecture of the Arts and Crafts. (He had published this diatribe in 1915.)[14] Had the Log Hut been designed under the influence of these sentiments? With the current strong swing to revivalist styles, had Walton felt the

213. Gate lodge of The Leys in white painted roughcast, built *c.* 1921-2.

same way? Perhaps he was not altogether disheartened when he heard of the razing of the site for a new Bank of England in 1928.

The apartment to which the Waltons had moved in 1920 could only be a temporary arrangement: with no studio, Walton had had to make arrangements to work elsewhere. His decision to take an office alongside Ernest Newton's at Gray's Inn Road in 1915, had proved over-ambitious: he had dropped it several years ago.[15] By mid-1921 it was becoming obvious that a house with a studio in Kensington was something he could no longer afford. Yet Walton was optimistic, for, probably with promise of further work from Wellington, this was the point at which he left the C.C.B.

By September Walton was drawing up plans for another small cottage almost identical to the Log Hut (pl. 211), which would mark a renewal of the client-patron relationship with his old friend J. B. B. Wellington.[16] It would be a new gate lodge for The Leys. The design for Davison had evidently proved successful. Walton made various refinements to Wellington's building: a slight increase in size meant three small bedrooms could be managed upstairs and, with no more need for the cabin bunks, a parlour below; reorientation of the stairs allowed more conventional access through the hall; and a small extension provided the larger scullery and storage needed for permanent accommodation. Outside, the rendering and whitewashing of the chimneys, combined with the less symmetrical elevations, made the effect even closer to Voysey's cottage style, though there was a reminder of Scotland too in the turret-like gate posts.

Contrasts

Walton had worked with T. H. Kingerlee & Sons, the Oxford builders, on and off since 1908, perhaps before. The company decided in mid-1921 to build a modest row of speculative houses in Sterne Street, Shepherd's Bush (the less salubrious end of Holland Road) and asked Walton to help with the design. When it became clear that Walton was in need of accommodation himself, they agreed to let him make the end house (no. 53) suit his own requirements.[17] The arrangement was feasible for Walton only if he could have a studio: and with the Kingerlees' consent, part of the the adjacent garden was annexed to make room. It was a small house with only three cramped bedrooms upstairs. The stark contrast with the large terrace in Emperor's Gate where he had lived before the war was inescapable (pl. 181).

But all the same, the Sterne Street row had a character of its own. The tiny front gardens were fenced with concrete posts and palings. The modest fronts had a grid of the newly-popular metal glazing bars. In the curve of the window in the front door was a faint echo of more lavish Glasgow Style mouldings. The surfaces of the upper and lower storeys were treated differently, much as at The Leys, with brickwork below and rendering above, a division marked by a strong horizontal, repeated at the roofline. Yet how different was this roof from that of the Log Hut and The Leys' lodge! Low-pitched and hardly overhanging the eaves-line, the impression it gives of a flat roof is strengthened by the low parapet sweeping round the corner to the side. Can a knowledge of recent work in Amsterdam be detected?[18] Inside no. 53, the hall was as large as Walton

214. Edward outside the small house designed by his father at 53 Sterne Street, the Waltons' home from 1923-30.

could afford to make it, reducing the area of the front room but giving instead an airiness and spaciousness which belied the reality of the situation. By careful planning upstairs he made the most of what space there was, and in the process gave each room an individual character. Similarly, each of the ten houses in the row had a different plan, as if he were trying out several alternatives for the best arrangement – or simply hated them all to be the same. At no. 53 parquet flooring was somehow managed; the small square garden had elegant brickwork detailing. The studio made it all worthwhile. It was a delightful building, quite adequate in size, and the provision of side access meant it could even be used for parties without anyone having to go through the house.

The Walton family, George, Daphne, and young Edward, had moved into their new house by August 1923.[19] The site had had to be worked from scratch (there was drainage and road-making to do) and the houses themselves had not been started till a year before. In the interim there was an expedient commission from John de la Valette – top-to-toe treatment for his house in Mayfair – which took the most part of 1922. Kingerlee's was contracted for the work. The Mayfair interiors (of which there is now no trace) cost de la Valette almost half of Kingerlee's total expenses in building the whole of the Sterne Street Row.[20]

As Walton set up house in Sterne Street, building toy cupboards for Edward, fitting plaster casts on the studio wall, George Davison and Joan were settling in to their own 'Château' in the South of France in quite different style. Their daughter Doreen, born prema-

turely, was still, in 1921, in such a fragile state of health that the doctors thought she might not survive the rigours of another Harlech winter. J. D. Fergusson and Margaret Morris (now his wife) had a penchant for the south of France.[21] They assured Davison it would be just the place to spend the winter. A suite was booked at the Grand Hotel, Juan-les-Pins, and Joan, G.D. and Doreen set off. Davison liked it immediately, bought a small house by the beach as a temporary measure – the 'Villa Gotte' – then decided to stay. He was not always in the best of health himself these days, and what better than the fresh air, the bathing, the sun and the sea? There had been so much unpleasantness in the press as well, those malicious personal attacks in *John Bull*, calling him a 'fomenter of sedition', and 'a moral menace'. For all his earnest and charitable concern, they could make such gross charges: 'We ... are not prepared to sit idly by while young persons of both sexes are systematically debauched in mind through the display of lavish hospitality serving merely to deck out a corrupt and indecent propaganda'. These accusations did much to drive him away.[22]

But the 'Villa Gotte' would hardly do: at Harlech he had now quite an entourage. Nine of his East End waifs, 'orphans from the depths of London society',[23] had been permanently adopted – and of course there would have to be a school.

When G.D. set out to look for suitable accommodation, he was not looking for a three-bedroomed house. He bought a magnificent twenty-two acre site on the Cap d'Antibes with the shell of a building started half a century before by the King of the Belgians. Close to

215. George Davison's library at the Château des Enfants, Cap d'Antibes, with its Cholmondeley chairs: *c.* 1923-4.

Cannes, with its own private beach, it promised the most splendid living. A French architect was commissioned to complete the building, leaving the original high ceilings in the central part of the house for dining room, library and drawing room, dividing the remainder into two floors – for the rooms were enormous.[24] The move would be permanent, the children fetched and settled. Wern Fawr would have to be sold and the furniture shipped; Walton would be needed to design the interiors. There was a lot to do. G.D., Joan and Doreen did not move in until the summer of 1923.

G.D. left Wern Fawr with some regrets: he is even said to have wept as he waited for the train.[25] The visitors he could in a sense take with him – for who would

refuse a holiday on the Riviera? – but the house he could not. Many of the main rooms of the Château would be scaled-up reconstructions of the rooms he had left behind (either from Wern Fawr or Holland Park), but there would be scope for new work too.

Yet the Château rooms are often disappointing. The largest, attempting to reproduce the music room at Holland Park – the same wood-panelling around the organ, the same wall framing, the same light fittings, the same diamond-and-triangle patterning – shows just how ineffective a scheme can be rendered by a change of scale. The lumpish armchairs hardly help – so unlike Walton, were they perhaps brought in from the hurried furnishing of the Villa Gotte? In the dining room

216. The nursery at the Château des Enfants, with two of Walton's beautiful carpets displayed to advantage.

217. The Margaret Morris dancers among the pine trees in the grounds of the Château des Enfants, c. 1923.

there was the older furniture, a sideboard, an 'Abingdon' and a 'Beechcroft' chair. More at home with beaten copper and coloured glass, they looked lost against the vast plain walls. The rooms were just too big. Yet, in these oversize interiors, Walton's carpets come into their own. Shown to their best advantage, the simple, regular patterns are delightful, even in the black and white photographs which are in most cases all that is known of them today. Some of the newer designs are more geometric than his earlier patterns, but in every room it is the carpet – now the only remaining pattern in the room – which unites the whole, which brings the scheme together.

There were some more successful rooms. The library and study were both lined with white-painted cabinets to reproduce Wern Fawr's, with the hinges now revealed in a geometric pattern. They gave interest to the walls and drew the eye away from the high ceilings. A mixture of old and new furniture was used effectively to break up the spaces. And the nursery was cheerful and inviting: one of Walton's loveliest carpet designs, a rocking horse and a white-painted, doll's house cupboard combined to make it a room for children to remember.

With twenty-three bedrooms and its own school, the Château must have kept Walton busy for some time. The Margaret Morris dancing school was due to arrive for the summer of 1923, but put up at a nearby hotel as the rooms were unfinished. They used the hall for events, the grounds for their classes, then tripped down through the pine woods and across the rocks for sunbathing and the sea.

Elstree Idyll

If the grandness and high spirits at the Château made Walton feel uncomfortable as he returned to his diminished practice and Shepherd's Bush, he could think of The Leys. After the Château, The Leys would seem homely and unpretentious. Walton was always welcome and always felt at home. He could wander down to the cowsheds or watch the clouds drift by; and the Wellingtons were a comfort to him. They became Edward's godparents about this time and somehow, sensitively and imperceptibly, guardians of Walton, too.

The friends Walton made were held. Voysey later wrote of him: 'May one who has known George Walton for forty years intimately be allowed to testify to his lovable nature. He could not say an unkind word about any man. If there were any he did not like he was silent ... He was the most gentle of men with strong feelings always under control'.[26] As the difficulties of the twenties dragged on, it was as if any who had worked with Walton and knew him well could not bear to see him fall on hard times. It was not only his foremost clients, Wellington and Davison, who were loyal; there would be others.

Wellington & Ward had profited by the War and though business fell off somewhat afterwards they were not in difficulties. The Wellingtons themselves were prosperous, but had not changed. Wellington still enjoyed tinkering in his workshops as much as anything; if he was not there, he could be found testing out his

218. 'Refreshing Moments', c. 1913. George and his daughter Marguerite attired for one of J. B. B. Wellington's tableaux in the door of the morning room at The Leys.

electrical devices in the study, where, by a conglomeration of amplifiers and bakelite-mounted lamps, he fed wireless programmes to the chauffeur's house.[27]

Wellington knew Walton's need. And there were all sorts of things he could do. There had been the gate lodge already, but there were other projects in Wellington's mind. This was a good time to realise them.

First Walton was asked for ideas for a set of memorial windows in memory of Mrs Wellington's parents for All Saints' Church in Borehamwood.[28] It was a wonderful commission, returning Walton to a medium he had hardly touched for almost twenty years. In the fresh, idiosyncratic designs he produced, there is a sense of an enormous enjoyment, an explosion of jubilant colour. The glass was richer than Alma House and freer than Victoria Road. The quality of the main panels

219. Pen and wash design for the cusp of a lancet panel, for All Saints', Borehamwood, 1922, recalling a roundel at Drumalis of thirty years before (pl. 40).

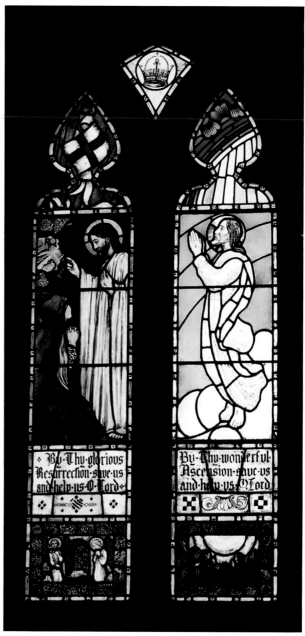

220. Stained glass window at the Church of All Saints, Borehamwood.

varies (Walton again lacking confidence with his figure work on show): it is the upper decorative panels and the lower almost sketch-like compositions which are so lively, some recalling earlier experiments at Drumalis. If it did not look forward like the strangely sparkling twenties glass of Harry Clarke, neither did it look back to the old days.

Then there were thoughts of a parish hall for Borehamwood: somehow Walton got the job of drawing up designs.[29] He came up with a curious conjunction of a simple late seventeenth-century Wren-like entrance front, an outside stair and a Voyseyesque low-roofed rear: perhaps a sign of the conflicting creative desires of a frustrated architectural imagination. The project fell through. And now Wellington had settled on a grander plan: the extension of The Leys. He wanted a new wing to house the billiards room, a library and new kitchens. Had his interest in billiards begun to wane or had it been too noisy in the centre of the house? Or perhaps it had been the kitchens which caused him most concern. There had been nearly two hundred guests at that Photographic Convention held in The Leys in 1913, which may first have put the idea in his mind; and he always liked his employees to have the best of conditions. The extension gave him more scope.

The new wing was built on to the north east, set

221. Pastoral scene at the base of a lancet panel,
Church of All Saints, Borehamwood.

back, a wall extending to form an enclosed courtyard space.[30] To contrast with the main block without dominating it, the elevation was open, with an arcaded loggia beneath and a balcony above. It was a successful solution. Inside the billiards room on the upper floor the rafters were, perhaps surprisingly, exposed, although the intention to transfer the long light fittings from the main house suggests why.

There was other connected work. The murals Walton had designed for the entrance hall in 1909 had for some reason never been executed. Now they were approved and £200 promised for the four. Stencilled decorations to the plain plaster frieze of the drawing room and the frieze and ceiling of the dining room may also have been carried out at this time, indicating a change in Wellington's taste (or possibly in Walton's?), a tendency to greater elaboration than had been intended at the start. Swing doors were added between the entrance hall and main hall, with finely carved lat-

ticework and an overflowing basket of flowers. Walton had not forgotten his joyful experience of designing for woodcarving work a decade before at Wern Fawr.[31]

Slump

Life had not changed much for either Davison or Wellington. Their business interests in their different ways had paid off. Davison from canny foresight, from making the right decisions at the right time, had quickly made his fortune. Wellington's venture had benefited from steady growth, from his good business sense. Neither was troubled with financial difficulty. Not so Walton. Like Wellington and Davison he had worked hard and had enjoyed life – thrown grand parties and mixed in the best circles – but he had done little to establish a secure base for the years ahead. At the time of the 1901 exhibition, Walton & Co. had been a well-established company with a future – if Walton had had the inclination to develop it. Walton & Co. had had seven years' start on Wellington & Ward and although photographic materials were in a more rapidly expanding market than furniture at that time, with the right moves he might almost have had a business like Wellington's by the 1920s. Heal's after all was doing well. Liberty's – even if it had reverted to the security of historic styles – would soon be planning its grand new Tudor-fronted building off Regent Street. A smaller concern along the same lines might not have been impossible. But wherever Walton's talents lay, it was not in making money. Walton's attempt to try out house-letting in the old Holland Street days, as Bolton remembered, had simply ended him up in court.[32] When Davison had offered him Kodak shares in payment for his work, Walton had turned them down ('he did not understand shares, he would rather have the money', as his son explained).[33] Walton's father had been capricious and a spendthrift. George had discovered his call-

222. The Leys, Barnet Lane, Elstree, Hertfordshire, with its new extension to the right added in *c.* 1923-4.

ing and stuck to it, but some of his father's character-istics were shared. Success had come simply because there were enough people with time and money to appreciate his sensitive, artistic abilities. Times had changed. The jobs Walton had gained since the war came erratically, had been neither big nor lucrative enough to return him to his pre-war prosperity.

While it is unlikely that all Walton's early commissions have been identified, a large collection of his later work was preserved by the family, so that now more is known of his work in the last decade of his life than in any other period.[34] Even with this biased evidence, the jobs of the twenties look thinly spread. In earlier chapters it has been possible to examine many (often large) commissions covered within a few months of each other. There were six or seven jobs in distant 1891, five in 1896 and six or seven in 1897. The more accessible twenties do not compare well. Since he left the C.C.B. there had been, in the first year, de la Valette's job, work on the Bank of England garden and the new gate lodge for The Leys; in 1922, the windows for All Saints' (that was the year the St David's Hotel burnt down, and his brother Edward's death had added to his burdens); since then, to put it bluntly, he had relied on Wellington's benevolence. And now, in the early summer of 1924, as he finished work on a fountain for the garden and some stained glass for the hall, where could he look for work?[35] Daphne was collecting references from former employers.[36] The future looked bleak. Two years previously *The Studio* had remarked that 'artworkers of practically all denominations are having a very bad time just now'.[37] There had been no improvement. Voysey, who had shared so closely in Walton's wartime experiences, was also struggling. The Mackintoshes, he heard, had moved to London, and having fared no better, had now moved on.

The last years of Walton's career would be besieged by difficulty. The general trend in furnishing and decoration in the post-war climate reflected the insecurity of the times, moving away from progressive work towards the revival of historic styles. Tudor and Jacobean pastiche or real antiques for those with resources would remain popular through most of the decade. The war had made Britain conservative in taste and the D.I.A. – the Design and Industries Association – was struggling with itself for a way forward. The backward-looking romanticism and preoccupation with handcrafts which had absorbed so many of Walton's contemporaries had prepared them to embrace neither revivalist styles, nor modernism – the route which led many European countries to a vital involvement in industrial design. For the type of meticulous, stylish work Walton had produced, now in itself old-fashioned, the bottom had dropped out of the market.

If he thought of Glasgow, things were no better –

the Glasgow Boys were old now and dispersed, the progressives not to his taste at all. Even Annan had given up his photography and was concentrating on dealing in fine art.[38] Prospects were certainly no better, and, anglicised as he was by now, it was too late to pick up the threads.

If we look on through the collection of Walton's later work left by his family, 1925 yields nothing, 1926 a few furniture designs, 1927 two small church commissions, 1928 a sideboard design and a tabernacle. Some time in these years Walton made alterations to a studio in London, and a proposal for a small house which was never executed. These paltry commissions, supplemented by a series of textile designs for James Morton, tell their own tale.[39]

Morton's: a lifeline

If it had not been for Morton, life would have been bleak indeed. Alexander Morton & Co. had moved most of their loom work to a disused mill in Carlisle in 1900, and the old friendship with James Morton had been revived in the war years when Walton was often in Carlisle.[40] The company had grown to include printed textiles in their range as well as the woven fabrics and carpets which were retailed in all the choicest outlets: Liberty's and Morris & Co. in London, Wylie & Lochhead in Glasgow. Walton's earliest textile design of the twenties is dated June 1926 and Morton's first recorded purchase 15 October. Surviving letters between Walton and Morton tell the story of his last years.[41]

At first Walton sent sketches from time to time. Morton took occasional designs for which Walton received £25 – more with alternative colourways – but as other avenues of employment closed up, Walton became increasingly anxious for some regular income and dependent on Morton as a source. In June 1927 he wrote:

> I should like to go on submitting designs to you and I feel confident that I can give you work of real use. To enable me to do this with a less anxious mind I would suggest that your firm should pay me some sort of retaining fee.[42]

To Walton's relief, £300 per year in monthly payments was agreed, though not without some hesitation on the company's part ('It is unfortunate that so far we have not had much success with any designs we have received from you').[43] Additional payment would be considered in twelve months' time if the work was of sufficient use to the firm, and in fact Walton received £500 at the end of each of the first two years. However, it was not a story of success. In the first year Walton went through various difficulties relating to his misunderstanding of the processes involved and the additional payments were not because his designs had been immediately useful. In July 1928 the sympathetic Morton wrote:

> When we started, of course, it was assumed perhaps that you would be having more architectural work than has evidently been the case ... More of your time has, therefore, been taken up on our work than was anticipated by either of us ... We have not been able to use as many of [your designs] as one would wish, but they ought to be useful in the future, and I should like to feel that you had been remunerated properly for the very fine work that you have given us.[44]

Nevertheless he was hopeful. He went on, 'The designs you are now developing will be, I think, in closer touch with the requirements of the trade than was previously the case in earlier stages'.

The range of designs Walton produced over these years is remarkable, and shows his earnest effort to arrive at a manner of work which would meet with approval.[45] First he produced some light, delicate patterns based on flower studies, like 'Peony and Lily' (pl. 224), and some elaborate landscapes with figures such as 'Fantasy' or 'Chinese Bridge' interspersed with a few more abstract designs. In 1928 there were some more conventionalised patterns like 'Cockade'. Various 'peasant' designs probably for block printing may also have come from this period. 1929 was a difficult year. Daphne was ill, possibly with an eye problem; in hospital for a month with 'her head between sandbags to prevent movement'. One of the deepest troubles this brought was the loss of income: 'she will not be working for another two or three months anyhow'.[46] But then there was an invitation to Antibes which Morton encouraged them to accept. The holiday was not without worries. Edward had reached the age limit at the school he attended and in order to decide on the next move, Walton needed to be sure of Morton's long term intentions. There had been some talk of the family moving to Edinburgh, so Walton wrote from Antibes to enquire ('I am sorry to trouble you with all this but I do not know what is in your mind with regard to my future work with you').[47] Walton had assumed the Edinburgh move would mean more work, but he was disappointed, and, after some hurried consideration as to comparative costs ('Schools: Edinburgh £18, London £46; Coal/Light/Heating: Edinburgh £12.10/-, London £25; Buss [sic]: (300 days at 4d) £6 5/-, London £20; Food: £150; Cleaning £26', and so on), they decided against.[48] There was worse to come; but before the crisis there was an interesting interlude.

Marguerite had always got on extraordinarily well with her cousin Margery, E. A. Walton's daughter. Margery had married a painter, William Oliphant Hutchison, and in 1922 they moved to London.[49] At first they lived in Chelsea, but two years later they were barely more than half a mile away from Walton at 72 Ladbroke Road near Holland Park. The Waltons, the Hutchisons and the Scotts were delighted with this opportunity to renew their intimacy. There was another benefit as the Hutchisons formed a further, if minor, source of work for Walton in this last, precarious decade of his career.

72 Ladbroke Road was a large terraced house just the other side of Holland Park Avenue from Davison's 32 Holland Park. When the Hutchisons had arrived in 1925, there had been a studio already, but they wanted alterations. It was the small job, previously mentioned, which must have been completed some time in the second half of the decade. Kingerlee's carried out the work: 'cutting out a small Bulls eye window in Brick Gable Wall & building a Cartwheel Window & other alterations'.[50]

Now in 1929 a larger job was offered. The Hutchisons had bought a disused vicarage from the Church Commissioners, a commodious house in the Victorian Gothic manner (a style seriously dated in the 1920s), and major alterations were intended from the start. Walton made several visits in October to talk over the possibilities and make plans of the existing layout.[51] It was hardly the best Victorian Gothic, but it had some good points, principally the brickwork, the proportions of the rooms and the setting – large gardens fringed by woodland – of considerable charm. But the driveway, inexplicably, approached the side of the house, so that the first glimpse was of the coal bunker tacked on the side. There were some ridiculous barge-boards. It would not do at all. If the Hutchisons were to be happy with this house, the changes would have to be drastic.

Walton conceived an imaginative scheme for reorientating the front ninety degrees from the northwest to the south-west, and a rather more dubious proposal to slap on a Georgian façade. What would Voysey say? And was this Walton, the lover of Georgian, throwing Arts and Crafts 'honesty' to the winds or was it a requirement of the brief? Whatever the case, the de-

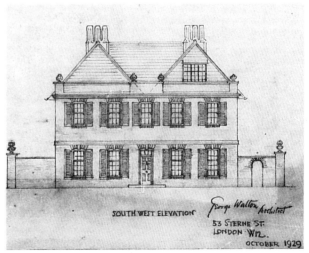

223. Proposed entrance front for The Old Vicarage, Letheringham, dated October 1929.

signs were accepted, with minor revisions, and the work went ahead.[52]

Walton's drawing for the front is certainly attractive – long shuttered windows, the neat roof tops behind, urns on the parapet and decorative garden walls. At the garden side the drawing (or living) room bay was removed and replaced by french windows so the guests could now spill from the dining room onto the lawn: for with the change in orientation the rooms had been rearranged.

Putting aside any questions of integrity, aspects of the proposal were cleverly thought out. Now the living room was more spacious and the hall enlarged and better lit, so that the house was considerably brightened by the change. Yet, to make a satisfying building from such a change-around is a tall order. Changing the style of a house as they might change a suit of clothes was a typical and much-criticised trait of the Victorians, and it was carried out convincingly only with a great deal of expertise and cash. The Old Vicarage had the benefit of neither. As might be expected of Walton, in the interiors, on the whole, he brought it off (though there something rather awkward about the shape of one of the bedrooms). Walton's experience of exterior conversions, however, was limited to that of the shopfront, which unfortunately is about the best way to describe the character of the operation here, for the finances allowed for no more than a face lift and this is all the Old Vicarage got. On the garden elevation, the pitch of the roof with its new square dormer abuts uncertainly with the abbreviated parapet of the front. The new round-arched studio window at the rear sits uncomfortably over the roof of an original bay. Even the pointed arch over the earlier entrance remains for all to see.

Some of the attractions of Walton's drawing were lost when it left the paper. He had been mistaken about the lie of the roof ridges, and they were too set back anyway to be seen from the ground; and some of the details, like the shutters and urns fell by the wayside. The house still has some good points – the neat shaping of the transoms on the front, Walton's sensitive handling of materials in the courtyard and garden (semicircular terracing and cobbles laid in patterns), a delightful summer-house – which go some way towards compensating for certain irregularities elsewhere.

While work at The Old Vicarage was going on, Walton continued with his efforts for Morton. Perhaps the parallel architectural commission had raised his spirits. Some of his strongest designs were produced in December 1929 and January 1930: 'Flowers of Paradise' which Morton thought 'very interesting from a decorator's point of view'; then a striking design with bird and sun rays in two colours on a buff ground; and another using the effect of folded paper cut-outs spread

224. Textile design: Peony and Lily, September 1927.

on a plain background (pl. 228). These imaginative designs contrast strongly with the more naturalistic floral patterns like 'Peony and Lily'. Walton was still searching for an idiom which would justify his employment.

Almost precisely as the thirties began, comments in Morton's letters began to signal difficulties. In January 1930 he wrote 'The trade is so uncertain ... just now that it is really difficult to gauge just what will sell'. In

225. Textile design: 'The Thistle, 1927-8. No. 7A'.

February, 'It appears to be more and more emphatic that there is not money available for expenditure on very high priced furnishing'.[53] In August Walton was notified that the block-printing department was temporarily closed due to lack of demand exacerbated by the development of cheaper 'surface-printing' by machinery. Morton added in his usual gentle manner:

> We have to cater to-day for a world of much smaller things in decoration – More "Bread-and-cheese" fare than big feasts. But we think the bread-and-cheese can be as good or better for people than the big feasts if it is Good Stuff.[54]

It was in September that things came to a head. By the thirteenth, Morton had reluctantly decided that he could no longer continue to offer Walton employment. Walton was understandably shaken:

> You will forgive me taking time to reply to your letter ... It was a shock and I don't know how to clear my

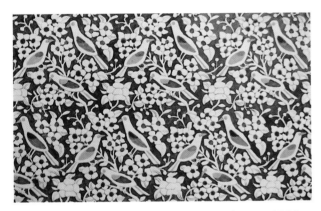

226. Birds and Blossom, textile design, February 1929.

mind as to the future. I cannot say however that I am surprised. I think I had it in the back of my mind that the trade was not going well but I have always been an optimist and it is a brunt when dreaming that the work I am producing is really useful ... I have as you say given my whole mind to the work and in this my whole heart. I think you know that prospects of getting work either architectural or other designing are practically non existent. The future will for me require a complete readjustment and it is difficult at this moment to see what form it will take.[55]

By November one thing at least was clear: 'I am unable now to keep up the studio and am negotiating to let it but hope to be able to retain the house'.[56] This does not appear to have been managed, and the Waltons moved in November to Hythe in Kent where living costs were cheaper. A desperate note arrived on Morton's desk one morning from Walton's second temporary address in Hythe:

> ... you can realise my anxiety to try and hold things together. There is no architectural work going. I have

strained in every direction for work of this kind. A past president of the RIBA wrote me the other day that he and many others had nothing to do and were only marking time ... Now I wish to ask you to reconsider your decision and if you can see your way to still keep me going in designing for you ... I have endeavoured to fall in with suggestions from you to the utmost of my ability and your expressions of approval of my designs from time to time gave me a feeling of security.[57]

Morton replied sadly to his old friend, 'Some of our best export markets have collapsed altogether', referring to the 'unpleasantness of having to close down certain of our more interesting and expensive things such a block printing'. He had other designers to worry about, though he did not say so – Voysey, Brangwyn, Sidney Mawson. It was simply not in the interests of his company to keep Walton on: 'as you know I personally like your type of design but it has been possible to use only a small proportion of what you have drawn for us'.[58]

If Walton looked back now at Morton's letters he might have remembered that some of the comments had not been so encouraging after all: Morton had thought 'Pink Blossoms' 'a fine old-fashioned thing, but I am not sure whether it may meet the particular demand they are after', or 'you have only partly caught the idea', or 'I am afraid they have not just as much sparkle or interest in them as I want for this new type of carpet'. Sometimes Morton had considered a design 'rather empty' or 'a trifle sad', or had had to admit that '[it] does not quite catch me'. Even Walton's political naïveté had sometimes let him down: in June 1927 'Old Russia' was returned 'because [Mr Morton] feels that any Russian design will not at present be looked upon very favourably by the trade'.[59]

The truth of it was that Walton had simply been unable to produce work which Morton could sell. It

227. The Dove, textile design, April 1929.

228. Unnamed textile design evoking paper cut-outs,
dated January 1930.

was not in his way of thinking to come up with the
rather brash bold designs appreciated by the twenties'
avant garde (though later he tried), nor could he bring
himself in all conscience to pander to the prevailing
taste for period furnishing. As he had sat those long
hours in his studio with his assistant Cassie Partridge,
counting the stitch numbers and working out the
points, it is understandable if he felt apart, somehow
disconnected. The fresh and vital patterns he had created in his youth – his silk and linen tapestry for
Buchanan Street or his innovative stencilwork – had
always belonged to an interior scheme: they had grown
from his feelings about the whole. They had never been
designed just for themselves, cut off from everything,
as these were.

A light in the darkness

As Walton sat with Daphne in the sitting room of
70 Seabrook Road, Hythe, where they finally settled in
March 1931, looking into the fire as his grandson remembered – or perhaps when he visited Voysey 'of fairly
advanced age' now, and like Walton 'not at all well off'
– he might have struggled to understand what went

wrong.[60] These last years had been agonising, but the
mistakes had all been made such a long time ago. There
had always been that expectation that the Gall money
would come; he had lived for the present, had never
really taken the future seriously, had always been an
optimist.[61] It can hardly have escaped his attention, as
he considered his years of decline, how unrealistic he
had been, how dependent he had allowed himself to
become on a few major clients; how in those halcyon
Holland Street days he had carelessly let the company
go – worse, recklessly thrown over his prospering practice to work for Davison alone, to become, in his later
years, humiliatingly, so dependent on the goodwill of
old friends.

And now Davison was dead. He had been in Exeter
last year, had quite suddenly chartered himself a special train to London, then a private coach all the way
to Antibes at the cost of £500; then died a few days
later on Boxing Day.[62] And, strangely, perhaps as
Walton brooded on the past, it was as if Davison came
to his aid. Within less than a month of Walton's final
appeal to James Morton he received a commission. Mrs
Joan Davison had decided to build a chapel in the
Château grounds – 'The Chapel of St George' – in his
memory. However inappropriate for G.D. (atheist and
anarchist) it was singularly apt that Walton's final work
should be to the memory of his greatest client.

229. Preliminary proposal for the Chapel of St George,
Cap d'Antibes, 29 April, 1931. Pencil and watercolour
on tracing paper.

In his work on the chapel, Walton overcame the stylistic difficulties of his immediate post-war years and, after toying with a star-shaped plan and dome (which suggests an eye to Lutyens's work at New Delhi), he settled on a simple oblong building with an apse for the altar.[63] The inspiration is early Byzantine, perhaps Romanesque, with semi-circular arches and a hidden dome; but the result is so elemental, so pared down (as Walton had always preferred his architecture to be) that the result is quite his own. The simple exterior is undecorated save for the careful contrast of roughly-cut stone against the smoother dressings of windows and doors. The semicircular arches eschew any suggestion of Classical order or decoration. The smooth internal walls accentuate form, void and solid, the play of light, just as they had at The Leys, effecting a quiet splendour, a peacefulness. And the marvellous woodwork – screens, doors, with copper wire gauze inserts like the Wern Fawr fireplace, and perforated symbolic carving – reaches out still to some new experience: never like Voysey looking back.

230. The Chapel of St George, Cap d'Antibes, built 1930-1.

231. The peaceful interior of the Chapel of St George,
Cap d' Antibes, Walton's last major work.
232. George Walton, *c.* 1932-3.

On his return from Antibes in October, there was a
last anguished cry to Morton. The main structure had
been finished and he was again needing work ('fees for
such a job don't go far in keeping the pot boiling').[64]

The final woodwork details for the chapel were
drawn up in January 1932. There is no record of any
further work. The last years were those that filled his
young son's memory with sadness and with a loyalty
to this gentle man who he knew had once been so filled
with creative force.

Walton took to ruminating by the fireside. He had
always been a reticent man, but now he sank into
longer silences, turning in on himself, filled with the
frustration of inactivity. The small collection of
glasswork and the residue of his furniture still kept
about the house, cramped in corners, were reminders
of another age.

EPILOGUE

Before George Walton died on 10 December 1933, John Betjeman, editor of *Architectural Review*, had sought him out, brimming with enthusiasm for an architect whom he saw as one of the early moderns. He began to plan an exhibition.[1] The project understandably came to nothing in the inauspicious climate of the mid-1930s, though Betjeman's interest in Walton brought about a perhaps more practical end: when he saw the desperate financial plight of Daphne, he set himself to procure for her a Civil List Pension.

The architectural historians of the thirties, among them John Betjeman, Raymond McGrath, F. R. S. Yorke, and Nikolaus Pevsner, in unison claimed for Walton the status of 'pioneer'. Pevsner thought Walton's designs 'amongst the most brilliant and historically most significant examples of the rapid and constructive progress of Britain away from William Morris towards a new style of the new century'.[2] For F. R. S. Yorke, Walton, with Mackintosh, Voysey and Edgar Wood, had made modern architecture possible by their 'struggle for a departure from revivalism, the acceptance of the machine by the artist, and the freeing of the plan'.[3] Betjeman claimed for his pioneers 'All Honour',[4] while the author of an article on the 'Edwardians' in *Architectural Review* of January 1934 pulled out all the stops: '[Walton] is more than merely representative of a great pioneer movement. He stands alone, like every genius'.[5] For Walton, recognition had come too late. Yet if he had been alive to read these words, he might have both smiled and shaken his head.

The White House (which had enjoyed no previous popularity among critics) was the focus of their attention for some very particular qualities: 'The balconies are uncommonly well designed in their delicate relation to the mass, and the glass doors stretching from floor to ceiling at the foot of the chief steps are very near to those glass walls facing on to gardens which are such a special point in most of our present day houses.' (pls 187, 188)[6] The author of 'Edwardians' makes much the same point, stressing Walton's use of 'contemporary materials' and adding 'Such a masterpiece as this is many years before its time'.[7]

Indeed, they had not been wrongly attracted to his work: Walton had played a part in, and extended, contemporary moves towards lighter interiors, towards trimming of ornament and an emphasis on form, had accepted the straightforward use of new materials and, it is true, had opened The White House to the garden by increasing the proportion of glass. In addition, he had never felt the antipathy to the machine registered by many of his contemporaries – perhaps as a result of his Glaswegian background – recognising that 'this is an age of machinery and keen competition and there is no reason why machinery in certain cases should not be used'.[8]

However, an open consideration of his work makes clear his interests did not lie in this direction. His search for refinement of form, for instance, did not lead to the geometric angularity of the Modern movement, of industrial form, but to a subtlety of expression which could only be realised by hand production. He could turn his hand quite competently to low-cost work, as he had at Sterne Street and in his work for the C.C.B., but this did not satisfy his more delicate sensibilities; he was too interested in the finest qualities of materials, in the most sophisticated modulation of forms, to find this type of work compelling. However much the balcony front of The White House is echoed in thirties buildings like the De La Warr Pavilion, Bexhill, by Eric Mendelsohn, his forms had come about not so much from yearnings for *Sachlichkeit*, or from concurrence with Le Corbusier (as the author of 'Edwardians' claimed),[9] not so much as the pioneering achievement of an isolated designer, but through a particular combination of circumstances: the past experiences of the designer, his artistic approach to his work (in which response to the site was paramount), and the interests and personality of a particular client. At the same time, these historians might have considered, he was building Wern Fawr.

As is now widely recognised, to see the work of Walton or any of his contemporaries in terms of its place in an evolutionary chain leading towards modernism, obscures too much. Certainly this approach has inhibited full understanding of Walton's work. The sudden interest in The White House demonstrates instead the preoccupation of British champions of the Modern movement in the 1930s with a search for origins of the new forms in their own architectural heritage, and reveals more of their interests than it does of Walton's intentions. Their interest in Walton's work in most cases (Pevsner being the prominent exception) started and stopped at The White House.

While the architectural historians of the thirties placed Walton with the moderns, more commonly in recent years his work has been classified as Art Nouveau. Considering that Walton made the following statement, this claim needs to be looked at carefully.

About 1892 while in Glasgow C. R. Mackintosh followed and our work was interesting the Dutch and later the Austrian architects and the type of work we were then doing would I think even today have been looked upon as modern, but unfortunately the movement after being distorted and twisted returned from Austria through Paris and finished in 'l'art nouveau'.[10]

Walton's own words make clear that he not only considered Art Nouveau different in its aims, but that he nursed a positive dislike for its productions. He was not alone in his feelings and it is necessary today not to let the passage of time obscure a distinction recognised decisively in the period. There were certainly flowing and expressive elements, even organic qualities, in Walton's work, from the metalwork signboard at Warneuke's gallery, the flowing hair of his figures in the early panels of glass, to the springy spirals of firedogs and leaded lines which typify the later productions of the firm. But these are merely components – as there were similar components in Ashbee's and Henry Wilson's designs – of the work of a designer always strongly controlled by symmetry and proportion, to whom the more Classical forms of his later years came quite naturally. There is no doubt that they were an important inspiration to the continental designers who developed Art Nouveau, but the character of Walton's own work must be clearly distinguished. In the end, the label Art Nouveau is as limiting as the label proto-Modern and leads as inevitably to a misunderstanding of the designer and his work. Although 'Glasgow Style' might seem a happier manner of identification, when it is considered that Walton's work can only be described as fully 'Glasgow Style' from the years 1896-1901, it is clear how unhelpful labels can be.

More likely to lead to understanding of his work and significance, is the attempt to understand him within his own context, exploring how much he was a creature of his time and situation, formed by the the pressures of life and circumstances of birth, and how much and in what ways he differed from his contemporaries. Inasmuch as these questions can be answered, they provide a broader platform from which to judge his achievements.

One of the most interesting aspects of George Walton is the way he does not quite fit into any convenient classification. He was neither modernist nor exponent of Art Nouveau, he was only sometimes Glasgow Style and however much in later years he became merged with the English Arts and Crafts, he never lost the more holistic approach he brought with him from elsewhere. His make-up was different, his outlook and motivations often contrasted with those of his contemporaries, enabling him to make an individual contribution to the arts of his times. From this sometimes unique position (as with his talent for unifying the interior) he became a force of bringing things together.

Walton was the first to plant the Glasgow Style firmly in English soil in the form of the Kodak shops, and so the fusion of the Scottish and English interpretation of the Arts and Crafts, the wooing with it of Liberty's and others, was begun. Similarly, if the English strayed to Glasgow before the opening of the School of Art and the emergence of Wylie & Lochhead's new line, it was Walton's less disturbing Glasgow Style which was most prominent. It was there in Miss Cranston's tea rooms – possibly also in the Cabin chain – and in Walton's scattering of other shops (Annan's, Warneuke's, Neilson Shaw & MacGregor's and his own showrooms). The impact of Walton's more easily assimilated Glasgow Style on the English (even if it cannot always be easily separated from the wider Glasgow Style), must not be underrated.

In taking on architecture as well as the crafts Walton again became a uniting force, epitomising the late Victorian search for unity of the arts, the fusion of architecture and the crafts, for which the Art Workers' Guild strove. In his unification of the whole house, as exemplified by The Leys, Walton reinstated the position of the 'minor arts' (and became literally and more fully Muthesius' *Wohnungskünstler* – the 'artist of the home'). At the same time, his atypical position brought about a curious reversal of their intention. While the arts and crafts of Ashbee's Guild were 'children of the mother art of architecture', in a curious way, for Walton, architecture was the child which had issued from his experience of the crafts.

This is not to imply that Walton worked from the inside out in his architecture: instead the work of building simply became another application of his craft. He designed a house as he might a sideboard – getting first the overall massing sorted out, ensuring that the surface and colour qualities of his materials were in perfect harmony with the form, attending to the craftsmanship and techniques of execution, and adding refinement, not so much in the form of outward ornament as in the finest handling of essential components – a delicate inset bone handle or an initialled lead waterpipe. Walton's arrival at architectural work by way of decoration and interior design singled him out from his contemporaries, gave him the motivation to integrate the details and structure of decorative work more fully into the building than many of his contemporaries.

His early 'training' in the school of the Glasgow Boys had a pervasive influence on his career. Walton absorbed the approach of a school of painting and applied it to design. Despite the mediocrity of his own forays into figure painting, his sharpened sense of colour harmonies, formal relationships, surface finishes and decorative qualities was the legacy of this training. The outlook of the Glasgow Boys not only led to his practical application of painterly skills in design work, it also informed his deeper motivations. In the work of Whistler and the Glasgow Boys a concern for beauty and decorative qualities was paramount. They were not concerned to surprise or disturb, nor to dominate; they were not concerned with eccentricity of form, nor to throw over traditional concepts of beauty. Walton operated from the same position and belonged more to this Glasgow 'school' than Mackintosh, whose inclination to distort conventional forms and proportions came from extra-Glasgow sources like Toorop and Beardsley. An alliance of painting and design is not unusual – aspects of the painting of the Pre-Raphaelites inspired the decoration of Morris's early furniture, that of the Cubists the productions of the Omega Workshop – but in many ways Walton brought about a deeper union.

In effect, Walton accomplished a marriage of Aestheticism with the practical philosophies of the Arts and Crafts. The outlook of the Glasgow Boys drew much from the 'Art for Art's Sake' doctrine of Whistler and Oscar Wilde. They had 'no proselytising creed', as Fra Newbery explained:

> they yet have a firm belief in one thing, which is that it is quite sufficient for Art to be Art and to be the most beautiful thing that the hand of man is capable of making her ... Art need neither be the teacher of religion nor the handmaid of literature, but ... is a quality which should have a place in the hearts of men, side by side with religion, literature, or any other of those great influences which enable mankind to express their gratification in creation.[11]

Or, as a writer in *The Quiz* explained more succinctly: 'No moral. No story. No nothing. But simply Art. And Colour.'[12] Walton concurred. He joined to his understanding of this view the emphasis on hand crafts, fitness for purpose, reformed views of decoration, and the respect for materials which had that quite different source in the more moralistic line of thought of Pugin, Ruskin and Morris. As the Glasgow Boys, from their gentler, less revolutionary position, in general turned away from the social comment of Courbet to the less ideological work of Bastien-Lepage, so Walton did not take on board the socialist aspects of the English Arts and Crafts movement. From his grounding with the Glasgow Boys, his standpoint was different from Mackintosh on the one hand, and different from Morris, Ashbee and Voysey on the other. And in some ways this softer, more eclectic, less theoretical outlook gave him a broader, more integrating, view.

Not least Walton combined the Whistlerian artist-decorator (his urge to decorate, his aim to touch the whole environment) and the Glaswegian entrepreneur. There was a dilettantism in Whistler's approach to decoration (in his somewhat superficial application of paint to articles designed by others) and a superiority in his attitude, which did not encourage the formation of a company, a linking with the Trade. Here Walton's thinking was stirred by other more immediate sources: the thriving industrial environment of Glasgow. And so he set up a business, and following Cottier's lead in Glasgow, helped to stimulate the growing interest in interior decoration in the city, laying the ground for Mackintosh's and Wylie & Lochhead's later exploits and by his company's success inspiring others to follow suit – Robert Paterson's and Stephen Adam's 'The Crafts' is only the clearest in descent. And when he left Glasgow behind, he took with him Whistler's breadth of vision and Glasgow's nerve. Largely unconcerned about lack of training, uninhibited by the conventions of any particular specialism, he did not balk at engagement with the new fields of houseboat or building design. This led on the one hand to surprising architectural achievements, on the other, to the dismal failure of some of his adventures in advertising graphics.

Walton's adoption of the Glasgow Boys' pragmatic 'creed' provided no defence against the attractions of professional prestige. Much as the Glasgow Boys in their later careers allowed themselves to be tempted by the rewards of Society portraiture and to be absorbed into the Academy, so Walton's progressive outlook was dulled by the desire for recognition, combined with his sensitivity to questions of status and the English Arts and Crafts snobbishness about the Trade.[13] These things led him to abandon his advanced interior decorating company for an established position as an architect. In London in the 1900s, he was no longer a leader; he became one amongst a much larger group who turned to Classicism as a means of expression. But he was not a spent force. His work remained inventive, was always freshly considered, and displayed much originality.

For Walton any theoretical undercurrents were undoubtedly subliminal. He made no claims and (other than the shifting goal of beauty) sought no ideals. He was not a reader, nor a theoretician, the flow of his creative thinking was for the most part undisturbed by the vicissitudes of ideology. But pragmatism has its strengths as well as its weaknesses, and like the Glasgow Boys, Walton was ultimately a pragmatist, picking and choosing his own way and resolving the dictates of his brief by setting himself only to reach the best possible solution, to the best of his ability. Walton was neither visionary nor revolutionary, he simply got on with the business of doing. And in the end it is better to take Walton on his own terms. His achievements were impressive, in glasswork, in furniture, in rising above the patchy English view of interiors, and in creating startling exhibitions and surprising buildings. They must stand on their own.

233. The doors from the music room to the conservatory at Alma House, Cheltenham.

NOTES

Abbreviations
A&CES: Arts and Crafts Exhibition Society
BJP: British Journal of Photography
GMAG: Glasgow Museums and Art Galleries
GWA: George Walton Archive
  The titles of books and articles listed in the Bibliography are given here in a shortened form.

I BEGINNINGS

1. Jackson Walton, born in 1809, married first Janet Young, who died leaving two children, and then Eliza Ann Nicholson, in 1844. Eliza bore twelve children of whom George was the youngest. Information from Edward Walton, George Walton Scott and Stephen Downs; *Glasgow P. O. Directories*; MacSporran, *Edward Arthur Walton* pp. 11-13.
2. Published later as W. Young, *Old Closes and Streets of Glasgow* (Glasgow 1900). On T. & R. Annan, see Margaret Harker, 'Annans of Glasgow', *BJP* 12 (1973) pp. 966-9; for J. C. Annan, see ch. II, n. 29.
3. For Helen Walton (1850-1921), information from Edward Walton. For her training, see Glasgow School of Art, *Annual Reports*. See also GMAG, *The Glasgow Style* p. 52.
4. Rupert Joseph Crawhall Walton to Vivien Hamilton, 15 Oct. 1989, Burrell Collection, Glasgow. On Joseph Crawhall senior, see Charles S. Felver, *The Newcastle Wood Engraver* (Newcastle 1972).
5. For E. A. Walton see Bourne Fine Art, Edinburgh, *E. A. Walton 1860-1922* (exhibition catalogue 1981); MacSporran, *Edward Arthur Walton*; Billcliffe, *Glasgow Boys*. For Joseph Crawhall junior see Vivien Hamilton, *Joseph Crawhall 1861-1913: One of the Glasgow Boys* (London 1990).
6. George Walton went to school at Sutherlands, Hillhead, 1874-6, and then Partick Academy *c.* 1876-1881. According to family sources, he started at the British Linen Bank, Glasgow, in 1881. This is confirmed by the census of 1881.
7. Billcliffe, *Glasgow Boys*.
8. Edward Walton in conversation with the author.
9. Date in Walton's hand on reverse of a photograph in the collection of G. W. Scott.
10. In his RIBA Nomination Papers, Walton said he trained at Glasgow School of Art and P. McGregor Wilson's School, although his name does not appear in School of Art records from the 1880s.
11. See n. 10 and *Glasgow P. O. Directory* for 1887-8 and 1888-9.
12. *Glasgow P. O. Directory* for 1881-2 and following.
13. The sisters did not distinguish their individual contributions; their infrequent signatures are simply 'H. W.'. For Hannah Walton (1863-1940), information from Edward Walton. See also Jonathan Kinghorn, 'China painting in Scotland', in *Aspects of Scottish Decorative Art in the Twentieth Century* (Scottish Soc. for Art History Yearbook 1988) pp. 61 ff.
14 Burkhauser, 'Glasgow Girls' pp. 165-74.
15. *St Mary's Glasgow Magazine* (1890) p. 98. For Constance Walton (1864-1960), see notes by her daughter Constance E. Ellis, April 1966 (GWA).
16. Helen's election to membership of the club coincided with her employment at the Glasgow School of Art. See Glasgow Society of Women Artists, *Lady Artists*; Burkhauser, pp. 47-8.
17. Cottier's firm had branches in Glasgow, New York and Sydney. See Girouard, *Sweetness and Light* pp. 210-11.
18. Christopher Dresser was born in Glasgow, though he left before he entered on his decorative career.
19. E.g., Leiper's Cairndhu House, Helensburgh in 1872-3, and Thomson's Queen's Park Church, Glasgow in 1869.
20. *Studio* 56 (1912) pp. 318-19.
21. *Cabinet Maker* 7 (1886) pp. 85-9; *Art Journal* (1887) pp. 295-8.
22. The Home Arts and Industries Association, founded in 1884, was dedicated to teaching and reviving home-based craftwork activities which included carpentry and cabinet-making.
23. See Aslin, *E. W. Godwin*; Pauline Agius, *British Furniture 1880-1915* (Antique Collectors' Club 1978) p. 64.
24. For 'Dado', information from Edward Walton. For Whistler as inspiration, George Walton to John Betjeman, 1 June 1933 (RIBA).
25. E.g. the butterfly pattern on a tea cup by Helen in GMAG shows the influence of a covered bowl by Eiraku Zenichiro, part of the 1878 gift to Glasgow. See Antonia Lovelace, *Art for Industry: The Glasgow Japan Exchange of 1878* (GMAG 1991).
26. It was Whistler's exhibition work which Walton particularly mentioned to Betjeman (see n. 24).

II GEORGE WALTON & CO., GLASGOW

1. See Kinchin, *Tea and Taste* p. 32, and Robertson, 'Catherine Cranston'.
2. See Kinchin & Kinchin, *Glasgow's Great Exhibitions*.
3. George Walton & Co. is first mentioned in the *Glasgow P. O. Directory* for 1888-9, suggesting that it was open for business by late spring, 1888.
4. See Billcliffe, *Glasgow Boys* pp. 207-27; and Kinchin & Kinchin, *Glasgow's Great Exhibitions*.
5. For Ashbee see below, p. 56.
6. For Scott Morton & Co. see below, p. 95.
7. In the possession of T. & R. Annan & Sons, Glasgow. George Walton is credited as the decorator of the illustrated Argyle Street rooms. As they are not known to have been redecorated by Walton between 1888 and 1898, it is assumed that the views shown are part of his earliest recorded commission. *Studio* 39 (1906) p. 33 records that Walton also worked on a smoking room in 1888, no illustrations of which have survived.
8. Lethaby's and Gimson's use of the device in the early 1890s is comparable. See Lethaby's inlaid staircase panelling at Stanmore Hall in Middlesex (part of a Morris & Co. job), illustrated in Cooper, *Victorian and Edwardian Furniture and Interiors*; the fall-front of Gimson's writing cabinet shown

by Kenton & Co. in 1891, now in the V&A. For later development of the Glasgow Rose, see Burkhauser, 'Glasgow Girls' pp. 102-6.

9. For Mallows' early acquaintance with Walton, see Walton's RIBA Nomination Papers.

10. *Studio* 39 (1906) p. 33.

11. For St Peter's (since demolished) see 'The Decoration of the Chancel of S. Peter's Church, Braid Street, Glasgow' in *St Mary's Glasgow Magazine* (Sept. 1890) p. 98 (the frontispiece of this issue is a line drawing of part of Constance's mural decorations); and *St Mary's Glasgow Magazine* (March 1891) p. 37. All quotations are from these articles.

12. Puvis de Chavannes was one of the artist-heroes of the Glasgow Boys.

13. Mrs R. Y. Pickering was probably related to Miss Ruby Pickering, an associate of the Macdonald sisters at the School of Art, who was involved in the entertainments at the Lady Artists' Fancy Fair (see below).

14. Hannah's exhibit (no. 505) was described as 'Plaque, underglaze and barbotine: "Angels". Designed after Benozzo Gozzoli. Executed by Hannah Walton': see A&CES, *Catalogue* 1890.

15. Edward Walton in conversation with the author.

16. For Robert Graham's exhibit see A&CES, *Catalogue* 1890, no. 636. An unnamed design featuring a lily and rose was registered in 1890 (Public Record Office, BT/50/144).

17. Walton's use of Morris & Co.'s textiles (and later of their 'Sussex' chair) and of Thomas Wardle's fabrics in his early interiors makes it probable that wallpapers were also available.

18. Glasgow Institute of the Fine Arts, *Exhibition of Works in Black and White and Pastels*, 1889. Walton's exhibit 'Music' was priced at 15 guineas.

19. The company was not listed as specialist frame-makers in the *Glasgow P. O. Directory* until 1896-7, but J. C. Annan recorded that Walton made frames for his photographs from 1890-95 (see n. 30). It is likely that they were made from the start.

20. 'Mr W. M. Warneuke, of Glasgow', *Amateur Photographer* 29 (1899) pp. 331-2. Mrs Warneuke was an occasional exhibitor at the Glasgow Institute exhibitions.

21. At the Exhibition, opened in Glasgow on 18 January 1890 at the Corporation Galleries, Walton could see copper and brass repoussé work by Ashbee's Guild, textiles by Morris & Co., Thomas Wardle (see n. 39), Voysey and Day, and frieze panels by Walter Crane. The St Peter's job was probably started in the summer, see *St Mary's Glasgow Magazine* (Sept. 1890) p. 98.

22. *Glasgow P. O. Directory* 1891-2. This expansion was probably completed in the early part of the year (see n. 3). St Peter's was reopened on 5 Feb. 1891.

23. Constance exhibited cartoons of her paintings at the Glasgow Institute in 1892 and 1893. Hannah first appears in 1890 as a teacher of painting and drawing, with Helen, at 2 Bothwell Terrace, Hillhead; see *Glasgow P. O. Directory* 1890-1.

24. Buchanan, *Mackintosh's Masterwork* p. 149.

25. Helen Law had employed Dora Walton as a governess to Lilian when she returned to painting after the death of her husband.

26. Undated programme, GWA. The performance must have taken place between E. A. Walton's marriage and George's as Helen and Kate are referred to as 'Mrs H. Walton' and 'Miss Gall'.

27. Information on the Gall family from Edward Walton and George Walton Scott. Details of George and Kate's marriage in GWA.

28. Rowntree was seven years older than Walton and had worked with the architects C. A. Bury and Edward Burgess before moving north: *Builder* (1927) pp. 88, 150. Helen Law's sister Mabel Henderson married a brother of Fred Rowntree's wife Mary Anna Gray (whose brother William became closely connected with Walton's firm). Information on Rowntree and Glasgow Quakers from Daniel Robbins. A large part of Stark's pre-1890 work was on churches and mission halls in Scotland.

29. W. J. Warren, *Amateur Photographer* (1899) pp. 251-2; William Buchanan, 'James Craig Annan: Brave days in Glasgow', in Mark Haworth-Booth, ed., *The Golden Age of British Photography 1839-1900* (London 1984), and Buchanan, *J. Craig Annan*.

30. Writing of 'I suppose about 1890-95', Annan recalled that Walton 'did a lot of work for our firm at that time in picture framing and in decoration of the premises. The frame mouldings were all his own design': letter from J. Craig Annan to John Betjeman, 21 Dec. 1933 (RIBA).

31. Annan seems to have had an agreement with Walton to photograph his interiors on a regular basis from 1889. Before 1952, Nikolaus Pevsner and Thomas Howarth saw a large collection of Annan's negatives of Walton's work: see Pevsner, 'George Walton' and Howarth, *Charles Rennie Mackintosh* pp. 234-5. Both refer to some locations of Walton's early work, and Thomas Howarth kindly supplied a copy of his notes listing negative numbers and descriptions. No company records or other documentation has survived from this period: since the loss of the negatives, Howarth's and Pevsner's written records have become a vital source of information on Walton's early career.

32. Walton's known commissions of 1891 are: interiors, The Glen, Paisley for Sir James Fulton, textile manufacturer (demolished); 15 Grosvenor Crescent, Glasgow for James Gardiner, shipping agent (interiors destroyed; window removed to GMAG); 5 Dundonald Road, Glasgow, for Frederick Gardiner, brother and partner of James Gardiner (windows and a possible Walton fireplace extant); interior decorations for E. A. Walton, probably at 203 Bath Street, Glasgow (destroyed); Thornton Lodge. 107 Sinclair Street, Helensburgh, for J. Whitelaw Hamilton, Glasgow Boy (interiors destroyed, Annan photographs at RIBA); shop for Neilson Shaw & MacGregor, silk merchants and drapers, probably at 40 or 44 Buchanan Street (destroyed); and, c. 1891-2, 7 Woodside Place for James Guthrie (some leaded windows, probably Walton's, remain).

33. Harrison, *Victorian Stained Glass*; Donnelly, *Glasgow Stained Glass*.

34. For Meikle & Sons and Adam, see Donnelly, *Glasgow Stained Glass*. Thirty-one Glass stainers, Embossers and Gilders were listed in the Trades section of the *Glasgow P. O. Directory* 1889-90.

35. See Donnelly, *Glasgow Stained Glass* pp. 26-7 and Billcliffe, *Glasgow Boys* pp. 265-7. For 'Three Musicians', see Fine Art Society, *Spring '86* (exhibition catalogue 1986) no. 138 (illus.).

36. See, e.g., 'Study for "Grandfather's Garden"' (illus. Billcliffe, *Glasgow Boys* p. 133), and 'Pink Geraniums' (illus. MacSporran, *Edward Arthur Walton* p. 43).

37. Howarth's comments on Frederick Gardiner's house show that Walton's decorations were quite unlike the window which survives: 'Generally he drew with broad precise lines' but 'in the hall at Sir Frederick Gardiner's house ... they approach the vigour of Horta's threshing, vermicular scrolls'. (*Charles Rennie Mackintosh* p. 234.)

38. Now in GWA.

39. Information on the fireplace from the late Mrs Purvis, daughter of J. Whitelaw Hamilton. The Wardle fabric was illustrated in *Academy Architecture* (1891) p. 64.

40. For James Morton and Alexander Morton & Co., see Morton, *Three Generations*. James Morton's collection of Italian textiles is now in the collection of Courtaulds plc.

41. Photographs of the Thornton Lodge drawing room at RIBA.

42. Walton's lecture notes, *c.* 1900 (RIBA).

43. Howarth, *Charles Rennie Mackintosh* p. 234.

44. Walton's lecture notes (RIBA). For Leiper's interior at Park Circus, see *Academy Architecture* suppl. (1891) p. 127.

45. See Nikolaus Pevsner, *Studies in Art, Architecture and Design* ii (London 1968) p. 184. Voysey seems the more likely influence, as Mackmurdo almost always set a background pattern against a main design which showed a good deal of movement.

46. See the background of a glass slide at the V&A of Walton's furniture (pl. 26), the ceiling design at Drumalis (pl. 35), the mosaic panel at Elm Bank (pl. 81), and elsewhere.

47. See n. 32.

48. Or red and brown, the tints of some of Annan's prints. Annan's beach scenes are clearly influenced by Whistler's watercolours of Southend, St Ives and the River Thames. See 'North Holland in Glasgow', *BJP* (1892) pp. 697-8; also William Buchanan, 'J. Craig Annan and D. Y. Cameron in North Holland', in Weaver, *British Photography* pp. 261-71.

49. The photographs of 230 Sauchiehall St in *Amateur Photographer* (1899) pp. 251-2 are taken to be the work of 1892 as the same early stencil from Thornton Lodge is used on the frieze. Annan wrote that Walton decorated T. & R. Annan & Sons' premises between 1890 and 1895 (n. 30).

50. *Amateur Photographer* (1900) p. 83.

51. *Amateur Photographer* (1899) p. 251.

52. *BJP* (1892) pp. 697-8. The reeded moulding referred to is on the frame of 'Dutch Dog Cart' (pl. 28).

53. The company's label has been found on the frame of one of Jackson Walton's paintings (coll. G. W. Scott). Several early paintings by Edward in their original frames have been examined. 'Sybilla' is in the collection of the Provinciaal Museum voor Fotografie, Antwerp.

54. 1892, when Warneuke moved his studio from 127 to 153 Sauchiehall Street, is the most probable date for the refurbishment: see *Glasgow P. O. Directory* 1891-3. For illustrations, see *Amateur Photographer* 29 (1899) pp. 331-2 and *Photogram* (1901) p. 244.

55. Although Howarth's description of the wall pattern at Dundonald Road suggests parallels (see n. 37).

56. A photograph of the gate (no longer *in situ*) was shown to the author by the late Mrs Purvis, daughter of Whitelaw Hamilton.

57. William Kellock Brown (1856-1934) was teaching at the Glasgow School of Art from 1887, but did not run a workshop until 1892 when he set up as 'Sculptor' at 138 Wellington St. See GMAG, *The Glasgow Style* pp. 13-14.

58. On the stair of 4 Devonshire Gardens, Glasgow, this window was probably designed in 1892. Part was shown at the Glasgow Institute exhibition in early 1893 (cat. no. 775), and the whole window was photographed by Annan in 1894 (RIBA). For Burrell see Richard Marks, *Burrell: A Portrait of a Collector* (Glasgow 1983). The lancet panel (photograph by Annan, 1894, at RIBA), was presumably for a church commission.

59. Peacocks were used on the company's hoarding at Buchanan Street (1896) (pl. 65) and on the company's seal (1896) and shopfront (1899) (pl. 97).

60. A fireplace in one room is marked with Sir Hugh Smiley's initials and '1893'. The windows in the hall are signed George Walton & Co. (suggesting a pre-1896 date as the company then became limited). In colour and design they are linked with the ceiling which appears stylistically to be early, and is likely to have been executed in 1893 with the other dated work. Much of Walton's stained glass, some door handles, the painted ceiling and a considerable amount of woodwork, assumed to be Walton's (see below) remain. Sir Hugh Smiley, married to a member of the Coats family of Paisley, was a patron of the Glasow Boys.

61. The brass floor plate on the swing doors to the billiards room is marked 'George Walton & Co. Ltd Glasgow', suggesting at least some work was carried out after 1896 when the firm became a limited company.

62. For Gray Dunn & Co.'s factory extension at 115 Stanley Street, Kinning Park, Glasgow, designed in 1893 and built 1893 and 1897, see John R. Hume, *The Industrial Archaeology of Glasgow* (1974) p. 242. The biscuit factory was a short walk from William Gray's home, Bedford House, 44, Maxwell Drive, which Walton later decorated. William Gray and George Walton were related by marriage through the Hendersons (see n. 28). Gray became a director of Walton's firm. Drawings by Stark & Rowntree for Neilson Shaw & Macgregor's shop at 56 Buchanan Street are in Strathclyde Regional Archives (Dean of Guild 1/3910).

63. *Hints on Household Taste* (London 1868).

64. Alan Calder, *James MacLaren 1853-1890: Arts and Crafts Architect* (London 1990) pp. 7-8.

65. For 'Furniture Warehouses', see *Glasgow P. O. Directory* 1891-2; for 'Cabinet Makers', see *Glasgow P. O. Directory* 1892-3.

66. Glass slides (V&A). The wallpaper behind the glazed cabinet (the company's registered design of 1890) suggests this photograph was taken at an early date. For Annan's spindleback, visible in the photograph of his showroom published in 1899, see *Amateur Photographer* (1899) p. 251 ('A Portion of the Reception Room and Gallery') (pl. 27). Howarth thought that, with few exceptions, the pre-1896 furniture was 'quite without distinction, revealing little evidence of the refined and elegant forms he eventually achieved' (p. 234). This implies that Walton's most characteristic designs, such as the 'Abingwood' and the Sheraton-inspired, black-caned chair, both used in his 1896 interiors, did not appear in the missing 1890-95 photographs.

67. For first entries for Cranston and Cochrane at East Park, see Slater's *Directory for Scotland* 1893. Parts of the scheme at East Park, Carlibar Road, Barrhead, are still *in situ*; see *Glasgow Herald*, 'Weekender' 6 June 1981, p. 7. Annan's photograph of the original interior can be dated 1894 by linking its negative number (11315) with the location list provided by Howarth: see *Amateur Photographer* (1899) p.

112 ('Decoration of a Drawing Room').

68. Fitted cupboards around the wall in one room at Drumalis show an earlier attempt to integrate furniture.

69. The only available photographs of this wall pattern, which is now papered over, are double-exposed. A photograph of Walton's piano design, taken by J. C. Annan, is in the collection of T. & R. Annan & Sons Ltd. The piano design was probably the one exhibited by Walton at the Glasgow Institute exhibition of 1895 (cat. no. 237/2).

70. Kate Gall later exhibited embroidery at the Arts and Crafts Exhibition of 1903 and completed work for Walton's Log Cabin houseboat, see p. 135.

71. The Exhibition was held from 6-11 April 1895. All quotations from *Glasgow Herald* 8 April 1895, p. 13; other information from the catalogue of the exhibition, designed by Walton (GWA).

72. De Courcy Lewthwaite Dewar, *History of the Glasgow Society of Lady Artists' Club* (privately printed 1950) p. 13. This history is written with hindsight, as Walton could hardly have been described as an architect in 1895. See also Glasgow Society of Women Artists, *Lady Artists*.

73. *Gentlewoman* 21 Dec. 1895, p. 849.

74. A note written by Voysey in 1933 records that he had known Walton intimately for forty years (RIBA).

III   TEA ROOMS AND INTERIORS, 1896-1897

1. There is no record of any involvement by the Walton sisters in the firm's interior work after 1891.

2. For Walton's 'Clutha' glass visible in his 1896 interiors, see p. 109 f.

3. *Glasgow P. O. Directory* 1893-96. 24 Renfrew St, for cabinet-makers, was set up c. 1893; 82 Sauchiehall Lane, for painters and paperhangers, was taken on c. 1895.

4. For instance, a Mission Hall and Institute for the Society of Friends in Scarborough, and Rowntree's Cocoa Factory (exhibition catalogues, 1890-5). Their Glasgow work included a temporary iron church (1891); the shopfront for Neilson Shaw & Macgregor (1895); Gray Dunn & Co.'s biscuit factory extension (1894 & 1897); and a competition design for the Glasgow Art Gallery (1892).

5. The Fancy Fair raised £2,777 3s 7d. The Lady Artists had occupied the building since 1893: the decision to purchase when the lease ran out in Nov. 1896 rested on the practicality of building a gallery extension. See *Bailie* 11 Dec. 1895, p. 2; Dewar (ch. II, n. 72); and Glasgow Society of Women Artists, *Lady Artists*.

6. In Strathclyde Regional Archives (Dean of Guild 1/4463).

7. The remaining work cannot be clearly dated because of a lack of early photographs, and a fire in May 1901. The style of surviving stained glass, fireplaces and metalwork is that of Walton's earlier period; so it is probable that in 1901 Walton & Co. was called in merely to reinstate the original.

8. For attribution of the fireplace, sometimes associated with Mackintosh, see *Charles Rennie Mackintosh Society Newsletter* 49 (1988) pp. 3-4. For the *History* see n. 5.

9. *Studio* 1 (1893) p. 216; 7 (April 1896) p. 155.

10. E.g. the fireplace by George Jack, made by Longden & Co., shown at the Arts and Crafts Exhibition of 1893 (where Walton also exhibited), illustrated *Studio* 2 (1893) p. 20.

11. Rowntree liked exposed timber, and went on using it. Other examples include the Friends' Meeting House, Scarborough (1896), the café for John Rowntree (see below), and three interiors illustrated in *Studio Year-Book of Decorative Art* (1907) pp. 68-9.

12. Much of the original woodwork remains at Glen Bank, Beechmount Road, Lenzie. Annan recalled that 'the dining room furniture, gate-table, chairs etc. were made by (Walton), and I have some other odd chairs': letter from J. C. Annan to J. Betjeman, 21 Dec. 1933 (RIBA). A high-backed, upholstered arm chair by Walton, similar to the one in the Ledcameroch drawing room (see pl. 73), which survived in the house until recently, may have been part of the original commission.

13. For the Frensham house, see the exhibition catalogue of Glasgow Institute of the Fine Arts, 1895; for Walnut Tree Farm, *Academy Architecture* (1895) suppl. p. 10. Rowntree exhibited his Glen Bank porch in 1898 at the Glasgow Institute.

14. Particularly Barry Parker & Raymond Unwin's garden village built for Joseph and Seebohm Rowntree from 1902.

15. For William Rowntree & Sons, see the company's archive in the North Yorkshire County Record Office, Northallerton; for John Rowntree & Sons, the records of the firm and surviving invoices from Walton, held by Richard Taylor; see also Moon, 'George Walton & Co.' For Scarborough, see Arthur Rowntree, *History of Scarborough* (London 1931).

16. Advertisement in the archive of William Rowntree & Sons (n. 15).

17. C. J. Taylor in records of John Rowntree & Sons (n. 15) Nothing survives *in situ*.

18. According to his son, Walton was a regular subscriber to *The Studio*. For Rowntree's interest in interior decoration, see his designs for a fireplace and door furniture at the Glasgow Architectural Association Exhibition of 1898, *British Architect*, 2 Dec. 1898.

19. M. H. Baillie Scott, 'The Fireplace of the Suburban House', *Studio* 6 (1895) pp. 101-8, from which quotations in this paragraph are taken.

20. For James Marshall's house, see below pp. 49 f. and n. 38.

21. *British Architect* 47 (1897) pp. 200-1.

22. For Walton's invoices, see n. 15.

23. *Amateur Photographer* (1899) p. 111.

24. David Park Curry, *James McNeill Whistler at the Freer Gallery of Art* (New York & London 1984) p. 22.

25. For Whistler's and Godwin's decorative schemes, see particularly, Aslin, *E. W. Godwin*; also Charlotte Gere, *Nineteenth Century Decoration: The Art of the Interior* (London 1989) pp. 279-80, 328-9.

26. See John Rowntree & Sons records (n. 15). Galleons were often used by William De Morgan and Ashbee. For emblems and symbols in the Arts and Crafts Movement, see Crawford, *C. R. Ashbee* pp. 221-31.

27. *Glasgow P. O. Directory* 1899-1900. Metalwork was included in the list of the firm's activities in 1897: see Memorandum of Association of George Walton & Company, Limited (Scottish Record Office BT2/3457/1) p. 1.

28. See, e.g., Nelson Dawson, 'Concerning repoussé metal work', *Studio* 2 (1894) pp. 195-9. Voysey's cabinet at the Arts and Crafts Exhibition of 1893 had prominent repoussé hinges.

29. For the history of Arts and Crafts metalwork, see Crawford, *C. R. Ashbee* pp. 313 ff.

30. *Studio* 5 (1895) pp. 66-74; *Art Journal* (1895) pp. 91-3; see also Crawford, *C. R. Ashbee* pp. 297-304.

31. The firedogs are now in the V&A.

32. Aslin, *E. W. Godwin* pp. 10, 33. For Walton's use of the *caquetoire* (or *caqueteuse*) and other Scottish forms, see Jones, 'Scottish furniture types'.

33. 'Abingwood' is Walton's name for the chair; see his Design Ledger (RIBA).

34. *Century Magazine* 56 (1912) pp. 505, 507. Some of Whistler's furniture can be seen at the Hunterian Art Gallery, University of Glasgow. See also Frances Collard, 'The Regency Revival', *Journal of the Decorative Arts Society 1890-1940* 8 (1983) pp. 7-18. For Walton's use of Sheraton arm construction and its place within the Scottish tradition, see Jones, 'Scottish furniture types'.

35. See John Rowntree & Sons records (n. 15).

36. Walton's tea room of *c.* 1897 was apparently on the ground floor of the main building; nothing remains of it, but there is a fireplace on an upper floor and stained glass in the extension, both by Walton; see *Decorative Kunst* 5 (1899-1900) pp. 139, 141, 144, photographs in RIBA and GWA, and a watercolour of the interior in the archive of William Rowntree & Sons (n. 15) (pl. 56).

37. Some rather clumsy leather-upholstered chairs were also used (photographs RIBA and GWA).

38. Marshall's room (so far unlocated) is illustrated in *Dekorative Kunst* 5 (1899-1900) p. 137 and Holme, *Domestic Architecture and Decoration* p. 195. Marshall was one of the firm's directors when Walton & Co. became a limited company in 1897; see also p. 57.

39. A photograph of this fabric, since covered by new upholstery, was kindly shown to me by Mrs D. Duncan, a previous owner of Glen Bank.

40. The Dean of Guild reported work on the interior from 26 Nov. 1896 (Strathclyde Regional Archives). The first date on the John Rowntree's bills is 31 March 1896; the final bill was submitted 9 Dec. 1896, five months earlier than Buchanan Street's opening on 5 May 1897 (*Bailie* 5 May 1897, p. 6). For a general discussion of the Buchanan Street tea rooms, see Kinchin, *Tea and Taste*.

41. E.g. from Glasgow Boy Alexander Roche, *Quiz* 15 Nov. 1894; see Elizabeth Bird, 'Ghouls and Gaspipes: public reaction to early work of the Four', *Scottish Arts Review* 14 (1975) pp. 13-16; Burkhauser, *'Glasgow Girls'* pp. 85-9.

42. See Howarth, *Charles Rennie Mackintosh* p. 124.

43. For Mackintosh's contribution to Buchanan Street and the division of work, see Gleeson White, 'Some Glasgow Designers and their Work (Part 1)', *Studio* 11 (1897) pp. 92-7; Billcliffe, *Charles Rennie Mackintosh: The Complete Furniture* pp. 38-41; Kinchin, *Tea and Taste*.

44. Gleeson White (n. 42) p. 97.

45. See Walton's lecture notes (RIBA) and p. 113.

46. His series of still-life paintings in the 'spindleback' dining room (pl. 61) are a modernised version of the historic Persian decorative form popular in the 1870s with designers like William Burges and Alfred Waterhouse.

47. The light fittings in this room were possibly by Mackintosh (see Billcliffe, *Charles Rennie Mackintosh: The Complete Furniture* p. 41), though in another room they are unquestionably Walton's: e.g. the elaborate spherical fitting, ingeniously linked in design to the murals in the 'spindleback' room, see *Dekorative Kunst* 5 (1899-1900) p. 146.

48. Clayre Percy and Jane Ridley, eds, *The Letters of Edwin Lutyens to his Wife Lady Emily* (London 1985) pp. 50, 56-7.

49. *British Architect* (1897) pp. 200-1.

50. For Voysey's wallpapers see, for example, *Studio* 7 (1896) p. 209; for the comparable Henry Wilson design, *Studio* 2 (1893) p. 22.

51. Richard Ellmann, *Oscar Wilde* (London 1987) p. 152; costume descriptions p. 157.

52. Was the large scale of Mackintosh's decoration in the Ladies' Room encouraged by Walton? It was unusual for Mackintosh to work on this scale, while Walton was convinced (through the advice of Morris) of the value of large-scale decorations. (See lecture notes, RIBA.)

53. *Studio* 2 (1894) p. 185; *Art Journal* (1892) pp. 132, 135.

54. The Ball took place on 4 Dec. 1896 at St Andrew's Hall in aid of the Scottish Artists' Benevolent Association: *Glasgow Herald* 5 Dec. 1896, pp. 4, 8. Warneuke set up a photo studio in an adjacent room and some of the artists present made sketches of the guests in costume.

55. Recorded by Janet Forbes on 18 Dec. 1896 (diary in the possession of Felicity Ashbee).

56. Letter from E. A. Abbey to E. A. Walton, 1 Dec. 1896 (album in the possession of Felicity Ashbee).

57. Muthesius, *The English House* p. 51.

IV TRANSITION

1. Minute of Agreement between George Walton and William Philp, 11 Feb. 1897 (Scottish Record Office BT2/3457/5).

2. See ch. II, n. 28.

3. Memorandum of Association of George Walton & Company, Limited, 8 March 1897 (Scottish Record Office BT2/3457/1) p. 1.

4. For the founders of the company see Memorandum of Association (n. 3) p. 4. Shareholdings are listed in Summaries of Capital and Shares (Scottish Record Office BT2/3457).

5. J. Bolton to Edward Walton, 17 Nov. 193(4?) (RIBA).

6. For Bolton, see Jill Lever, 'A. T. Bolton, architect', in John Newman, ed., *Design and Practice in British Architecture: Studies in Architectural History presented to Howard Colvin (Architectural History* 27 [1984]) pp. 429-42.

7. Kelly's *P. O. Directory* for London 1898-1901, after which time he was listed under 'Architects'.

8. *Century Magazine*, 61 (1912) p. 501, and Taylor, *Whistler* p. 90.

9. C. R. Ashbee, 'The Ashbee Memoirs' vol. 1, *c.* 1938 (unpublished typescript, V&A). For 'The Architect as Artist', see Mark Girouard, *The Victorian Country House* (rev. edn, London & New Haven 1979) pp. 67-8.

10. H. J. L. J. Masse, *The Art-Workers' Guild 1884-1934* (Oxford 1935) p. 7; see also Royal Pavilion, Art Gallery and Museums, Brighton, *Beauty's Awakening*.

11. For all details of Walton's contract with the company, see Minute of Agreement between George Walton and William Philp (n. 1).

12. A. C. R. Carter in *Photograms of 1900* (1900) pp. 109-10. For The Linked Ring, see Harker, *The Linked Ring*.

13. 'Selector', in *Linked Ring Papers: An Intermittent Journal* 10 Nov. 1896 (Royal Photographic Society, Bath).

14. *BJP* (1897) p. 645.

15. *Photography Annual for 1898* (1898) pp. 318-19.

16. For a detailed description, see *Photography Annual for 1898* (n. 15).

17. Quotations in this paragraph from *Photograms of 1897* (1897) p. 94; *BJP* (n. 14); and *Photography Annual for 1898* (n. 15).

18. *Photography Annual for 1898* (1898) p. 319; *Amateur Photographer* (1897) p. 322.

19. *Photograms of 1897* (1897) p. 94.

20. Taylor, *Whistler* p. 107.

21. George Walton to John Betjeman, 1 June 1933 (RIBA). For Whistler's exhibitions see Taylor, *Whistler*, and Jan Hunt 'J. M. Whistler as a Designer and Decorator' (Birmingham Polytechnic Dissertation 1976).

22. *Photography Annual for 1898* (n. 15).

23. *The Photogram* (1897) pp. 318-19.

24. Davison moved to Beechcroft, The Park, East Molesey (now 19 Spencer Road) in 1897 and Walton probably decorated the house then: Walton called the chair used in 1898 in the hall at Elm Bank the 'Beechcroft' (Design Ledger, RIBA). The Beechcroft interior has gone, but a photograph of the high-backed settee in one room (pl. 142) is in GWA .

25. For Davison, see Brian Coe, 'George Davison: Impressionist and Anarchist', in Weaver, *British Photography* pp. 215-41; and Ronald Davison 'The Family Record' (manuscript in possession of David Davison, 1953).

26. Reviews in *The Photogram* (1897) pp. 372-4; *Amateur Photographer* (1897) p. 375; *BJP* (1897) p. 697; *The Practical Photographer* (1897) pp. 368-70; *Camera Notes* (1898) pp. 98-9.

27. *Amateur Photographer* (n. 26).

28. *The Photogram* (n. 26). For attendance figures, see the 'Portfolio of Royal Pictures shown at the Eastman Exhibition' in the collection of Kodak Ltd.

29. A picture book by William Nicholson bought for Marguerite was inscribed by Kate in Glasgow on 20 Dec. 1897. (In the possession of George Walton Scott.)

30. *Building News* (20 Jan. 1899) pp. 91, 94-5, 9, 98-9; *Academy Architecture* 13 (1898) pp. 70-2. The house has been demolished.

31. For Voysey connections, see Pevsner, 'George Walton' p. 105. For the Hans Road staircase, see *Studio* 1 (1893) p. 225.

32. Howarth, *Charles Rennie Mackintosh* p. 236.

33. The Cabin was at 105 St Vincent St, The Anchor at 40 Gordon St, The Orient at 91 Hope St, and The Mecca at 17 Bothwell St. The Mecca opened in January 1897; the others were described as having been 'lately carefully overhauled' in *Bailie* 28 April 1897, p. 12. Walton & Co.'s work is evidenced by Howarth's list of Annan photographs (see ch. II, n. 31)

34. Probably Bedford House, 44 Maxwell Drive, Pollokshields, Glasgow, now demolished. See W. Gray to J. C. Annan 27 Dec. 1933 (RIBA).

35. For Brahan, Perth, see p. 111.

36. Sidney Leetham bought Elm Bank for £10,000 on 18 April 1898 (title deeds in possession of the owners, 1980). As Walton's work was executed during 1898 (date on the dining-room fireplace), planning may have started before the sale was completed. The job may have come through Rowntree, as Leetham was a Quaker.

37. For a full description of Elm Bank, from which this quotation comes, see *Studio* 22 (1901) pp. 36-42.

38. See *Builders' Journal and Architectural Record* 12 (1900) pp. 267 ff.

39. For the Davy Hall Restaurant, see *Architectural Review* 10 (1901) pp. 38-9.

40. Thomas Howarth, 'The Arts and Crafts Revival', in W. A. Singleton, ed., *Studies in Architectural History* (York 1954)

p. 73. Howarth attributes the interior of the Davy Hall Restaurant to Walton; wrongly, as the list of contractors in *Architectural Review* shows (see n. 39).

41. The design was awarded a National Gold Medal at South Kensington in the same year: see *Building News* 76 (1899) p. 233.

42. *Academy Architecture* 5 (1893) p. 41.

43. Walton's lecture notes, *c.* 1900 (RIBA).

44. Jack's use of stringing is discussed in Morris, *Inspiration for Design* pp. 145-7.

V 'DECORATOR-IN-CHIEF TO PHOTOGRAPHERS'

1. For a description of the 'new Palace of King Kodak', 41-3 Clerkenwell Road, see *BJP* (1898) p. 357. Original photographs of the Kodak shops are in the archive of Kodak Ltd and at the National Museum of Photography and Film, Bradford. Many are illustrated in Hermann Muthesius, 'Die Kodak-Läden George Waltons' pp. 201-21.

2. Walton later registered a very similar chair, known as the 'Cholmondeley'. (Public Record Office, Register of Designs BT50/459, No. 389,022).

3. The showroom was probably open by mid-1898. The hoarding was still up in April: see *Amateur Photographer* 27 (1 April 1898) p. 242, where the extent of the work is also mentioned; and *BJP* (8 April 1898) p. 219.

4. Edward Spenser (*sic*) 'afterwards connected with an Art Guild' is mentioned as Walton's assistant in a letter from J. Bolton to Edward Walton, 17 Nov. 193(4?) (RIBA). Edward Spencer was later a member of the Artificers' Guild and a prominent Arts and Crafts metalworker.

5. For St Stephen's National Schools, Paddington, see *Building News* (1900) p. 807, and drawings in RIBA.

6. *Building News* 76 (1899) p. 233; *BJP* (n. 3).

7. For distribution and marketing of furniture, see Pat Kirkham, Rodney Mace and Julia Porter, *Furnishing the World: the East London Furniture Trade 1830-1980* (London 1987).

8. *Amateur Photographer* 27 (1898) p. 242.

9. *Building News* 76 (1899) p. 233.

10. *Architectural Review* 14 (1903) pp. 80-1.

11. *Amateur Photographer* (1898) p. 270; *The Photogram* 5 (1898) p. 270.

12. *BJP* (1898) pp. 265-8.

13. *Photograms of 1898* 4 (1898) p. 20.

14. *Amateur Photographer* 28 (1898) p. 790.

15. *BJP* (1898) p. 644.

16. *Amateur Photographer* 28 (1898) pp. 790-1.

17. *Amateur Photographer* (1898) p. 375.

18. *Photograms of 1898* (n. 13).

19. *Amateur Photographer* (1899) p. 111.

20. *Photograms of 1898* (1898) p. 48.

21. R. C. Davison to Tom Jones, 17 July 1941 (Coleg Harlech Library, Harlech)

22. Walton had worked on Parkinson's premises, 50-1 High Street Doncaster *c.* 1898, though none of his work there has survived. (See RIBA Nomination Papers.) For Parkinson's shop, see T. G. Manby, *Doncaster Yesterday: No. 1 About the Town* (Doncaster 1980). For the Brussels front, see Muthesius, 'Die Kodak-Läden George Waltons' p. 216 and Horace Dan and E. C. Morgan Willmott, *English Shopfronts Old and New* (London 1907) plate 51.

23. *Architectural Review* 14 (1903) p. 83.

24. For shops in the 'Queen Anne' style including Deighton & Dunthorne's, see Girouard, *Sweetness and Light* pp. 197-201.
25. *Architectural Review* 14 (1903) pp. 79-80.
26. Dan and Willmott (n. 22) p. 34.
27. Register of Seisins for Glasgow.
28. Dean of Guild plans, Strathclyde Regional Archive (B4/12/1/7204). See also pp. 93-4. The building survives in a radically altered form, and the extension has disappeared.
29. Photograph in the V&A.
30. See *The Photogram* (1901) pp. 198-9; *Scots Pictorial* (1898) p. 165.
31. Both are reviewed in *Amateur Photographer* 30 (1899) pp. 408-9.
32. *Amateur Photographer* 30 (1899) p. 409.
33. *BJP* (1900) p. 631.
34. *Amateur Photographer* 32 (1900) p. 262.
35. For Dawson's slightly later shopfronts in Edinburgh and Glasgow for Jaeger, see Dan and Willmott (n. 22) pls 19, 23. He produced graphic work for Elliott & Sons and for *The Amateur Photographer*, and may have known Walton through Elliott & Son.
36. Dan and Willmott (n. 22) p. 36.
37. *Amateur Photographer* 34 (1901) p. 24. The hoarding is illustrated in Muthesius (n. 1) p. 202. Colin Campbell, *William Nicholson: the Graphic Work* (London 1992).
38. Alexandria was in emulation of Walton's style. See p. 81.
39. For Wellington & Ward's regular advertisements in *BJP*, see volumes for 1899-1900.
40. RIBA Nomination Papers (n. 22). The Milan showroom, *c.* 1902, was at 34 Corso V. Emanuele and the Vienna showroom, *c.* 1902, at Graben 29; the Moscow branch, which was at Grachev House, Petrovka, was refurbished between 21 July and 6 Oct. 1903 (unsigned drawings survive in the Moscow Historical Architectural Archive).
41. Muthesius, 'Die Kodak-Läden George Waltons'.
42. In Dublin the agent's name, Hurman Ltd, was retained on the shopfront for some years.
43. *Architectural Review* 14 (1903) p. 83.

VI   J. B. B. WELLINGTON AND THE LEYS

1. C. J. Todd 'Memories of Wellington & Ward Ltd' (manuscript in the possession of Sam Welford). See also Sam Welford, 'J. B. B. Wellington (Part 1)', *The Photo Historian* (Summer 1991) pp. 44-6; and Graham Balfour 'J. B. B. Wellington', in W. A. Boord, ed., *Sun Artists* (London 1891).
2. Walton designed an exhibition stand for Elliott's in 1900, possibly through Wellington's recommendation; see pp. 78-9.
3. Walton's lecture notes (RIBA).
4. *BJP* 44 (1897) p. 645.
5. Walton's lecture notes (RIBA).
6. Edward Walton in conversation with the writer.
7. For The Leys, see Muthesius, *The English House* p. 54; Margaret Richardson, *Architects of the Arts and Crafts Movement* (London 1983) pp. 123, 126-7. For illustrations of the interiors, see GWA, RIBA, and W. S. Sparrow, *The British Home of Today* (London 1904) pls C11, C13 & E13.
8. Mark Girouard, *The Victorian Country House* (revd edn London & New Haven 1979) pp. 46, 78-9. For Scott, see J. D. Kornwolf, *M. H. Baillie Scott and the Arts and Crafts Movement* (Baltimore & London 1972).

9. Muthesius, *The English House* p. 90.
10. Cited in Girouard (n. 8) p. 46.
11. Muthesius, *The English House* p. 90.
12. Howarth, *Charles Rennie Mackintosh* p. 238.
13. Broadleys was illustrated in *Studio* 16 (1898) p. 158.
14. For Shaw, see Andrew Saint, *Richard Norman Shaw* (New Haven & London 1976).
15. See Service, *Edwardian Architecture*; Girouard, *Sweetness and Light*.
16. Compare, for instance, his hall at Bedford, illustrated in *Academy Architecture* (1895) no. 1585. (Pl. 109)
17. *Studio* 21 (1900) pp. 242-3.
18. 25 Cadogan Gardens, London. The architect was Mackmurdo, the fittings made up in Japan. See *Studio* 17 (1899) pp. 170-8.
19. Walton's lecture notes (RIBA).
20. For Belcher's hall, see *Academy Architecture* 13 (1898) p. 39.
21. RIBA. GWA and Muthesius, *The English House* p. 54.
22. These, a revival of seventeenth-century detailing, were popular with progressive architects at the time.
23. Walton's lecture notes (RIBA).
24. Plans for Ault Wharrie, Leewood Road, were submitted to the Police Commissioners of the Burgh of Dunblane on 26 June 1900. Some of the glass, woodwork and other details of Walton's interior remain.
25. The door handles, designed by Voysey for Thomas Elsley Ltd, were illustrated in *Catalogue of Thomas Elsley Ltd: Designs by C. F. A. Voysey, Architect* (undated) p. 11, in the Voysey collection at the RIBA. Elsewhere, Walton specified cast-iron fireplace margins from Longden's catalogue (Design Ledger, RIBA); a surviving margin at The Leys, identical to the one Walton used at The Long Croft, Helensburgh (also 1901), may have been ordered from this firm.
26. C. R. Ashbee, ed., *Transactions of the Guild & School of Handicraft. Vol. I.* (London 1890) p. 27. The dining room is illustrated in Muthesius, *The English House+*, p. 178.

VII   THE COMPANY: PROSPERITY AND PASSING

1. A. T. Bolton to his wife, 7 and 8 March 1899 (RIBA).
2. J. Bolton to Edward Walton, 17 Nov. 193(4?) (RIBA).
3. 35-7 Buccleuch St was recorded as the new Registered Office on 7 June 1900 (Scottish Record Office BT2/3457/14).
4. For shareholders lists, see 'Summary of Capital and Shares', 30 Dec. 1899 (Scottish Record Office BT2/3457/13). The artisans James Wright and Stephen Downie, painters, and Duncan McLean, smith, appear as a group together with the known employees John Shedden and James Paterson for the first time on the shareholders list of 1899. McLean, who worked on his own as a smith until 1899, may have joined the company during this year. The promotion of Shedden, Wright and McLean to the status of 'Foremen' can be followed in the lists of subseqent years.
5. Agreements between George Walton & Co. and J. S. Cox (31 May 1899) and J. D. Laird (28 Oct. 1899), Register of Seisins for Glasgow.
6. Dean of Guild plans, Strathclyde Regional Archive, B4/12/1/7204. For further discussion of the plans, see p. 77 f.
7. The tile-making industry in Glasgow was insignificant: Stoke, the centre for tile-making in Britain, was the main source of the tiles used in Glasgow at this time. See Eliza-

beth Aslin, 'Tiles in the Nineteenth Century', in Jon Catleugh, *William De Morgan Tiles* (New York & London 1983) pp. 9-34. For Walton & Co.'s styling as Tile Makers, see 'Memorandum of Association of George Walton & Company, Limited', 8 March 1897, p. 1 (Scottish Record Office BT2/3457/1). A possible Walton & Co. tile design was included in a fireplace at 5 Dundonald Rd, Glasgow.

8. Walton & Co. installed parquet flooring, e.g., at Long Croft, Helensburgh for A. N. Paterson in 1901 at a cost of £8 15s. 6d (manuscript record of contractors in possession of Paterson's daughter in 1980); also at John Rowntree's (John Rowntree Archive in possession of Richard Taylor).

9. Memorandum of Association (n. 7).

10. *Studio* 11 (1897) p. 94. For Guthrie & Wells, see *British Architect* 49 (11 March 1898) p. 161-2, reviewing the 'just published' Guthrie & Wells catalogue (copy in Hunterian Art Gallery, University of Glasgow); see also GMAG, *The Glasgow Style* pp. 24-5.

11. For Scott Morton & Co., see Elspeth Hardie, 'William Scott Morton', in *Antique Collector* (March 1988) pp. 70-9, and 'Tynecastle Tapestry in the United States' (May 1989) pp. 108-15; and Elizabeth Cumming, 'A Gleam of Renaissance Hope: Edinburgh at the Turn of the Century', in Wendy Kaplan, ed., *Scotland Creates: 5000 Years of Art and Design* (London 1990).

12. Kinchin, 'Wylie and Lochhead' pp. 4-16.

13. Crawford, *C. R. Ashbee* p. 29, where the ethos of the Guild of Handicraft is explained.

14. Naylor, *Arts and Crafts Movement* p. 117.

15. Crawford, *C. R. Ashbee* pp. 30-1.

16. Harrison, *Victorian Stained Glass* p. 57.

17. Ray Watkinson, *William Morris as a Designer* (London 1967) p. 39.

18. Harrison, *Victorian Stained Glass* pp. 57-8. For Cottier's stained glass, see also Donnelly, *Glasgow Stained Glass*.

19. Gauld's 'Music' panels: see ch. II, n. 35. The influence of Japanese prints probably reinforced Walton's and Gauld's interest in outline and linear qualities combined with flat areas of colour.

20. For Stewart's window, see Donnelly, *Glasgow Stained Glass* p. 18; a photograph in RIBA provides a glimpse of the Thornton Lodge window.

21. There has always been some difficulty with the dating of this commission, but it is now clear that the rooms we know from *Studio* 39 (1906) pp. 32-4, were considered new by the public at the end of 1899 and could not have been completed by the widely accepted date of 1897. *Glasgow Advertiser and Property Circular* 24 Oct. 1899 reports the imminent completion of the Argyle Street premises ('Decorators have just put the finishing touches ...'), describing in detail the Luncheon Room, Billiards Room and Smoke Room as illustrated later in the *Studio* article of 1906. Miss Cranston's faith in Walton had not faltered over the years since she last employed him in 1896-7: she had bought £100 of the company's shares in the previous year.

22. *Studio* 39 (1906) p. 33.

23. *Glasgow Advertiser and Property Circular* 24 Oct. 1899. It is surprising to find, on the Argyle Street toilet doors, a leaded window copied almost directly from one by Baillie Scott in *Studio* 5 (1895) p. 21.

24. According to Donnelly, *Glasgow Stained Glass* p. 22 and n. 101, much of Walton's glass prior to 1898 was executed by James Benson at Blythswood Stained Glass; I have not

been able to verify the reference for this.

25. According to the occupiers of 1980 who saw the lower panels before they were destroyed.

26. Walton's lecture notes (RIBA): see p. 52.

27. See Gow, *Scottish Interior*.

28. Middlesex Polytechnic, *A London Design Studio 1880-1963: The Silver Studio Collection* (London 1980).

29. 28 Kensington Court was possibly designed for Louis Samuel Montagu, J.P.: the surviving contents of the interior, originally bought by The Fine Art Society, are now in a number of, mostly private, collections. For the Argyle Street billiards-room fireplace, see *Art et Décoration* 21 (1907) p. 166.

30. For Glasgow's metalworking skills as displayed at the 1888 and 1901 International Exhibitions, see Kinchin & Kinchin, *Glasgow's Great Exhibitions*.

31. For Arts and Crafts metalwork, see Crawford, *C. R. Ashbee* pp. 306-7, 313-44.

32. For a survey of the Victorian interior, see Cooper, *Victorian and Edwardian Furniture and Interiors*.

33. Walton's lecture notes (RIBA).

34. For Thomson, see Ronald McFadzean, *The Life and Work of Alexander Thomson* (London 1979).

35. All quotations in this paragraph from *Studio* 39 (1906) pp. 33-5.

36. See Mary Comino, *Gimson and the Barnsleys: 'Wonderful furniture of a commonplace kind'* (Evans Bros 1980).

37. Girouard, *Sweetness and Light* pp. 130-8.

38. Parry, *Textiles*.

39. For Alexander Morton & Co., see Morton, *Three Generations*. A piece of this fabric is now in the V&A.

40. Walton's lecture notes (RIBA).

41. Ill. in Taylor, *Whistler*, pp. 82, 132.

42. Walton's lecture notes (RIBA). See Malcolm Haslam, *Arts and Crafts Carpets* (London 1991).

43. For James Couper, see Brian Blench, '"From Coffee Machines to Clutha Glass": Notes on Couper's City Glassworks, Glasgow', in *Scottish Art Review* 17 (1991) pp. 12-15. For Dresser's Clutha glass, see Widar Halén, *Christopher Dresser* (Oxford 1990) pp. 192-6.

44. Halén (n. 43) p. 193. For the Liberty connection see also Barbara Morris, *Liberty Designs: 1874-1914* (London 1989) pp. 70-2.

45. See GMAG, *The Glasgow Style*; Burkhauser, *'Glasgow Girls'*; and Buchanan, *Mackintosh's Masterwork*.

46. Walton's lecture notes (RIBA).

47. *Builder* 75 (1898) p. 215.

48. See a photograph of the interiors in *Dekorative Kunst* 6 (1902) p. 96.

49. *Dekorative Kunst* 6 (1902) pp. 92, 96.

50. Papers and furniture relating to this commission are now in GMAG.

51. Paterson's daughter, the late Miss Paterson, kindly showed me the record of contractors made by her father. The attribution of the stencils to Walton, but not the furniture, is made on stylistic grounds.

52. M. H. Baillie Scott, *Houses and Gardens* (London 1906) pp. 202-6; see also Muthesius, *The English House* p. 165.

53. Furniture pricing from the Paterson papers, see n. 51. For Walton's contract terms, see 'Minute of Agreement entered into between George Walton and William Philp' 27 May 1897 (Scottish Record Office, BT2/3457/5). The commission figure, based on the 1897 contract agreement, is

likely to have been raised by 1900 when the Bickley work was carried out.

54. For the Glasgow Style and its designers, see GMAG, *The Glasgow Style*; Burkhauser, *'Glasgow Girls'*; Larner, *The Glasgow Style*.

55. For MacNair, see Roger Billcliffe, 'The Mackintosh Circle Part IV: James Herbert MacNair 1868-1955', in *Charles Rennie Mackintosh Society Newsletter* (1982) no. 33; and *Studio* 11 (1897) pp. 225-36.

56. For the Macdonalds, see Studio 11 (1897) pp. 86-100; Pamela Reekie, 'The Mackintosh Circle Part II: Margaret Macdonald Mackintosh', in *Charles Rennie Mackintosh Society Newsletter* (1981-2) no. 31; and Hunterian Art Gallery, University of Glasgow, *Margaret Macdonald Mackintosh 1864-1933* (exhibition catalogue 1983).

57. *Studio* 11 (1897) p. 232; pp. 225-36 cover various aspects of Morris's work. For his work for Blackie Books, see Gerald Cinamon, 'Talwin Morris, Blackie and the Glasgow Style' *Private Library* 10 (1987) pp. 3-47.

58. Colin White, *The Enchanted World of Jessie M. King* (Edinburgh 1989).

59. MacFarlane & Arthur, *Glasgow School of Art Embroidery*.

60. Holme, *Domestic Architecture and Decoration* pp. 143-6 and facing p. 40.

61. Billcliffe, *Charles Rennie Mackintosh: The Complete Furniture*. The few simple, abstract, stained-glass panels of Mackintosh's earliest furniture, *c.* 1893-4, cannot be compared to contemporary work by Walton, either in power or in quality, and Mackintosh appears to have made no significant contribution to stained glass until his Munich commission from H. Bruckmann of 1898. His later glass, with that of Oscar Paterson, E. A. Taylor and others, was important in forming the fully 'Glasgow Style' glass of post-1900, particularly as Walton's presence in Glasgow began to wane.

62. Howarth, *Charles Rennie Mackintosh* p. 126

63. *Cabinet Maker* 23 (1903) p. 190.

64. Buchanan, *Mackintosh's Masterwork*.

65. 'Proceedings of the Glasgow Architectural Society', 26 Feb. 1900; see also *Glasgow Herald* 27 Feb. 1900, p. 6. These reports suggest that Walton's lecture notes in the RIBA almost certainly relate to this occasion. Some of the slides Walton showed at this lecture may be among those now in the V&A.

66. *Studio* 39 (1906) p. 33.

67. Kinchin, 'Wylie and Lochhead' pp. 4-16; *Art Journal* (1901) pp. 237-43; Kinchin & Kinchin, *Glasgow's Great Exhibitions*.

68. *Art Journal* and Kinchin & Kinchin (n. 67).

69. For Walton's display, see *Art Journal* (1901) pp. 239-40, 275, and *Dekorative Kunst* 8 (1901) pp. 492-4. The style of Annan's picturesque exhibition building suggests it was designed by Walton.

70. *Builders' Journal and Architectural Record* 17 (1903) pp. 126-7, also describes the series of later tea rooms, as does Kinchin, *Tea and Taste*.

71. *Amateur Photographer* (1897) p. 322.

72. According to the late Miss Marjorie Dick, James Dick was more closely involved in the company than his brother Robert (Miss Dick's father), even though Robert was acting as chairman in 1905 (Miss Dick to the writer, 16 Aug. 1988). Robert Dick's house, Armadale, has lost its Walton contents. James Dick's Glasgow home, 11 Kelvin Drive, re-

tains some of Walton's interior woodwork and some fittings. Both houses were refurbished *c.* 1902. For Finnart House, see pp. 119 f.

73. Walton & Co.'s work on Hous'hill, amounting to £42 5s. 6d., is recorded in two entries (21 July 1904 and 3 Feb. 1905) in Mackintosh's job books (copies at the Hunterian Art Gallery, University of Glasgow). For Hous'hill, see Robertson 'Catherine Cranston'. A postcard of the John Rowntree Coronation decorations survives in the John Rowntree Archive held by Richard Taylor.

74. For Walton's career with the company, Scottish Record Office BT2/3457.

75. Scottish Record Office BT2/3457/23. See also *Edinburgh Gazette* (7 July 1905) p. 681.

76. 'Minute of Agreement entered into between George Walton and William Philp', 11 Feb. 1897 (Scottish Record Office BT2/3457/5).

77. Walton's lecture notes (RIBA).

78. Howarth, *Charles Rennie Mackintosh* p. 237.

79. Cited in David Park Curry, *James McNeill Whistler at the Freer Gallery of Art* (New York & London 1984) p. 67.

80. *Glasgow P. O. Directory* for 1900-4 shows that an additional workshop was set up at Dalhousie Street *c.* 1900; and new showroom at Mains Street *c.* 1903.

81. For the market in Arts and Crafts artifacts at this period, see Crawford, *C. R. Ashbee* pp. 144-5.

82. William Gray: J. Craig Annan to John Betjeman, 21 Dec. 1933 (RIBA). Robert Dick: Special Resolution of George Walton & Co. Ltd, 30 June 1905 (Scottish Record Office BT2/3457/23).

83. John Buchanan Dick: Gill Butler to Daniel Robbins, 15 Nov. 1992 (GMAG).

84. Edward Walton to the writer, 9 April 1981.

85. Local directories suggest the York office was closed *c.* 1901-2.

VIII HOLLAND STREET, 1901-1905

1. J. Bolton to Edward Walton, 17 Nov. 193(4?) (RIBA).

2. *Academy Architecture* 13 (1898) pp. 70-2; *Building News* (20 Jan. and 17 Feb. 1899); *Dekorative Kunst* 5 (1899-1900) pp. 132- 46; *Studio* 22 (1901) pp. 36-42; Holme, *Domestic Architecture and Decoration* pp. 195-206.

3. Walton's Design Ledger (RIBA); some drawings originally from this ledger are in GWA.

4. Jones, 'Scottish furniture types'.

5. For Mr Flausch, see p. 130.

6. Photographs of 44 Holland Street in RIBA and GWA; see also Muthesius, *The English House* p. 198; W. S. Sparrow, *The British Home of Today* (London 1904) pls C23 and C27. Two stained-glass panels in the house are highly uncharacteristic figure studies (plus an almost equally unusual design of flying birds), the only known figure panels between 1894 and 1922. The composition strongly recalls Burne-Jones's designs for Morris & Co. tiles, and painted details and shading, rarely used after 1894, are an essential part of the design.

7. Finnart House, 156 Oatlands Drive, Weybridge, Surrey has recently been demolished. Only photographs of the dining-room scheme have survived, see Muthesius, *The English House* pp. 172, 184, and GWA. It is not known whether the unusual rough-cast gate house was by Walton.

8. At The Phillippines, now Care Village, Ide Hill, Sevenoaks,

Kent, parts of the drawing room scheme remain (including the fireplace and frieze stencil). For photographs, see GWA and *Studio Year-Book of Decorative Art* (1907) pp. 79, 117.

9. Alma House, 73 Rodney Road, Cheltenham contains stained glass, fireplaces, architectural woodwork, metalwork, stencils, painted panels, etc. in much the same quantity as Elm Bank, York and Drumalis, Larne. Photographs in RIBA and GWA; see also *Studio Year-Book of Decorative Art* (1907) pp. 76-8, 99 (below), 116, 118. Sketches of furniture used at Alma House are in Walton's Design Ledger (see n. 3); also in a small group of colour sketches at RIBA, see Jill Lever, *Architects' Designs for Furniture* (London 1982) pp. 102-4.

10. See p. 28.

11. For the Ball exhibition, see *Berliner Architekturwelt* 8 (1906) figs 25, 31, 133-4, and pp. 26-8; *Deutsche Kunst und Dekoration* 16 (1905) pp. 396, 400, 402, 412, 414-17. See also Walton's 'Lancelot' series of designs (RIBA), and a 'Cabinet for Professor Alfred Grenarda' (*sic*) in Ledger sheets in GWA (n. 3).

12. For 11 Kelvin Drive see ch. VII, n. 72.

13. Stark suffered a breakdown in health and was drinking heavily when the partnership was dissolved; information from David Walker.

14. See, e.g., Sparrow (n. 6).

15. For Voysey's dislike of Classicism, see p. 165.

16. *Art Journal* (1901) p. 240.

17. *Cabinet Maker* 23 (1903) p. 190.

18. *Amateur Photographer* (1897) p. 322. For Gleeson White's articles, see *Studio* 11 (1897) pp. 86-100, 225-36; Muthesius, *The English House* p. 51.

19. Clayre Percy and Jane Ridley, eds, *The Letters of Edwin Lutyens to his Wife Lady Emily* (London 1985) p. 50; see pp. 54-5.

20. *Cabinet Maker* (March 1903) p. 266.

21. Elizabeth Aslin, 'Sir George Donaldson and "Art Nouveau" at South Kensington', *Journal of the Decorative Arts Society 1890-1940* 7 (1983) p. 11.

22. *Magazine of Art* (1904) p. 212.

23. H. J. Jennings, *Our Homes and How to Beautify Them* (1902).

24. Muthesius, *The English House* pp. 51-2.

25. *Dekorative Kunst* 5 (1899-1900) p. 133.

26. Muthesius, *The English House* p. 53.

27. *Amateur Photographer* (1900) p. 83.

28. George Walton to John Betjeman, 1 June 1933 (RIBA).

29. Elizabeth Aslin, *The Aesthetic Movement: Prelude to Art Nouveau* (London 1969) p. 65.

30. Walton's lecture notes (RIBA).

31. Cited in E. P. Thompson, *William Morris: Romantic to Revolutionary* (London 1977) p. 109.

32. For the stand, see *Dekorative Kunst* 6 (1903) p. 201; advertising material in the collection of Kodak Ltd.

33. For Judd's office, see *British Architect* 59 (1903) pp. 403-4. The studio was in Regent Street, where these 'Links' were both based in 1900, the date to which the interior can be stylistically dated.

34. Hermann Muthesius, *Das Englische Haus.*

35. *Dekorative Kunst* 5 (1899-1900) pp. 132-146; 8 (1901) pp. 489-96; 6 (1903) pp. 201-21.

36. *Berliner Architekturwelt* 8 (1906) p. 27; see also n. 11.

37. Goshawk's name appears on a photograph (RIBA) suggesting a domestic commission, although the photograph is of the Vienna showroom; his private residence has not been traced.

38. Morris, *Inspiration for Design* p. 72.

39. A copy of the Walton-decorated catalogue is in the V&A. For the exhibition, see Juliet Kinchin, 'Glasgow - Budapest, 1902', *Charles Rennie Mackintosh Society Newsletter* (1985) no. 41 pp. 4-6. For Walton's exhibits, see *Magyar Iparmüvészet* (1902) pp. 202, 207, 210.

40. *St Mungo* (13 May 1897) p. 4.

41. Cited in Gyöngyi Éri-Zsuzsa Jobbágyi, *A Golden Age: Art and Society in Hungary 1896-1914* (London & Miami 1990) p. 37.

42. George Walton to J. Radisics, 5 Dec. 1902 (National Museum of Applied Arts, Budapest).

43. For details of the purchase, see Jones 'Scottish furniture types' p. 66.

44. *Dekorative Kunst* 7 (1903) pp. 95-7, 100; *Innen-Dekoration* 15 (1904) p. 186. Walton's drawings of the 'Lovat' chair and related designs are in GWA; see pl. 153.

45. A client from Mainz might well have sought to emulate the Grand Duke of Hesse's furnishings at neighbouring Darmstadt. For Walton's design see the Design Ledger sheets (GWA).

46. For the 'Brussels' and 'Jordaens' furniture, see the Design Ledger (GWA and RIBA).

47. In order of mention: *Dekorative Kunst* (1901) p. 347; *Innen-Dekoration* 17 (1906) pp. 151, 161; Larner, *The Glasgow Style* ill. 28; *Dekorative Kunst* (1904) p. 68.

48. The Birch cost books are in the Chair Museum, High Wycombe, Bucks. Birch also had an office in London.

49. A note on Walton's drawing of the 'Jordaens' settee is inscribed 'made by Burch' (*sic*) and 'Drawing supplied to Mr. J. S. Henry' (see Ledger sheet in GWA). For the Arts and Crafts Exhibition 1903, see *Studio* 28 (1903) p. 29; for the Judd office, see n. 33.

50. *Cabinet Maker* (1903) p. 266.

51. See A&CES, *Catalogue* 1910; and *Studio Year-Book of Decorative Art* (1907) p. 98.

52. Photograph of a fireplace marked Elsley & Co. in RIBA.

53. *Art Journal* (1905) pp. 129, 284.

54. Now in the V&A.

55. Examples of Walton's glass are in the V&A and GWA. For the influence of historic examples at the V&A, see Morris, *Inspiration for Design* pp. 164-70.

56. Sketches in RIBA.

57. Notes by Edward Walton in GWA.

58. For the Goodyers connection, see *Studio Year-Book of Decorative Art* (1906) p. 26. For Liberty's, see particularly, 'Liberty Handbook of Sketches' p. 75 (V&A Library, 788/36/2).

59. Graham Balfour, 'J. B. B. Wellington', in W. A. Boord, ed., *Sun Artists* (London 1891).

60. Balfour (n. 59) p. 20.

61. *Amateur Photographer* (1897) p. 322.

62. Balfour (n. 59) pp. 20-1.

63. For Davison in this and the following section, see the sources quoted in ch. IV, n. 25, and Harker, *Linked Ring*.

64. See ch. IV, n. 24.

65. Davison, 'The Family Record' (n. 63).

66. R. G. M. Baker & G. Baker, *Thameside Molesey: A Towside Ramble from Hampton Court to Hampton Reach* (Barracuda Books 1989).

67. The Log Cabin houseboat is difficult to date. Ronald

Davison's 'Family Record' gives two conflicting dates, but 1902-3 fits more clearly into the general account. R. C. Davison to Tom Jones, 16 July 1941, suggests that the houseboat was in use before his trip to Harlech in 1905 (Coleg Harlech Library, Harlech). A drawing in RIBA, inscribed 225 High Street Kensington (Walton's address *c.* 1906), was probably made for the *Studio* article of June 1907 (pp. 62-3). All quotations in this section are from the *Studio* article. Photographs in RIBA, GWA, and in possession of David Davison.

68. Walton notes on the Log Cabin drawings 'The awning and fixings are to be similar in every respect to those on the "Alcedo".' (RIBA)

69. A photograph in GWA is so marked. A&CES, *Catalogue* 1903.

70. The dinner card is now in GWA.

71. J. Bolton to Edward Walton, 17 Nov. 193(4?): 'I believe that Walton moved to Kensington & tried to let a house, which involved him in a Lawsuit as I saw in the paper' (RIBA). Details of the lawsuit have not been traced.

72. Robert Paterson left George Walton & Co. *c.* 1901-2, and set up on his own as a 'cabinet maker, upholsterer, designer and decorator: stained and leaded glass' (*Glasgow P. O. Directory* 1903-4). In 1905 he joined forces with Stephen Adam jnr (from the stained glass firm of that name) to form The Crafts, at 302 Sauchiehall St, premises recently given up by Walton & Co. (*Glasgow P. O. Directory* 1905-6). This venture seems only to have lasted for a year. For the work of The Crafts, which plainly shows Walton's influence, see *Studio Year-Book of Decorative Art* (1907) pp. 65, 92-3.

IX ARCHITECT ALONE

1. R. C. Davison to Tom Jones, 17 July 1941 (Coleg Harlech Library, Harlech). There is some uncertainty in Ronald Davison's two accounts, of 1941 and 1953, as to when the Davisons first went to Harlech. See ch. IV, n. 25.

2. See Allan, 'George Walton at Harlech'.

3. Davison, 'The Family Record' 1953. See ch. IV, n. 25.

4. As this was Crown Land, Harry More would have been involved.

5. The site plan of Plas Wern Fawr, showing the house blocked in, refers to Mr Bowen-Jones's plan of the new road dated 2 Oct. 1906, but is not itself dated (RIBA). No other plans of Wern Fawr have survived. The house was not built until 1908, the date on a rainwater pipe on the building, corroborated by Ronald Davison's accounts.

6. See ch. VIII, n. 72.

7. For Spencer's later work, see *Studio Year-Book of Decorative Art* (1913) pp. 106-9, 111, and (1914) pp. 82-3.

8. For Elmdon & Co., see their catalogue in the V&A, and *Art Journal* (1905) pp. 188-9. The company was presumably named after Elmdon Hall, Warwickshire, which belonged to the Spooner family.

9. Plans dated 14 Jan. 1907, in the possession of the St David's Hotel in 1981. See also, 'Memorandum and Articles of Association of the Harlech Hotel and Land Development Syndicate, Ltd.', 6 June 1907, p. 5 (draft copy in Dolgellau Area Record Office, Gwynedd).

10. *Studio* (June 1907) p. 62.

11. Allan, 'George Walton at Harlech' p. 75.

12. Edward Walton in conversation with the author, 1980.

13. RIBA and GWA have many photographs of Wern Fawr;

see also *Studio Year-Book of Decorative Art* (1910) p. 86.

14. Photographs in GWA and RIBA.

15. Walton's lecture notes (RIBA), see p. 90.

16. *Architectural Review* 74 (1933) p. 151.

17. Muthesius, *The English House* p. 40.

18. Walton's signed plans for The White House are in RIBA: it is probable he was drawing up his own plans at this stage.

19. For the contemporary reception of The White House, see below and p. 179.

20. Jennifer Sherwood pointed out this connection in J. Sherwood & N. Pevsner, *The Buildings of England: Oxfordshire* (Harmondsworth 1974) p. 757.

21. Joanna Symonds, *Catalogue of the Drawings Collection of the RIBA: C. F. A. Voysey* (1976) p. 9.

22. British contemporaries, in particular; the use of exposed structural metalwork on domestic buildings was accepted in France at an earlier date.

23. In his later work at Glasgow School of Art, he would add two fire-resistant staircases, one of them with a bowed cantilevered platform which resembles the balcony of The White House. (Designed from 1907, the School was not formally opened until December 1909.)

24. For Walton's drawing of the 'Thames' sideboard, see Ledger sheets in GWA. A set of photographs of The White House interiors is in the National Monuments Record.

25. One of these carpets is now in the V&A.

26. C. H. Hosken, Kingerlee's cost clerk, gives the clue: 'Previous to my association with T. H. Kingerlee & Sons ... I believe we carried out some works at Harlech, Wales and at Thames Valley'. (C. H. Hosken to the *Architectural Review*, 9 Jan. 1934, in RIBA.) A contract, probably for The White House, specifies Kingerlee's as the builders, who agree to execute the building for £3,044 (GWA).

27. Raymond McGrath, *Twentieth Century Houses* (London 1934) p. 80.

28. The surviving plans are dated 10 Jan. 1909 (RIBA). The date on the rainwater head is 1910.

29. Information on Miss Du Pre from R. E. Brinton of Carisbrooke Castle Museum.

30. Sketches, notes, contracts, photographs and records of meeting in GWA. The house was extended at a later date, and, later still, dismantled and removed to Perranarworthal, Cornwall.

31. Or was it at her instigation? Had Walton fallen under its spell? Whatever the case there is no doubt Osborne House stood behind the design that emerged.

32. Ronald McFadzean, *The Life and Work of Alexander Thomson* (London 1979).

33. For Elmdon Hall, see Roy Strong, Marcus Binney and John Harris, *The Destruction of the Country House 1875-1975* (London 1974) pl. 103.

34. See p. 24.

35. Nomination Papers (RIBA).

36. Sketch books in GWA.

37. Drawings for the frieze in the entrance hall, The Leys (RIBA).

38. A sketch by Walton records the guests, pl. 193 (GWA).

39. See n. 9 above.

40. For 1907 plans see n. 9 above; 1908 plans in RIBA.

41. For 72-5 Cheyne Walk, see Crawford, *C. R. Ashbee*, pp. 241-50.

42. Only photographs of the front elevation survive (RIBA). The hotel was greatly altered after a fire in 1922.

43. Contract in GWA gives detailed specifications, plans in RIBA show layout of furniture and rugs.

44. The Wern Fawr extension, particularly its interior, is well recorded in RIBA, GWA and the collection of Doreen Leslie Smith. See also *Studio Year-Book of Decorative Art* (1913) pp. 75-8.

45. Messrs Giddy & Giddy, Auction Brochure for the sale of 'Wernfawr Hall' on 18 July 1923 (Coleg Harlech). The house became Coleg Harlech, and Arthur Penty later made alterations to it. (Drawings in RIBA).

X UPHEAVALS

1. Photograph in RIBA.

2. The Phillippines mural survives in the original building, now Care Village, Ide Hill, Sevenoaks, Kent.

3. For the Beggarstaff Brothers, see ch. V, n. 37.

4. Original designs in RIBA.

5. Edward Walton in conversation with the author. For murals and the Art Workers' Guild, see Royal Pavilion, Art Gallery and Museums, Brighton, *Beauty's Awakening*.

6. Photograph in RIBA.

7. *Studio Year-Book of Decorative Art* (1910) p. 86.

8. Nomination Papers in RIBA; certificate in GWA.

9. For details of the Licentiateship scheme, see Barrington Kaye, *The Development of the Architectural Profession in Britain* (London 1960).

10. McIsaac was probably the eldest son of James Robertson McIsaac, a shipowner and Provost of Saltcoats, on the Ayrshire coast. The stained glass can be seen in photographs of the garden taken when the garden work was recently completed (GWA and RIBA). The external ironwork parallels that on the Duchy of Cornwall Estate, Kennington, of 1909 onwards. Most of the work described remains *in situ*.

11. Walton's plans, of c. 1909-16 to judge by Walton's address, include the furniture layout on the ground floor; drawings of the furniture are in the Design Ledger (RIBA). The interior has been destroyed.

12. Opening reported in *BJP* Feb. 1914. Photographs in RIBA and GWA.

13. Harker, *Linked Ring* p. 83. Sources for Davison in this chapter are as ch. IV, n. 25, and Margaret Morris, *The Art of J. D. Fergusson* (Glasgow 1974) (often inaccurate).

14. Judith Collins, *The Omega Workshops* (London 1983) p. 34.

15. 'The Insurgent Virus' (photocopy from an unrecorded source in the possession of D. Davison).

16. Letter from George Eastman to Davison, 25 June 1912, quoted in Weaver, *British Photography* p. 238.

17. Morris (n. 13) p. 133.

18. For Arbuthnot see Melinda Boyd Parsons 'Malcolm Arbuthnot: Modernism and the end of Pictorialism', in Weaver, *British Photography*.

19. C. H. Hosken to the *Architectural Review* 9 Jan. 1934 (RIBA). Photographs of the interiors at the Musical Museum, Brentford. Little survives *in situ*.

20. Hosken (n. 19).

21. Davison to Tom Jones, March 1913, cited in Coe (n. 13) pp. 238-9.

22. Cited in Victoria and Albert Museum, *British Art and Design 1900-1960* (London 1983) p. xviii.

23. George Bernard Shaw to Henry Wilson, cited in Elizabeth Aslin, 'Changing Taste and Influences, English Design 1900-1940', *Bulletin of the Decorative Arts Society 1890-1940* 1 (no date) p. 6.

24. *Amateur Photographer* 12 June 1916.

25. A list of Walton's surveys for the C.C.B. and photographs of his pub interiors are in RIBA. For the C.C.B. scheme see John Hunt, *A City Under the Influence* (Carlisle 1971); Basil Oliver, 'English Inns', *RIBA Journal* (14 May 1932) pp. 545-62; and Basil Oliver, *Renaissance of the English Public House* (London 1947). Little of Voysey's or Walton's work appears to have survived.

26. For Redfern's contribution to public house design see the titles by Basil Oliver in n. 25.

27. Hunt (n. 25) p. 19; Oliver, 'English Inns' (n. 25) p. 549.

28. Some of Voysey's designs are in RIBA.

29. All quotations are from Oliver, *Renaissance* (n. 25).

30. Note written at the time of Walton's death (RIBA).

31. The location of the Lion and the Lamb is not recorded: Walton's furniture drawings for the C.C.B. are in RIBA.

XI OLD FRIENDS

1. She worked for Louise Creighton on the Women's Advisory Committee; for her character, see job references in GWA.

2. In Chelsea Registry Office; marriage certificate in GWA.

3. George Davison to Tom Jones, March 1914, cited by Brian Coe in Weaver, *British Photography* p. 239.

4. Eugene Goossens,*Overture and Beginners* pp. 135, 137. Davison would play his mechanical organ 'at fantastic speed, producing unheard-of effects' which 'bewildered everyone, including the composer, who would rush to the organ and pull the control lever hard over to decelerate the headlong pace of his opus' (p. 137). For Davison in this chapter see also Margaret Morris, *The Art of J. D. Fergusson* (Glasgow 1974); Allan, 'George Walton at Harlech'; Coe (n. 3); Cyril Scott, *My Years of Indiscretion* pp. 238-41; correspondence with Edna Williams, in possession of the author, and with David Evans, in the possession of GMAG.

5. For Boult and Goossens, see Goossens (n. 4) p. 156; for Arbuthnot, Morris (n. 4) pp. 135-6.

6. In favour, Morris (n. 4) pp. 132-6; against, *BJP* 2 Jan. 1931, p. 5.

7. Information from title deeds in possession of the present owners; Davison's correspondence in Coleg Harlech library shows his concern for Walton.

8. Plans in RIBA.

9. The original church was in Braid Street, but a new church was built in Gardner Street in 1899, and Walton's reredos would have been installed there; both buildings have been demolished and the reredos is untraced. Photographs and drawings in RIBA; newspaper cuttings in GWA; C. H. Hosken to the *Architectural Review*, 9 Jan. 1934 (RIBA).

10. From a memorial pamphlet, *The Old Lady of Threadneedle Street*, Dec. 1921, in GWA; contract, specification, photographs and other papers in GWA. Holloway Bros of London did the work; Kingerlee's had not tendered.

11. For friendship with Grahame, author of *The Wind in the Willows*, see notes by Edward Walton in GWA.

12. The Stablers had been friends of the family for several years.

13. For Voysey and Classicism, information from John Brandon-Jones.

14. All quotations from *Individuality* (1915; repr. Shaftesbury

1986).

15. Kelly's *P. O. Directory* records Walton at 4 Raymond Buildings, Gray's Inn Road in 1915-16, and his residence at 43 Bullingham Mansions, Kensington Church Street, in 1920.

16. Gate lodge at The Leys: drawings at RIBA.

17. For the Sterne Street houses, which still stand, see the papers of T. H. Kingerlee & Sons.

18. The curving corners suggest his knowledge of this work.

19. Address on a drawing of this date for a loggia at The Leys (RIBA).

20. 12 Little Stanhope Street, Mayfair has been engulfed by a rebuilding programme. Sources include a letter from de la Valette of 1933 (RIBA), and Kingerlee's accounts. For John de la Valette, see Fiona MacCarthy, *All Things Bright and Beautiful* (London 1972) p. 106.

21. Fergusson had just settled at Cap d'Antibes when war was declared, forcing his return. See Crawford Centre for the Arts, St Andrews, *J. D. Fergusson* (exhibition catalogue 1982) p. 9.

22. *John Bull* 10 Sept. 1921, pp. 10-11; 21 Oct. 1921, p. 6.

23. Peter Stead, *Coleg Harlech: The First Fifty Years* (University of Wales Press 1977) p. 23.

24. Sale catalogue in the possession of Doreen Leslie Smith.

25. Edna Williams to the author, 20 Sept. 1980.

26. Voysey testimonial to Walton, 1933 (RIBA).

27. Edward Walton to P. J. Kendrick, 23 Nov. 1980 (GWA).

28. Drawings at RIBA. The glass may have been made by Lowndes & Drury of the Glass House, Fulham as a demand for payment addressed to Walton at 53 Sterne St survives.

29. Plans and elevations at RIBA.

30. Drawings at RIBA. Photographs by Wellington at Royal Photographic Society, Bath. As Hosken of Kingerlee's recalled, 'a nice job but we did not get it. I believe Long and Son of Bath carried out the work.' (Hosken, n. 9). Walton wrote a note on costs c. 23 Sept. 1924: 'Contract agreed for £5,626; extras amount to £1,082.2.5 - total = £6,708.2.5.' (GWA) The extras were steps and a fountain.

31. Details of 1920s projects for Wellington, including photographs of dining-room frieze and ceiling decorations, are at RIBA.

32. J. Bolton to Edward Walton, 17 Nov. 193(4?) (RIBA); see also ch. VIII, n. 71.

33. Edward Walton in conversation with the author.

34. The principal sources are in RIBA and GWA.

35. See n. 30.

36. References in GWA, one dated 1924.

37. Martin Battersby, *The Decorative Twenties* (London 1988) p. 23.

38. Buchanan, *J. Craig Annan*.

39. Furniture designs, 1926 and 1928; reredos for St Anne's, Derby, 1927; tabernacle for St John's, Lichfield, Staffs, 1927; proposed house at Stoke Park, Bucks for Mrs R. Hutchison (RIBA); textile designs now in V&A and some related drawings, sketches and photos in GWA.

40. Morton, *Three Generations*.

41. The letters are divided between GWA and the Morton Collection, V&A Archive of Art and Design.

42. Walton to David Craig, June 1927 (GWA).

43. David Craig to Walton, 24 June 1927 (GWA).

44. James Morton to Walton, 3 July 1928 (GWA).

45. All original designs for textiles are in V&A.

46. Walton to James Morton, 28 June 1929 (GWA).

47. Walton to James Morton, 25 July 1929 (GWA).

48. Note attached to a letter, Walton to James Morton, 22 Aug. 1929 (GWA).

49. Hutchison (1889-1971) was a portrait and landscape painter, who had studied in Edinburgh.

50. Hosken (n. 9).

51. Notes of travel expenses jotted on sketch plan. Drawings and photographs for The Old Vicarage, Letheringham, Woodbridge, Suffolk are in possession of the RIBA and the Hutchison family.

52. The contract went to a local firm, rather than Kingerlee's. Other Arts and Crafts architects, such as Ashbee and Percy Worthington, were also quietly Georgianising Victorian Gothic houses.

53. James Morton to Walton, 20 Jan. and 13 Feb. 1930 (GWA).

54. James Morton to Walton, 5 Aug. 1930 (GWA).

55. Walton to James Morton, 16 Sept. 1930 (V&A).

56. Walton to James Morton, 28 Nov. 1930 (V&A).

57. Walton to James Morton, 13 Feb. 1931 (V&A).

58. James Morton to Walton, 2 March 1931 (V&A).

59. James Morton to George Walton, 16 Sept., 23 Nov. 1927, 4 April, 25 Jan. and 21 April 1928; for 'Old Russia', David Craig (a Morton employee) to Walton, 21 June 1927 (GWA).

60. Noted by James Morton, 1929 (V&A).

61. Walton received very little money from the will of Kate Gall's parents.

62. *BJP* 2 Jan. 1931, p. 5.

63. Drawings for the Chapel of St George, Cap d'Antibes, in the RIBA; photographs in RIBA and GWA.

64. Walton to James Morton, 19 Oct. 1931 (V&A).

EPILOGUE

1. Correspondence relating to the planning of this exhibition is in RIBA.

2. Nikolaus Pevsner, 'George Walton' p. 543. Pevsner aimed that this article should remedy his omission of Walton from *Pioneers of the Modern Movement* (1936).

3. F. R. S. Yorke, 'The Modern English House: Introduction', *Architectural Review* 80 (London 1936) p. 237.

4. John Betjeman, 'There and Back: 1851 A.D. to 1933 A.D.: A history of the revival of good craftsmanship', *Architectural Review* 74 (1933) p. 6.

5. 'Edwardians', *Architectural Review* 75 (1934) p. 1.

6. Raymond McGrath, *Twentieth Century Houses* (London 1934) p. 81.

7. 'Edwardians' (n. 5), caption to plate I.

8. Walton's lecture notes (RIBA).

9. 'Edwardians' (n. 5).

10. George Walton to John Betjeman, 1 June 1933 (RIBA).

11. Francis H. Newbery in the introduction to David Martin, *The Glasgow School of Painting* (London 1897).

12. *Quiz* 16 Feb. 1893.

13. Betjeman expressed this viewpoint clearly in *Architectural Review* (n. 4) p. 8: on the failure of the 1912 Arts and Crafts Exhibition, a group of artists and craftsmen suggested a shop be opened in a place like Bond Street, but the Arts and Crafts Exhibition Society felt (as Betjeman explained) 'This would be competing with commerce on its own ground. The idea was rejected. Gentle folk can have nothing to do with the trade.'

BIBLIOGRAPHY

Note on sources

For many years, the chief source of available material on George Walton's life and work has been the collection of photographs and architectural drawings, with some related papers, passed by his surviving family to the RIBA. Walton's son, Edward, retained an even greater quantity of documents, sketch books, photographs and objects. It was his wish that this material should be freely available for use in the exhibition of 1993 at Glasgow Museum and Art Gallery, Kelvingrove, and in this book.

Edward Walton's collection, The George Walton Archive, will pass to the Victoria and Albert Museum's Archive of Art and Design, where it will be available to researchers. It will join the Museum's already significant collection of objects which includes furniture, table glass and vases, drawings for textiles, and objects in other media, reflecting Walton's broad range of design activities.

The collections at the RIBA and V&A will then form the two main archives for the study of Walton and his work. Documents relating to the company in Glasgow are held in the Scottish Record Office in Edinburgh. The archives of Kodak Ltd contain photographs and some documentary material which are an important source for Walton's work in exhibition and showroom design.

Books and articles

Allan, Ian, 'George Walton at Harlech', *Journal of the Merioneth Historical and Record Society* 10 (1985) pp. 71-84

Aslin, Elizabeth, *E. W. Godwin: Furniture and Interior Decoration* (London 1986)

Billcliffe, Roger, *Charles Rennie Mackintosh: The Complete Furniture, Furniture Drawings & Interior Designs* (third edition, London 1986)

Billcliffe, Roger, *The Glasgow Boys* (London 1985)

Buchanan, William, ed., *Mackintosh's Masterwork: The Glasgow School of Art* (Glasgow 1989)

Buchanan, William, *The Art of the Photographer: J. Craig Annan* (Edinburgh 1992)

Burkhauser, Jude, ed., *'Glasgow Girls': Women in Art and Design 1880-1920* (Edinburgh 1990)

Cooper, Jeremy, *Victorian and Edwardian Furniture and Interiors* (London 1987)

Crawford, Alan, *C. R. Ashbee: Architect, Designer & Romantic Socialist* (New Haven & London 1985)

Cumming, Elizabeth & Kaplan, Wendy, *The Arts and Crafts Movement* (London 1991)

Donnelly, Michael, *Glasgow Stained Glass: A Preliminary Study* (Glasgow 1981)

Girouard, Mark, *Sweetness and Light: The 'Queen Anne' Movement 1860-1900* (Oxford 1977)

Gow, Ian, *The Scottish Interior* (Edinburgh 1990)

Harker, Margaret, *The Linked Ring: The Secession Movement in Photography in Britain 1892-1910* (London 1979)

Harrison, Martin, *Victorian Stained Glass* (London 1980)

Holme, Charles, ed., *Modern British Domestic Architecture and Decoration* (Studio Special Summer Number 1901)

Howarth, Thomas, *Charles Rennie Mackintosh and the Modern Movement* (second edition, London 1977)

Jones, David, 'George Walton's revival of Scottish furniture types', in John Frew and David Jones, eds, *Scotland and Europe: Architecture & Design 1850-1940* (St Andrews 1991) pp. 59-66

Kinchin, Juliet, 'The Wylie and Lochhead Style', *Journal of the Decorative Arts Society, 1850-Present* 9 (1985) pp. 4-16

Kinchin, Perilla & Kinchin, Juliet, *Glasgow's Great Exhibitions: 1888, 1901, 1911, 1938, 1988* (Wendlebury 1988)

Kinchin, Perilla, *Tea and Taste: The Glasgow Tea Rooms 1875-1975* (Wendlebury 1991)

Larner, Gerald & Celia, *The Glasgow Style* (London 1980)

MacFarlane, F. C. & Arthur, E. F., *Glasgow School of Art Embroidery 1894-1920* (Glasgow Museums and Art Galleries 1980)

MacSporran, Fiona, *Edward Arthur Walton* (Foulis Archive Press, Glasgow 1987)

Moon, Karen, 'George Walton & Co.: work for commercial organisations, the Rowntree firms', *Journal of the Decorative Arts Society, 1890-1940* 5 (1981) pp. 12-22

Morris, Barbara, *Inspiration for Design: The Influence of the Victoria and Albert Museum* (London 1986)

Morton, Jocelyn, *Three Generations in a Family Textile Firm* (London 1971)

Muthesius, Hermann, *The English House* (London 1979), a shortened edition, translated by Janet Seligman, of *Das Englische Haus* 3 vols (Berlin 1904-5)

Naylor, Gillian, *The Arts and Crafts Movement* (London 1971)

Parry, Linda, *Textiles of the Arts and Crafts Movement* (London 1988)

Pevsner, Nikolaus, *Pioneers of the Modern Movement* (London 1936), subsequently revised and reissued as *Pioneers of Modern Design: From William Morris to Walter Gropius* (Harmondsworth, various dates)

Pevsner, Nikolaus, 'George Walton: his life and work', *RIBA Journal* 46 (1939) pp. 537-47

Robertson, Pamela, 'Catherine Cranston', *Journal of the Decorative Arts Society, 1850 - Present* 10 (1986) pp. 10-17

Service, Alastair, *Edwardian Architecture: A Handbook to Building Design in Britain 1890-1914* (London 1977)

Taylor, Hilary, *James McNeill Whistler* (London 1978)

Weaver, Mike, ed., *British Photography in the Nineteenth Century: The Fine Art Tradition* (Cambridge 1989)

Exhibition catalogues

Glasgow Museums and Art Galleries, *The Glasgow Style 1890-1920* (1984)

Glasgow Society of Women Artists, *A Centenary Exhibition to Celebrate the Founding of the Glasgow Society of Lady Artists in 1882* (1982)

Royal Pavilion, Art Gallery and Museums, Brighton, *C.F.A. Voysey: Architect and Designer 1857-1941* (1978)

Royal Pavilion, Art Gallery and Museums, Brighton, *Beauty's Awakening: The Centenary Exhibition of the Art Workers Guild* (1984)

INDEX